CW01369205

21 Centuries of Marine Pilotage
The History of the United Kingdom Maritime Pilots' Association

By
Harry Hignett

PUBLISHED 2012 BY THE
UNITED KINGDOM MARITIME PILOTS' ASSOCIATION

Published by the United Kingdom Maritime Pilots' Association

UKMPA
128 Theobald's Road
London
WC1X 8TN

chairman@ukmpa.org

First published 2012
Text © Harry Hignett
Images © as attributed

ISBN: 978-0-9574917-0-0

The moral right of Harry Hignett to be identified as the author of this work has been asserted.

All rights reserved. No part of this book may be reproduced in any form or by any means without prior permission in writing from the publisher.

Designed and printed by
Jeremy Mills Publishing Ltd
www.jeremymillspublishing.co.uk

Cover Illustration
Follow the Leader by J.Witham 1882
During a severe gale and pilots were wind-bound in the River Mersey about a dozen vessels were off the Mersey Bar, attempting to enter the river. The pilot cutter Leader flying the signal "Follow me" sailed past the ships and conducted them safely in to the river 1881.
© Merseyside Maritime Museum

The Early Steam Cutters

THE TYNE PILOTS were probably the first to use steam cutters, initially hiring one to tow their cobles out to sea in bad weather around 1852. Later they chartered a steamer for longer periods, although not exclusively for pilotage work: This was the *Pilot* which was taken on by Newcastle Trinity House for inspection of lights and navigational marks. However the *Pilot* was not a cruising pilot cutter in the conventional meaning. A similar system was used in the Mediterranean approaches to the Suez Canal in 1867 two years before the opening of the Canal.

In 1876 the Sydney Harbour authority moored a steam pilot cutter just inside the Heads as accommodation for pilots – the Sydney Heads were approached by mainly 12 miles of unpaved road, and the pilots normally travelled to the pilot station by rowing boat.

Also in 1876 the Weser pilots chartered a steamer to cruise off the entrance in place of their schooners which were threatened by the French Navy during the 1870–80 war.

The steamer was withdrawn in 1877 at the end of hostilities. Also in 1876 the Maryland pilots, whose base was Baltimore some 50 miles south from the entrance to Chesapeake Bay, stationed a steam cutter for the use of the pilots. It was the first real cruising cutter in the World.
Image © UKPA

Contents

Acknowledgements	vii
Foreword	ix
Chairman's comment	xi
Introduction	xiii
Presidents	xv
Abbreviations	xvi

Part One
The Early Days	1
19th Century the Coming of Steam	24
Modern Administration	30

Part Two
The Origins of the Association	43
1895–1900	59
1901–1941	68

Part Three
Pilotage Act 1913 & After	81
Reductions in Earnings: Economic Depression	90
1940s Membership splits to T&GWU	97
End of Hostilities	100

Part Four
New Legislation	107
Large vessels and Pilot Hoists: Modern times	113
National Pensions Fund	117
Steering Committee on Pilotage	118
1973 Health Study Proposals	120
1975 Human Factors study	126

Advisory Committee on Pilotage	132
Pilotage Commission	134
Deep Sea Pilots	145
UKPA(M)	158
Pilotage Act 1987	161
Personal Safety Concerns	175
SEA EMPRESS incident	177
First decade of 20th Century	180
Effects of 1987 Act	181
Humber contracts cancelled	182
AZIMUTH	198
Pilot Exemption Certificates	200

Part Five
Summary	203
1956–2001	206
Limitation of Liability	218
With B. Youde's Legal Points	222

Appendix
Appendix A – S.C.O.P.	237
Appendix B – P/Commission	245
Appendix C – Helgoland	251
Appendix D – AZIMUTH	255
The Author	259

Acknowledgements

TO JOHN RICH (Bristol) for research into the origins of the UKPA John Herbert (Bristol Seafarers Centre). Nick Cutmore and Caron James (IMPA). John Clandillon-Baker (editor of *THE PILOT*). Nic White (Liverpool JM University). Louise Bloomfield (Lloyd's Register Information Group), Barrie Youde (solicitor, Liverpool), Kevin Vallance (Deep Sea Pilots), South Tyneside Libraries, Merseyside Maritime Museum, National Maritime Museum.

Foreword

Lord Tony Berkeley, Honorary President

IT GIVES ME great please to introduce this excellent updated version of the History of the UKMPA which chronicles the story of this unique band of people who ensure the safety of our ships around our ports and navigation channels.

Pilots are often the unsung heroes who guide masters of all kinds of ships, from the largest to quite small ones, advise on safety and operational improvements both their own work and for navigation generally. They have to work alone in often difficult circumstances. Whereas 100 years ago their skills were fully if no doubt grudgingly recognised, now pressures on costs and competition issues often cause governments and industry to question their need or professionalism.

So the creation of the UK Maritime Pilots' Association, and their work with the European and International associations provides an essential forum to discuss their concerns and interests, and enables them to represent these clearly and strongly to maritime organisations, governments and the European Commission.

It is also important for pilots to take politicians and legislators on regular pilotage duties, so that they can witness first-hand the importance of the pilot's job, the challenges, the risks and responsibilities that go with it.

There is no substitute for such collective working by the UKMPA in preserving (indeed enhancing) the highest professional standards in an era where maritime skills generally are in decline. This includes the preservation and maintenance of navigational safety, environmental protection, and commercial efficiency of port traffic movements. Pilots also have to adapt, to technical innovation and work with Governments and other agencies and bodies to improve the competitive efficiencies of the sector as well as protecting the standards of the profession.

The success of the UKMPA in this work is a tribute to a long line of UKMPA chairmen.

I am honoured to be the Honorary President of UKMPA. It is of special importance this year as we host the 21st IMPA conference.

Comment from the UKMPA Chairman

In 1884, Commander Cawley founded the organisation which has over the years evolved through many guises to become the UKMPA which exists today. His original objective was to influence the development of Pilotage and Associated Regulations, including Acts of Parliament, and to help those members around the country who found themselves in difficulty. That goal is as relevant today as it was then. In this rewrite of his original 1984 work, Harry Hignett provides an insight into some of the challenges and developments that pilotage and indeed individual pilots have experienced, endured and overcome over the last century and a quarter.

I am very privileged to be the latest in a long line of pilots who have chaired this highly respected professional body. Particularly so in the year which has seen UKMPA members host the International Pilots' Association congress, the European Association's football tournament, take on the role of Master of the Honourable Company of Master Mariners, command the royal barge during the Queen's Diamond Jubilee river pageant and of course facilitate the publication of this book.

With 95% of UK (indeed the world's) trade being carried by sea and almost all of it being conducted through UK ports on ships piloted by UKMPA members, the importance of pilots to the safety and efficiency of our ports cannot be over-stated. I believe that the UKMPA can look forward to a long and productive future mirroring its history described in this book.

Don Cockrill
Chairman,
June 2012

Introduction

THE PLEASURE AT being able to bring the original history three decades up to date was matched only by the surprise when finding that the problems engaging the attention of the UKPA officers differed little from those over the previous century. Trinity House had primarily administered the pilot services in many of the smaller ports, mostly in the south of England. In other ports, pilot administration was conducted by local authorities, public corporations having elected members. From 1980 administration has been conducted by public commercial businesses, whose principal concern was financial profit. The Trinity House of Deptford Strond (Thames), and those of Hull, Newcastle and Leith etc were no longer concerned with pilotage services.

Pensions for pilots had become a problem, the earnings of the individual ports and the smaller ports had insufficient funds to provide adequate pensions. Shipowners, pilots and port authorities discussed difficulties of pension provisions. Pilotage rates must be adjusted.

Increasingly dangerous boarding equipment and apparatus brought problems. Lack of proper maintenance of pilot ladders and pilot hoist development requires international crew training. Links with European Maritime Pilots' Association and the International Maritime Pilots' Association are essential to achieve improvement.

The membership in 1971 was about 1600. After the early retirement system the numbers dropped to 650 in 1986. Five years later when the Humber pilots' contracts were not renewed the numbers dropped to 520. By 2004 the membership was steady at 493.

It has been apparent in this research that, over the several decades, where pilots have maintained good relationships with the authorities, they have been more successful in achieving their aims.

The number of categories that Section Committee members have to cope with grows continually and the discussion and meetings arising occupies far more time and energy than evermore. Because of the complexities of the work, I have added a summary of the latter part of the history from about 1970 as Part Five. It includes an explanation, by a former pilot, of major developments (and faults) arising from the 1987 Pilotage Act. The UKPA remains a very necessary organisation for the wellbeing and safety of its members.

Harry Hignett

UKPA badge 1961

Presidents

1884–1910	Commander George Cawley (Founder President)
1910–1923	Mr. Michael Joyce MP (Limerick) licensed pilot
1923–1925	The Hon.J.M. Kenworthy MP (Hull Central)
1925–1942	Lord Apsley DSO MC MP (Bristol Central)
1946–1947	Admiral Lord Mountevans KCB DSO
1949–1962	Captain Sir Peter MacDonald KBE MP
1963–1976	The Rt Hon. James Callaghan PC MP (Cardiff South East)
1978–1990	The Rt. Hon. The Lord Strathcona and Mount Royal
1991–1997	Lord Stanley Clinton-Davis
1998	Lord Tony Berkley

UKPA original badge 1884

Abbreviations

ABP	Associated British Ports
BLL	Solicitors Blake, Lapthorne, Linnell
CHA	Competent Harbour Authority
CHIRP	Confidential Hazard Incident Reporting
DAS	Group Legal Protection Insurers
DfT	Department for Trade (also DoT)
ETCS	Education, Training, Certification and Standards
H&SE	Health & Safety Executive
IALA	International Association of Lighthouse authorities
IMO	International Maritime Organisation
IMPA	International Maritime Pilots' Association
ITF	International Transport Federation
MAIB	Maine Accident Investigation Board
MCA	Marine & Coastguard Agency
NOS	National Operational Standards
P&I	Protection and Indemnity Insurance
PEC	Pilotage Exemption Certificate
plc	public limited company
PMSC	Port Marine Safety Code
PNPC	Pilots National Committee for Pensions
SOLAS	Safety Of Life At Sea
STCWS95	Standards, Training, Certification & Watchkeeping
TWGU	Transport & General Workers Union
VTS	Vessel Traffic System

PART ONE

PART ONE

Pilotage: The Early Days

IT IS NOT easy to define the work of a marine pilot, the tasks vary according to the trade over different periods of time. Pre 1500 multiple-masted ships were rare. From 1600 ships with two or more masts became more efficient as more sophisticated rigging was available. The introduction of steam power with iron or steel hulls brought about larger, safer and faster ship but also introduced added challenges of scale and manoeuvrability. Again the pilots had to adjust their training and experience to the modern technology.

Today the term is applied to the person with local knowledge who, not being a member of the crew, acts as a guide to ships in their own specific and limited district. Nevertheless it is difficult to confine the work to anything so specific: we must include pilots working along the coasts, in rivers and estuaries, harbours and docks.

At Dover in 1496 the "Fership (fellowship) of Passagers" was given a formal recognition as providing a ferry service across the Channel to France and the low countries. This service had been in existence from Roman times and was subject to a system approved by local authorities from the mid-14th century.

The system operated in a similar way to a local taxi service; the first traveller to arrive in Dover would take the first vessel on the quay, independent of route or destination. In 1496 the court was held in Dover Castle with the Constable of Dover Castle in the Chair. The names of 16 vessels and their owners were listed: all agreed to carry passengers and goods to Germany and the Rhine and Maas Delta havens to the east and as far as the Bay of Biscay and Cadiz to the West. The agreement: a mutual insurance covered a voyage from the time of clearing Dover to the return to Dover. Any damage or loss would be covered by the 16 members. The vessel on 'turn' would take the first customer and charge accordingly. As the fares varied it was considered that the income from each fare would average out. No vessel was allowed to get more than three 'turns' ahead of the others.

In 1516 the "Fership of Passagers" convened a court in Dover Castle to establish the Lodmanage of the Cinque Ports with an almost identical operating system. The former shipmasters and owners having noticed a tremendous growth in traffic along the Channel, were now pilots.

The Cinque Ports' pilots conducted shipping from the Channel into the Cinque Ports and the Thames' ports which continues to this day. They have also taken ships to the more northerly waters of the British Isles and were often asked to pilot ships along the European coast as far as the Baltic. They do this currently and for the purposes of this chapter they are the pilots who work in a defined district but not necessarily confined to that district.

The earliest description of a marine pilot's work comes from the *Periplous of the Erythraean Sea*, a merchant's guide to the northern Indian Ocean and the Red Sea. Written about 64 AD, it is not unlike the present-day *Admiralty Sailing Directions*, or, as they are often called, Admiralty Pilots. The writer, a widely travelled Greek-Egyptian merchant, describes the port of Barygaza, in northern India, the modern Broach at the mouth of the Narbuda River in the Gulf of Cambay:

'The passage is difficult because of the shoals at the mouth of the river. Because of this, the native fishermen in the King's service go up the coast to Syrastrene to meet the ships. And they steer them straight and true from the mouth of the bay between the shoals with their crews and they tow them to fixed stations going up with the flood and lying through the ebb at anchorages and in basins. These basins are deeper places in the river as far as the port, which lies about 10 stadia up from the mouth.'

In this extract we can recognise the work of an estuary or river pilot from the earliest times. Sailing, rowing and drifting with the current, using the anchors to hold and manoeuvre the vessels whilst waiting for the next tide is still practical: mention is made of towing. Pilotage and towing have always had something in common.

Before 1000 AD there is little evidence for activity of marine pilots. Although in 280 AD Carausius was appointed commander of the Classis Britannica, (the Roman British fleet) to seek out and destroy pirates preying on cross-channel traffic. Some historians consider he was in league with the pirates, possibly because he stemmed from Menapia (Flanders) and was also reputed to be himself a channel pilot. The earliest recorded pilot in Britain was a Roman military man based at York between 250 and 300AD. An inscription on an altar stone reads "Marcus Minucius Audensis …Gubernator of the VI Legion". The word 'Gubernator' was normally applied to the person in charge of the navigation of the ship. Audensis was probably employed conducting shipping along the River Ouse between York and the Trent.

There are indications that a base for mariners was established at Flaxfleet, opposite the confluence of the Trent with the Humber.

Before the 15th century the term pilot was practically unknown on the northern coast of Europe. It had its origins in the Mediterranean in classical times and arrived in the British Isles towards the end of the 15th century defined as meaning a navigator

– the man who held the book of sailing directions. The older northern European term for pilot was 'lodesman', derived from the old English word 'lád' = to lead or guide. The word changed from 'ládman' to 'lodesman' between 1000AD and 1300AD and in the latter form remained in use until the middle of the 19th century. To this day the term in northern Europe remains 'lods' (Scandinavian), 'lotse' (German) and 'loods' (Netherlands). In 1513 the petition for the charter for the Trinity House of Deptford Strond uses both words in the same phrase 'Pilottes and Lodesmen'. The French used 'lomant' or 'lamans', and even in the 20th century 'pilote-lamaneur' was prevalent.

The Spaniards and Portuguese brought the word 'pilot' to Britain shortly before 1500 possibly from the Mediterranean area. It seems to have been derived from the Greek 'periplous' (peri meaning around, plous meaning navigation) a form of sailing directions. The 'plous' probably modified to 'pilous', thence 'pilout' and so to 'pilot'. There is no evidence to support the belief, prevalent on the Continent, that 'pilot' derived from the Germanic words 'peil' (sounding) and 'loot' (lead).

Godric of Walpole, an early English pilot, was born in 1084, the year that the Domesday Book was compiled. He was first a travelling salesman, then a maritime merchant sailing along the coast between Scotland and Denmark. Godric was so renowned for his knowledge of the routes he sailed that he was asked to pilot the ships. After some 25 years at sea he retired to a hermit's cave not far from Durham, and on his death was canonised as Saint Godric, the Hermit of Finchale.

Perhaps the earliest written reference to a guide or pilot in Britain appears in a poem by the East Anglian abbot Ælfric who wrote about 1000AD: 'You should go to the West. I be your l dman.' There is no indication of pilots being involved with the fleet of William the Conqueror in 1066, but surely several were needed to guide so large a fleet. William's administrators must have known the need for pilots for, when the Domesday Book was compiled, it was stated that, at Dover, the King's Messenger hired one of the passage craft at a specific rate, and that there was an obligation on the town to provide a 'stiremannum et unum alia adjutor'. This seems to apply to a pilot and an assistant.

As the Viking raids diminished trade continued to increase. The Hansa ports aided the growth in trade. Bergen was exporting large quantities of salt fish (stockfish). In 1274 Norwegian national laws laid down pilotage fees generally between ports; being coastal pilotage of up to 150 miles. Two years later an increase in traffic caused the Bergen authorities to order that any shipmaster taking a pilot was required to pay the designated fees.

In the 12th century Alexander Neckham described the magnetic compass indicating that it had been in use for a number of years. It was a major factor in the tremendous increase in maritime trade during the 12th and 13th centuries. One important trade route was the carriage of wine from Bordeaux to Britain and Flanders, leading from the Gironde past the Isle d'Oleron towards Ushant and the Channel. The island became a nodal point where ships sheltered from adverse winds, exchanged information and occasionally formed convoys against piratical attacks. Richard I of England is reputed to have visited this mother, Queen Eleanor of Aquitaine, in 1199 at Oleron, and ratified the set of maritime laws that came to be known as the Role d'Oleron. From their complex and comprehensive nature it is obvious that they derived from earlier maritime laws, perhaps even from the sea-laws of Rhodes (400 BC). Two of the articles relate to pilotage:

> XIII A ship is freighted at Bordeaux, or at Rochelle, or elsewhere, and arrives at her place of discharge and has a charter party, towage and petit lodemanage fall upon the merchants. On the coast of Brittany all those whom they take after they have passed the Isle de Batz are petit lodesmen.
> XXIV A young man [= knave = mate = pilot] is pilot of a ship and he is hired to conduct her into the port where she

ought to discharge, it may well happen that the port where the ships are placed to discharge is a closed port .....and the pilot has well done his duty when he has brought the ship safely to her berth, for so far he ought to conduct her and thenceforth the duty is on the master.

It is evident from a study of the charter-parties between 1200 AD and 1450AD that at the end of the Middle Ages maritime trade was a developed industry with a complex structure. In this stage of pilotage the pilots were the men who had gained experience and memorized the sailing directions, customarily for a specific channel or sea coast. Charts were not easily drawn and not carried on many of the primitive vessels. Books were even more difficult to carry and preserve. There is little evidence of any organisation of harbour pilots and pilotage was irregular; indeed in most ports facilities and regulations were few.

Prior to the organisation of pilotage, pilots had to understand and keep in mind the various currencies. In Britain there were about seven varieties of coinage: guinea, pound sterling, noble, crown, florin, shilling, groat and penny. But there were other currencies French, Netherlands, German, Danish, and so on. An important currency mentioned in 12th to 15th century charters was the Lübecker pound. Lübeck at the southwest corner of the Baltic Sea was the centre of Hansa commercial transactions.

The sea pilot was familiar with at least one port, his home port, and on the return voyage he would be invaluable in the event of a lack of pilots at the approaches to the port. But he might have left the vessel en route, as occurred in 1465 at one English vessel where a pilot was exchanged for one who was familiar with the Irish Sea. But how were pilots obtained or chosen? It is likely he would have been waiting near the Customs House or applying for work through the shipmens' guilds.

Almost invariably shipmens' guilds were closely allied to religious institutions and dedicated to religious figures and, being of a charitable nature, provided an almshouse for their own aged and infirm mariners and shelter for other distressed seamen. A few of the guilds were formed by and for the benefit of shipmaster/merchants and in the course of time admitted other maritime bodies to membership. The guilds may have attempted to control pilotage by ensuring that pilots were sufficiently competent for their respective ports but there is no direct evidence for it. It is likely that the Shipman's Guild of Great Yarmouth, formed in 1207, is the earliest such society in Britain. With the express permission of King John of England a guild for mariners was formed at Bayonne in 1215. A similar guild was formed at Bordeaux in 1462 by local seamen and boatmen, some of who were also pilots. In the 15th century York, Kings Lynn, Boston and Bristol, each had a similar guild.

Among the earliest laws established for the safety of life and property on the seas in Europe are the Maritime Laws of Oleron. Issued in the twelfth century they stated that 'for a ship from Bordeaux or La Rochelle having a (sea) pilot on board, all those taken on after passing the Isle de Batz (off Roscoff, Brittany) are 'petit lomans'. Similarly a vessel from Normandy taking on a pilot on passing the Strait of Dover would take a 'petit lodesman'. In 1344 a law of the Commune d'Oleron defined 'petit lomant' as one who 'stations himself at the entrance to ports and havens knowing the danger of the ports and of the havens'.

About thirty years later, at the Inquisition of Queenboro (Medway), the Royal legal advisors stated:

> In right of lodemanage or pilotage the aforesaid jurats doe say that it seems to them in that case that they know no better ad vice or remedy but that if it be from this tyme henceforth used and done in the manner which is contained in the role d'Oleron ......and lett inquiry [examination?] be made to lodesmen who doe take upon themselves piloting which they know not how to perform, whereby a ship is sunk or a man killed.

The advantage of internationally recognised laws or conventions must have been in operation when, in 1388, a ship of Stralsund (Germany) on a voyage from La Rochelle to Ireland called at Falmouth to obtain a pilot for the Irish Sea.

We know that pilots were paid fees for pilotage in 1300 when Edward I, travelled from Harwich to Brabant (Flanders) on a ship for which John Jolif, lodman of Sandwich, was employed. Jolif received 26s. 8d. a day for the voyage to the Scheldt; the crew and officers were paid a daily rate. Jolif's fee indicated the distinction between the pilot and members of the crew.

Occasionally it was thought necessary to carry more than one pilot and on several voyages to Prussia, between 1390 and 1393, the future Henry IV of England sailed on a ship carrying three pilots, each receiving 40 shillings for the outwards voyage. On one of the return voyages there were only two lodesmen, their names were given as Robert Hayden and Edward Thorne, each receiving 5 pounds sterling. A deep-sea lodesman was customarily given an advance of fees. In 1465 Earl Hawkins hired a lodesman for a Baltic voyage, the account books showing that he made 'covenant with John Yonge of Deptford beside London that he shall be lodesman of my said master's shippe into Sprewse (Prussia) and he shall have for his labour xl shillings and thereof my master toke him in hand xii shillings.'

The international aspect of pilotage can be seen in the account of the *Kattryn* of Hull in 1457, paid to Rychard Symson for lodmonage to Selland (Zealand) £3,10s. 9d. A similar account for 26s. 8d. appears for pilotage of the *Godes Knecht* of Westenchouwen (Netherlands) about 1450.

Pilotage in the Thames estuary was an occupation for some mariners in the early 15th century. Thomas Franke of Harwich began working as a pilot about 1410 at the age of 21, probably in the North Channel approaches. He appears in several official proceedings and his death is noted in an inquest on Franke, 'lately lodysman of the *Mary Knight* of Dansk in Prussia' held in the City of London in 1417:

> On Thursday, 5th August last, between the hours of two and three in the afternoon the aforesaid ship, by the negligence and undue steering of the steersman and mariners therein, was sent and lodged upon a certain shelf, called Rantesbourne Shelf near West Greenwich (Deptford), within the liberty and franchise of the City of London; and that they had let go one of their anchors, the more speedily to get the ship off such shelf at the next flow of the tide, when then and there the said Thomas Franke went outside of the ship and stood upon another anchor that was hanging from the bow of the ship, and, taking in his hands a certain staff commonly called a "spek", he thrust the staff into the knot of the rope by which the other anchor, which before had been let down, was fastened; and while with such staff he was exerting himself with all his might to loosen and let out the rope aforesaid, the anchor, upon which he was standing swayed so greatly, to and fro, that it turned over, upon which the said Thomas Franke fell into the water, striking his head, in so falling, against the iron peak and sharp end of that anchor, which penetrated through his forehead to the brain; the ship in the meantime and for long after standing fast and without any motion.

Lodemanage in the Thames in 1437 comes to light in the account books of a shipmaster produced at a Hansa Court Inquiry:

> to the losmanne who sailed me into the Temse   *10s. 6d.*
> to the man who led the shippe through the bridge   *8d.*
> to the man who led the shippe into the dock   *6d.*

This compares with the later system of estuary, river and dock pilotage.

The success of the guilds in providing some control over pilotage, both on the continent and on the Humber (see below), probably led to the founding of the Trinity House on the Thames. Its charter of incorporation was issued to the Guild of the Holy Trinity and St. Clement of Deptford Strond in 1514, eventually known as the Corporation of Trinity House. There were initially, 40 members (mostly pilots), eight assistants, four wardens and the master, (corresponding to the usual numbers in the pack of cards – 52 and the joker) and many of the trade's guilds of the day had the same composition. For the first 50 years the Corporation was to all intents and purposes, exclusively concerned with pilotage and most of the senior members were important naval officials, shipmasters or both. The first master of Trinity House, Sir Thomas Spert, was master of the King's ship *Henry Grace à Dieu* who, before he died in 1542, became one of the controllers of Henry's Navy; this in addition to owning two merchant ships. The Corporation was asked, in the 1560s, to undertake other duties including buoyage of the Thames and the establishment and maintenance of lights and seamarks along the coasts.

The founding of Trinity House was followed in 1527 by a more formal recognition of the pilots at Dover working under the Lord Warden of the Cinque Ports. The Dover organisation was the Court of Lodemanage of the Cinque Ports, all officers and members being serving pilots and the officers elected by the members with the approval of the Lord Warden. The first master was Richard Couche, later to become Mayor of Dover. That the pilots of Dover had the confidence of the King's advisers can readily be understood from their action in selecting Couche to undertake a secret surveying mission to the Zuider Zee prior to sending ships to Gelderland to bring Anne of Cleves to England. From its foundation the court was to be inextricably linked to the Corporation on the Thames, which carried the fastest growing maritime industry of the time.

By 1457 the Trinity House of Hull had become an exclusive maritime organisation and in 1512 passed an ordinance that only members of Hull Trinity House could pilot ships between Hull and the mouth of the Humber. The rule was difficult to enforce however, and when Henry VIII visited the port in 1541 he asked to meet the pilot of a ship berthing nearby. The pilot was a Scot, which irked Henry for he was not too pleased with Scotland at the time. The incident may well have been stage-managed to support the request of the elder brethren for a charter. A charter was granted to the Hull Trinity House, just as one had been granted in 1536 to the Trinity House of Newcastle.

Pilots were active around the Bristol Channel, in 1525, when the Bristol Council dismissed a seaman from his office of 'Towing and Lodesmanship'. Across the Bristol Channel on the River Towy at Llanstephan, near Carmarthen, Leland noted, in 1536 'before the havin mouth liith a barre so that shippes lighteli cum not in owt a pylot'. On the south coast an Exmouth pilot was arraigned in the Admiralty Court in 1573 for negligent pilotage in grounding a vessel, thereby causing the loss or damage of 18,000 salt fish. He was ordered to pay damages of some £300, an enormous sum. A few years later, in 1580, Southampton Town Council laid complaints in a local Admiralty Court against nearby villages whose inhabitants were undertaking unauthorised pilotage on the Solent.

Before the end of the 16th century there was strife between the Dover pilots and their Trinity House counterparts because, when they disembarked from the Cinque Ports, the Corporation pilots attempted to offer their services to inward bound ships. The boating services were, however, in the hands of relatives and friends of the Dover pilots who were understandably reluctant to offend any Cinque Ports pilots. This forced the Corporation pilots to travel home by land, a journey of at least two days on horseback via Canterbury to Gravesend and thence by boat to Deptford. Naturally the Cinque Ports pilots found difficulty in obtaining vessels to pilot from the Thames outwards. There was criticism of one-way pilotage as being wasteful and inefficient, but in the days of sail, shipping often arrived without warning in great numbers according to the winds and travelling in company as a precaution against pirates and enemy ships. Pilots living near the pilot station had the advantage. So began the Thames pilotage system; Trinity House outwards, Cinque Ports inwards.

Pilots working in the Thames approaches in the early years could be subject to claims for damages. In 1563 William Holland was pilot of the *Pellikan* of Hamburg a vessel of 400 tons with a light draft of 12 ft outward from London. The last of a group of six ships sailing in company she ran aground off Reculver, Kent having taken a channel to the north of that taken by the other 5. The strain of grounding caused the mast to break and fall, killing the ship's boy who was the master's nephew. A long court case ensued and Holland was fortunate enough to be absolved from blame. A year later John Lisse of Harwich piloted *The Nicolas* of Danzig through the North Channel. When the ship grounded, Lisse's boat, with two crew, was alongside at the time and he tried to escape the wrath of the master by jumping into the boat. The master however, grabbing hold of the boat's mast, was able to prevent him escaping and report him to Trinity House. Having such as boat was an expensive pastime and it can be assumed that the sea pilotage was to a certain extent subsidised by income from fishing. A century later Francis Merrit, one of the Elder Brethren of Trinity House and a choice pilot for the East India Company refused to move one of their vessels because it was likely to move during the fishing season. About the same time the Netherlands pilots were threatened with suspension if, during the herring season, they did not attend their pilot stations.

The East India Company, founded in 1600, grew to become the largest trading company the world had ever known. From the outset vast profits enabled the Company to use the finest ships available and to offer good income to the most competent and experienced commanders, officers and crews. The Company even employed its own pilot for the river Thames between Deptford and Gravesend. One of these pilots in 1635, was Captain William Swanley, one of the Elder Brethren of Trinity House, He also acted as 'master-pylott' to superintend the employment of labour for shifting ships Thames to and from the wharves and dry-docks and repairing rigging. Swanley also conducted the ships downstream from the Deptford base to Erith or Gravesend, where, after taking on more cargo, the Trinity House pilot joined to take them to the Downs. Inward bound, the Cinque Ports pilot brought the ships into the Downs and thence to Gravesend, where they lightened before the river pilot organized the passage up river to Deptford. Swanley was one of the panel who, when the *Mary* arrived home in 1636, arranged for the cargo to be lifted out of her, as due to her age, the draft made her unsuitable to 'pass over the Flatts' into the Thames.

Samuel Pepys as Master of Trinity House, wrote a memorandum on the shortage of pilots for Royal Naval vessels. These were navigators that specialised in sailing through their own districts and are better called 'Sailing Masters'. For some time Trinity House pilots were recruited but there was no standard of rank for them, despite a proposal about 1750 that they should be treated as warrant officers.

Transport packets between Harwich and Elbe-Hannover ports, each carried two pilots each way,

In 1654, Leith pilots were provided with a pilot boat at the expense of the Town council. This was by no means usual, and only one other town council, Hamburg on the Elbe, a few decades earlier, did the same by offering a loan to the senior pilot for building a galiot to be reclaimed via the pilotage fees.

Trinity House officials wrote to the Admiralty when, in 1745, six pilots were ordered to the *Royal Sovereign* at the Nore, for conducting H.M. ships to the Downs or overseas. The six thought they would be on a roster, but a Cinque Ports pilot was placed aboard HMS *Hound* to take her to the Downs: the six had been there for a fortnight, the Dover man one night. One asked the Captain where he could sleep, but "the Captain did not care" and there were no orders for beds or bedding; "which is a great hardship upon them to lye anywhere like dogs with heir cloaths on exposed to the cold or what else shall happen, for which reason many of them get coulds and sometimes even death itself."

The Elder brethren complained about pilots and their apprentices being impressed into naval service: at the beginning of the 18th century several apprentices were taken into naval service both from the Thames and the Humber. In 1755, at Liverpool, it was reported in evidence to a court that a Liverpool pilot had warned the crew of an inward bound vessel he was piloting that the Press Gang were waiting out of sight near at the entrance to the Mersey.

There were many complaints against pilots by naval officers, often justified, but in 1826 a Tyne pilot was reported for refusing to pilot a naval vessel into the Tyne. The complaining officer did not explain that the pilot had informed him that he was engaged in piloting a merchant vessel and was taken by the naval crew while he was sounding the bar.

Wars severely affected pilot services too and even without war pilots could suffer, as at Southwold in 1742 when a Dunkirk vessel appeared off the port making signals for a pilot. A small boat rowed by six men carried a pilot out, but nearing the vessel, (a privateer) it was fired on and four men killed. 54 years later a Southwold pilot cutter was captured by a French frigate off Yarmouth and the pilots and crew taken prisoner. In 1728 the pilot galiot cruising off the Weser had been taken by a corsair: the master and crew carried off to it was presumed slavery. Also in 1728, in response to the strife between the several (up to 6) pilotage groups along the Gironde estuary, a new set of laws was issued by the French Admiralty to smooth the contentions. In that year a Netherlands shipmaster applied to the French courts for the return of the pilotage fees after his vessel was grounded by an incompetent pilot. It then appeared that the pilots were charging more than 50% over the ordained rates. The result of the new law was that the Gironde pilots were unable to increase their fees for more than four decades.

Wars with the Dutch before and after 1799, and the Napoleonic Wars drove maritime trade into the northern ports of Britain. Liverpool, having gained financial benefit from the London merchants hurt by the outbreak of the Plague in 1665, and the Great Fire of London of London in 1666, was in a position to exploit this trade and make important connections with the West Indies and North America. Liverpool privateering added more to the wealth of its citizens who were able to build the first enclosed dock in Britain in 1715. In 1765 the Liverpool town council obtained an Act of Parliament enabling it to establish a pilot service.

By the 1630s regular sailings allowed the East India Company to forecast the arrival of each homeward-bound East-Indiaman. At the appropriate time the directors would commission a small vessel to cruise between the Scillies and Ushant, carrying the Cinque Ports pilot, and extra anchors, cables and spare rigging for the expected arrival. John Culmer of the Cinque Ports was such a pilot in 1636 when he was awarded an extra £20 for bringing an inward-bound East Indiaman into the Downs in difficult circumstances. He had not always been in such good standing: a month after being appointed a pilot of the lower class (up to 100 tons) he grounded a vessel of 300 tons near the Pool of London, and in 1638 he brought an inward bound vessel into the Downs and took ashore eight rolls of calico, bought from the Captain. The "Farmer" of the Customs caught him and reported him to the East India Company who demanded the name of the person who sold the calico. Not only did Culmer tell them, he asked for the return of the money it cost to transport the material between Dover and London.

Each succeeding monarch renewed the charter granted to Trinity House by Henry VIII, but the Court of Lodemanage had no such basis, being supported only by the diminishing powers and importance of the Warden of the Cinque Ports. In about 1600 the pilots at Dover formed a local Trinity House and unsuccessfully applied for a charter. Even so, economically, conditions improved for the Dover pilots until, in 1685, James II came to the throne. He appointed a friend, Sir Edward Hales, as Warden of the Cinque Ports. Hales immediately dismissed the elected Master and Wardens of the Court, putting in his own nominees in place to manage the pilots' administration and, of course, milk the pilotage income. This state of affairs lasted until William of Orange came to the throne in 1689. The pilots appealed to William who restored their ancient rights, but they had learned a lesson and took steps to ensure that a similar situation could not arise. It was a long process, lasting more than 25 years, until they finally obtained what they wanted – a Pilotage Act.

The Pilotage Act 1717

The first major parliamentary legislation on pilotage. Its main provisions delineated the Cinque Ports pilotage district, made unlicensed pilotage an offence and laid down penalties for offenders. The Act, nevertheless, exempted masters, mates and owners of vessels residing in the Cinque Ports from the obligation to use pilots officially licensed; this section led to much abuse and caused a considerable amount of litigation (owners of foreign-flag vessels appointed seamen from the Cinque Ports as mates of their ships and entered the district as 'exempt vessels'). There was also a section in the Act that dealt with claims for salvage and the recovery of anchors and cables by Deal Boatmen, who, as we have seen, were not unconnected with the pilots. The Court of Lodemanage was the arbitrator in these matters.

The Dover pilots now had something that Trinity House had not. The obvious advantage of parliamentary legislation encouraged the elder brethren to apply for their own. The next Pilotage Act, passed in 1732, included and confirmed the provisions of the 1717 Act and, whilst giving the same powers to the Corporation, gave exemption to the Trinity Houses of Hull and Newcastle wherever their respective jurisdictions overlapped. This act was the first legislation covering the Trinity Houses and the first to include more than one port or district. It can be considered as the beginning of British Pilotage.

From 1770, pilotage regulation became widespread. More ports and harbour authorities recognized the need for better pilotage and better control. The Government produced a clause regarding pilotage that could be inserted into new local authority Parliamentary legislation.

By the middle of the 18th century the West Indian and North American trades began to rival that of the East Indies, bringing about an increase of traffic along the northern side of the English Channel. Establishing longitude at sea remained a difficult matter and many shipmasters feared to approach the Isles of Scilly, with their myriads of small rocks that made the area a noted graveyard for ships. The fishermen of the Scillies now began to take up pilotage, meeting the vessels well out of sight of land and guiding them past the Isles toward the Lizard, Start Point or the Isle of Wight. The boats used were about 30 ft long and 5 ft in the beam; tiny frail craft for such waters. Ships occasionally asked for stores, or to be piloted into the harbour of St. Mary's. By 1800 there was an officially recognized pilot service conducting ships to all parts of the British Isles and the coasts of France and Belgium.

The East Indian Company financially the most important British concern had their own "choice" pilots for conduct their vessels from the Channel to London and vice versa. There were seven pilots named, from about 1790 to 1808.

List of pilots who are accustomed to take East India ships from Gravesend to the Isle of Wight

Blyth, Mr Philip, 12, Hereford Place, Commercial Road.
Johnson, Mr. James, 3, Turner Street, Commercial Road.
Meek, Mr. James, 6, St. George's Place, St. Georges East.
Park, Mr. Thomas, 5, Whitehouse Place, Commercial Road.
Rees, Mr. Moses, 8 Church Lane, Whitechapel.
Seabrooke, Mr. Johnathan, Gravesend.
Thomas, Mr. Daniel, 54 Gainsford Steet, Horsly Down.

River pilots who take the east india ships from london to gravesend and back

Bell Mr. Henry, 36, Brunswick Street, Blackwall.
Clippendale, Mr. John, Brunswick Street, Blackwall.
Ferguson, Mr. John, 226 High Street, Poplar.
Lockwood, Mr. William, Colton Place, Poplar.
Nevill, Mr. John, Fisher Lane Greenwich.
Powell, Mr. Richard T. near the Victualing Office, Deptford.
Ross, Mr. Richard, Junr, Bull Lane, Deptford.
Ross, Mr. Thomas, Greenwich
Slaney, Mr. John B. Church Street, Greenwich

From the records of Newcastle Trinity House in 1795 there is a listing of pilots that not a few serving pilots will humorously recognise that appears occasionally. The eleven town pilots on the register were listed:

Name	Address
Isaac Thomson	not traceable
William Gibson	in gaol
William Hall	not traceable

Thomas Hedley	not traceable
George Redhead	Hebburn
Edward Robson	not traceable
Thomas Henzell	not traceable
Thomas Smith	Howden Pans
George Taylor	not traceable
Joseph Pringle	St. Antoins
Joseph South	not traceable

From 1795, French troops under Napoleon swept along the northern coasts of Europe from Holland, to the Danish parts of the Jutland peninsular. In reply the British Navy blockaded the Netherlands and German coasts, and also ensured that Denmark no longer controlled the entrance to the Baltic. And to further the blockade Helgoland Island, in the approaches to German ports, was occupied by troops, who were, in fact, Hannover troops under the control of a governor appointed by the British government. Surprisingly this was not unpopular with the islanders, in fact, the Danish overlords taxed heavily the income of the pilotage based on the island.

Helgoland, at the entrance to the German Bight, was on the path for ships makng for the Weser and Elbe rivers and ships arriving in the area with the prevailing northwest winds sought pilotage assistance to the Elbe. The Helgolanders, to the annoyance of the Elbe Sea-pilots, readily accepted the work and often sailed past the Elbe station and handed over pilotage to the river Elbe pilots; the sea-pilots losing the income.

This was an unusual situation: from 1807 to 1890 the island was considered British, with the Helgoland flag had the union flag inserted into the centre. The British Governor encouraged the islanders to become smugglers, thereby annoying the French occupiers. The islanders had British passports and were quite unhappy when the governance of the Island was ceded to the German government in exchange for the Island of Zanzibar in

1871. Many of the residents held their passports until World War I. (Appendix C)

The successful application of parliamentary legislation led to further local Pilotage Acts, including those for Boston (Lincs) in 1774 and Hull in 1800, which were older established port. Nevertheless new industrial ports in the late 18th century such as Swansea had its first pilotage regulations in 1791. It was so important that local authorities were able to obtain a section requiring concerning compulsory pilotage. This was a new factor that would have important effects in marine litigation. Another featured a section laid down the system of cruising cutters to be operated in Liverpool Bay. The Act stipulated that there were to be nine cutters, four on station between Anglesey and the Isle of Man, one cruising between Hoylake and the Nor'west Lightfloat and the remaining four servicing ships in the river and taking off pilots from the outward-bound vessels at the Bar.

It was obvious that additional legislation was necessary by 1800 to control the many ports and districts not covered by separate legislation. The first comprehensive Pilotage Act was placed on the stature book in 1808; 'An Act for the better regulation of Pilots and of the Pilotage of Ships and vessels navigating the British seas'. The most important provisions were the establishment of compulsory pilotage in all districts where licensed pilots were available, and the authority given to the Trinity House of Deptford to form pilotage districts where it was deemed necessary to control pilots and regulate pilotage. Almost immediately 35 Trinity House outports appeared around the coast of Britain.

Section IX and schedule C of this Act continued the ancient regulations of the Court of Lodmanage, by requiring the master and wardens to swear an oath:

> "That I will diligently and impartially examine and inquire into the capacity and skill of .. .. in the Art of piloting ships and vessels over the Flats and round the Longsand

Head, and up the rivers of *Thames* and *Medway*, and into *Ramsgate, Dover, Sandwich,* and *Margate* Harbours, and also upon the coasts of Flanders and Holland; and will make true and speedy Return thereof to the Lord of the Cinque Ports for the time being, or his deputy, without favour, affection, fee or reward. So help me GOD".

As the 1808 Act was only to be in force for four years, further legislation was required to replace it. The Pilotage Act 1812 re-enacted most of the provisions of its predecessor and gave the Trinity Houses of Hull and Newcastle the powers they had exercised previously in addition to 'any ports or harbours or places within the limits of their respective jurisdictions'. An entirely new section required that all pilots to execute a bond for their good behaviour in the sum of £100. This requirement has been carried through to the present day with the sum also remaining unchanged. An important section of the Act attempted to define the responsibility and rights of the shipowner, master, and owner or consignee of the cargo, with regard to any damage to ship, goods or persons occurring through 'neglect, default, incompetency or incapacity of any pilot taken under the provisions of the Act'. This section also gave rise to a considerable amount of litigation. Another Pilotage Act was passed in 1825 and seems merely to have prolonged the existing situation, without easing the litigation problem that had already given the industry extra worries.

An example of the complications that could arise in the 1830s can be found in the movements of a sailing vessel bound for the Thames, which, on approaching Margate, found the pilot cutter busy servicing other vessels. The master was obliged to keep way on the vessel to avoid other ships, and eventually passed the cutter and found difficulty in making way to windward in confined waters. He decided to sail on without a pilot and on arrival at Gravesend consulted his agent and a solicitor. Taking the latter's advice to pay the statutory penalty, the money was sent to the Cinque Ports office in Margate. Meanwhile the Warden at Margate had informed Thomas Paine, solicitor and pilots' agent at Dover. Paine issued a writ for the amount due and sent it on to Gravesend, but the vessel had already sailed for Hartlepool. The writ was forwarded to Hartlepool and the vessel was arrested, incurring some 14 days delay. Similar difficulties led to complaints that were the cause of the Court of Lodemanage being dissolved, in 1853, to become one of the Thames pilotage districts administered by Trinity House.

In 1835 there were several renewed approaches to the problem of pilotage. A Parliamentary Bill was introduced, specifically to allow the steam vessels plying the Irish Sea, usually, ferries between Liverpool Dublin, Belfast and Derry, to sail without pilots. It failed 2 to 73. However in the same year, a Royal Commission was instituted to look into the 'existing laws, regulations, and practises under which pilots are appointed, governed and paid in the British Channel and the several approaches to the Port of London, and also in the navigation connected with the other principal ports in the United Kingdom.' It was the first major inquiry into pilotage. One of the main items in the findings and report of the Commission was the recommendation that there should be a central body to control all pilotage affairs. Unfortunately the ensuing Pilotage Act of 1836 did not take up this far-reaching proposal.

It is perhaps surprising that Southampton, a great and ancient port, did not really have an organized pilotage at its approaches until it was established as a Trinity House outport under the Act of 1808. There were at least 38 pilot cutters based on the Isle of Wight. Other Trinity House outports were the Scilly Isles and Falmouth. The advent of larger cutters caused the steady decline of the Scillies pilotage which ceased to be of importance in Channel pilotage by 1890.

There were further inquiries into pilotage in 1860, 1870 and 1888. The inquiry by the Parliamentary Select Committee of 1888 was the idea of Joseph Chamberlain, a brilliant but erratic politician, who used the objection of compulsory pilotage to promote his

Parliamentary standing. This was particularly significant as it was specifically instituted to study the problems of compulsory pilotage.

Evidence placed in front of the 1888 Committee showed that 51 British Chambers of Commerce objected to the principle of compulsory pilotage. Of this number 23 came from the following districts:

Batley, Birmingham, Coventry, Darlington, Derby, Dewsbury, Halifax, Heckmondwike, Holmfirth, Huddersfield, Kendal, Leeds, Luton, Macclesfield, Morley (nr Leeds), Northampton, North Staffordshire, Nottingham, Rochdale, Sheffield, Wakefield, Wolverhampton, Worcester. (Holmfirth, by the way, was the site for several hundred (TV) episodes of *The Last of the Summer Wine*)!

The 1888 Committee developed into a major study lasting about 3 months investigating all aspects of pilotage. The members voted by a majority of one to recommend the abolition of compulsory pilotage, but parliament noting the narrow majority wisely took no action. The Merchant Shipping Act of 1854 included and consolidated most of the existing legislation on pilotage, as did the Merchant Shipping Act of 1894.

By the end of the 19th century it was again obvious that the existing legislation was outdated an inadequate and, after a searching inquiry in 1910/11, the Pilotage Act of 1913 came into being, however the First World War delayed its implementation in many districts for over 5 years. After the end of the Second World War there were several minor inquiries and attempts to devise a new Pilotage Act. This came to fruition in 1974. A Special Committee on Pilotage 1978 (SCOP) was instituted and the Advisory committee on Pilotage ACOP each investigating the changes necessary to bring the administration of pilotage to match the current economic and political situation – i.e. in the Thatcher era.

The Nineteenth Century: The Coming of Steam

The years from 1800 to 1914 were the most difficult any pilots have had to face. The new technology of steam power enabled the development of many improvements in safety and work practices. Iron ships, screw propulsion and the electric telegraph all made their appearance about mid-century, improving standards and speeds but carrying new problems for pilots in handling ships up to eight times as large with single screw propulsion. Perhaps these challenges discouraged pilots from introducing steam-powered cutters before the 1890s.

When shipowners realised that ships were no longer dependent on wind and tides they suggested that pilots were no longer as important and proposed reductions in pilotage tariffs. It was also claimed that vessels being towed by steam tugs did not need pilots.

Opening the century at peace, by 1803 Britain and France were once again at war and with a break of a few months, in 1811, the war continued until the Battle of Waterloo in 1815. There was peace in Britain for the next 100 years or so, but anything but peace and contentment for pilots. The effect of hostilities lasted little more than a couple of years after the armistice, but the effects of legislation were to last for the remainder of the Century.

The Pilotage Act of 1808 promoted a wider regulation of pilotage than previously and Trinity House was empowered to establish pilotage districts in places and ports where there had been no prior authority. Pilots at Southampton came under regulations for the first time in 1808. The Act also made provision for general compulsory pilotage, and which provision was included also in another pilotage act four years later. But the later 1812 Act included an extra paragraph:

"No owner or master of any ship shall be answerable for any loss or damage for, or by reason of, any neglect, default or incompetence of any pilot taken on board of any such ship under or in pursuance of the provisions of this Act".

A somewhat simple idea, but the interpretation of this clause by the courts brought chaos for shipowners and pilots alike, and fortunes for the lawyers in the Admiralty Courts.

The clause gave absolute freedom to ships under compulsory pilotage from claims for any damage done to other vessels or property. If ship 'A' under compulsory pilotage collided with ship 'B', a barge or any other vessel not subject to compulsory pilotage, ship 'A' was free from liability, even when, under normal circumstances she would be at fault. Under this clause ship 'A' was also free from liability for damages after striking a shore installation. In 1910, almost a century later, an inward bound cargo steamer struck the Wallasey Ferry Landing Stage. The owners claimed freedom from liability under this clause and won the ensuing court action. The incident was the subject of a complaint to the 1910 Departmental Committee on Pilotage. An inward bound tanker in the Mersey struck the Egremont Landing Stage to completely destroy the structure. The stage was never replaced. The owners of the vessel claimed freedom from restitution as she was under the control of a compulsory pilot.

During the Napoleonic War, pilots had other problems to contend with as the following letter demonstrates:

> To the Minister of Marine, Dept of Prisoners of War, Paris. We the Master and Wardens of the Society or Fellowship of Pilot of the Cinque Ports, beg leave to solicit of the French Minister of Marine his attention to the following request:
> On their hearing there were two French Pilots in confinement as prisoner of war, they petitioned the Honourable Commissioners for the Transport Service, to liberate and send home the two pilots vis. A. Delpiere captured in the prame *"La Ville De Lion"* and Jacques Equinet captured

in the brig "*No20*", pilots of Calais but being informed by the Transport Board that these pilots cannot be released whilst English pilots are detained in France and there being now Thomas Atherdon of this port, pilot of the gun brig "*Inveterate*", Lt George Norton, wrecked at Dieppe on the 18th February 1807 detained at Verdun and Barrington Edgerly also of this place, pilot of a Swedish brig captured and carried into Calais on the 6th December 1805 now in prison in Givet.
These Cinque Port Pilots now earnestly request those English pilots may be liberated in order that the two French pilots also imprisoned may also be returned home to their country and friends.

The Court of Loadmanage had other albeit minor problems, not least from among the characters appearing from the ranks of their own members, one Sherlock, for instance. In the 1820s he left a vessel at Gravesend but did not return to the rota for several days. His excuse was that he had found his father as mate of a vessel berthed nearby and as they had not met for a number of years they stopped for a drink. The following year he was seen leaving a certain hostelry a little unsteadily and at a time when he was required for a rota turn. At the subsequent proceedings he claimed he had been leaving the shop next door where he had purchased a remedy for the malady that had made him rather dizzy.

Larkins was another character. About the same time as the above charge was made against Sherlock, Larkins was before the Court of Loadmanage for assaulting the Senior Warden who was making an inspection trip to the cruising cutter off Folkestone. He had not been aboard long before Larkins came from below and according to the charge "caught me by the collar and all the bad language possible threatened my life and frequently repeated the words, 'you old bugger as you are fond of writing I have given you a fine opportunity and you old bugger you may make me pay'".

PILOTAGE: THE EARLY DAYS

There were several Larkins working as pilots in the Cinque Ports, not all of them as noteworthy at the above. But the name appears quite often in the Court's *Accounts and Returns*; and one letter written by the Warden to their Secretary at Dover catches the eye:

> "You will perceive that Larkins can get home for 17 shillings. I think that he cannot eat by the way and perhaps he belongs to a temperance society."

There were occasional complaints that the Court was not acting properly in the matter of proceedings against the Deal boatmen who acted as salvors when ships were aground on the Goodwins, or recovered anchors lost, or supplied stores to ships at anchor in the Downs (they were also not averse to a certain amount of smuggling). The Wardens of the Cinque Ports were adjudicators in cases of dispute between the boatmen and shipowners or captains.

Whenever a pilot was accused of negligent pilotage, the Court was presided over by the Lord Warden of the Cinque Ports and with him was a local magistrate as well as one of the Wardens. In 1817 when the East Indiaman *WARREN HASTINGS* grounded in the Downs, the pilot, Samuel Taverner, was suspended sine die. Supporting an appeal against the suspension, the whole service petitioned the Lord Warden for mitigation of sentence. Taverner had served in the Navy between 1780 and 1809, first as a midshipman, later as pilot. He claimed that the leadsman had given imperfect soundings and that although the ship had grounded the boatmen who had assisted received only a small reward. Taverner 'humbly requested that his Lordship's humanity would be extended to a poor and wretched man, the prime of who's life had been expended in the service of his country and who's advanced time of life (57) will not admit him capable of obtaining other employment. The punishment already received has reduced him to poverty and want'.

Pilots elsewhere were called before the local pilotage boards as at Liverpool where John Creary was fined 7 guineas in 1807 for carrying a gaff topsail whilst on station, making it difficult for an approaching vessel to catch up with the cutter. At the same meeting he was fined 2 guineas for striking another vessel with his cutter at Ravensglass (Cumberland) whilst on a survey trip. A month earlier another pilot had been fined £10 for running a ship ashore on a sandy beach 3 miles north of Liverpool. Later that year in the same district a pilot was fined 3 guineas for 'abusive language to a Gentleman on the quay'! Discipline amongst the Liverpool pilots must have been difficult in the 1840s when there were 3 Owen Owens, 4 Edward Edwards, 3 Griffith Griffiths, 4 William Williams and two Hugh Hughes. There were also Owen Hughes, and Hugh Owens and more than one Owen Griffiths, Griffith Owens and so on. It must be explained that the Liverpool Pilotage Committee minutes contain frequent rewards for outstanding services to shipping in difficulties.

Similarly Leith pilots were praised in February 1816 when an approaching vessel flying distress signals was boarded by a dozen pilots from two cutters and who successfully laboured for 7 days to save the ship and cargo. In June of that year, during a furious gale, a Swedish brig with two anchors, down drove to within 2 cables of Inchkeith Rocks. Nine pilots saw the distress signals flying and set of in their boats through a short steep sea. Three managed to board the ship and found the master preparing to cut away the masts. The pilots stopped him and took over the ship. Cutting the port cable and setting the for'd staysail, they caused the ship to sheer towards a gap in the rocks. They then cut the remaining cable and steered the ship to safety. The rewards were £50 each for the first incident and £105 for the second.

Another Pilotage Act in 1824 replaced the 1812 Act, a section of which made it possible for a non-British vessel to enter or leave British ports without pilots. A further section gave new security to pilots by stating that a pilot who had executed a bond would not be liable for damages of more than £100 'arising from negligence or want of skill'. During a court case several decades later it was decided that this section did not apply to non-Trinity House pilots.

In the 18th century it was customary for pilots to be taken out to ships by boat from Deal or Dover. After 1812, 2 large pilot cutters either anchored or cruised off Dungeness, waiting for ships coming up channel. The *Argus* cutter was purchased in 1824 by two Deal pilots, Thomas Thompson and Robert Sherwood, and sold 5 years later to George Clendon senior, a warden of the Deal pilots, 'in trust for all and every the pilots for the time being...' The master in 1829 was William Gosley, also a pilot. A crew of 7 worked the vessel and the ships' boats, and up to 20 pilots were carried aboard at a time. The *Registry of British Shipping* for Deal shows that this ship was built in Hastings in 1812. She was 76 tons burthen, 58 ft in length an 18 ft in the beam. The image shows part of the registry entry for 1824.

At the entrance to the English Channel, the coasts of Devon and Cornwall have claimed many wrecks, as have the Isles of Scilly, many of them, due to the inability of mariners to find the longitude. In the 19th century the increasing traffic from the new lands in the West enabled a viable pilot service to establish itself. The former fishermen met vessels well out of sight of land and conducted them past the Scillies toward the Lizard, Start Point of the Isle of Wight. Their open boats were about 30ft long, 5ft wide, rowed by 8 men – tiny, frail craft for those waters. The pilots conducted ships as far as Cardiff, Hull and Rotterdam. This pilotage lasted until the 1860s when the larger cutters of Falmouth and the Isle of Wight extended their cruising ranges and even cutters from the Elbe, Weser, Rotterdam and other places were seen between the Lizard and the Scillies. As steamers began passing the Scillies the men turned to cruising cutters, but with dwindling success. A few of the open boats were known, in fine weather, to have rowed to the coast of France on smuggling expeditions!

The Scillies pilots were described by the mate of the yacht *America* on passage from New York to the Isle of Wight to take part in what was to become known as the *America*'s Cup' race in 1851:

"This channel beats everything and all conception that I had of its extent and magnitude. The pilot boats beggar all description, they are about 40ft long, sloop-rigged or cutter as they call them. Most of them carry only one or two pilots and these as dirty as chimney sweeps. The first thing they ask is, "Do you want a pilot?" if answered in the affirmative they ship over the side a small boat and board you.

The pilot steps aft and is introduced to the Captain. They make a bargain as to the amount. He next asked, "Have you a bottle of spirits aboard for the boat?" I will give you the words that passed between our Captain (himself a New York pilot) and the pilot. In answer to the first question the Captain said "No!" "Have you any pork?" The Captain told the steward to get some of each kind and give it to the boats. "Could you spare some tea and coffee? We have been out on this trip three weeks last Tuesday" Here the Captain filled away and the boat had to leave. The pilot told me that he spoke and boarded every vessel he met and asked the same questions. He told me that he supplied a ship last Wednesday with 200 lbs of beef and port, besides other things for which they received £3 sterling. They are without any exception the damnedest beggars I ever fell in with".

Modern Administration

During the early part of the 19th century British vessel entering and leaving the Tyne enjoyed preferential rates of pilotage. The advantage over foreign vessels was ended by the 1824 Act that gave equal treatment to foreign vessel wherever their governments gave similar treatment to British vessels. To compensate the Tyne pilots for the loss they would have sustained they were to be paid, by the Treasury, Reciprocity Money, viz. the difference between the

Liverpool pilot swings aboard. (Image © The Liverpool Pilots' Association)

old and the new tariffs for foreign vessels. Newcastle Trinity House claimed the full difference for all vessels entering the Tyne although many never went above the entrance, but the pilots were paid only on the ships they piloted. The unclaimed pilotage was then allocated to the Superannuation Fund, although the pilots disputed the right of Newcastle Trinity House to retain the money and demanded a full distribution of the amounts involved. Newcastle Trinity House refused and was unwilling or unable to account for the money. The pilots later proposed that Trinity House use the funds for building cottages for retired pilots. The Elder Brethren agreed but nothing came of it. Another suggestion was that Trinity House should assist in providing a steamer for pilots in weather unsuitable for their cobles. This was also refused, and in 1852 the pilots themselves bought a steam vessel for their own use, probably the world's first steam pilot vessel.

In 1861 the Treasury discontinued Reciprocity Money, but as compensation the pilots were to receive for a ten-year period, a sum equal to the Reciprocity Money paid in 1861. Every year £6,400 was handed over to Trinity House at Newcastle but only £3,200 was given to the pilots. The latter commenced legal proceedings against the Elder Brethren who in turn sent for the pilots' leaders and ordered then to bring their Branches with them. Two pilots refused to attend and were threatened with dismissal. Trinity House began to examine and license local fishermen.

The two senior pilots, John Hutchinson and Robert Blair, went to London to put their case to the Board of Trade and eventually before Parliament. In 1863 an order by Parliament forced Trinity House to publish the accounts that showed a balance of more than £20,000, although further unclaimed pilotage of over £3,207 was not shown in the accounts. The pilots successfully petitioned Parliament for the establishment of another pilotage board. A long legal battle with Trinity House at Newcastle ensued from which the pilots emerged victorious and a new body, the Tyne Pilotage Commissioners, was formed in 1865. It was finally proved that Trinity House had withheld over £24,000 from the pilot whose average wage was about £180 per annum, The Elder Brethren claimed £3,500 for expenses incurred in opposing the Parliamentary Bills and other legal proceedings. The final amount distributed to the pilots was £15,000 after making provision for pensions for Trinity House officials.

Of the pilots, Hutchinson and Blair were to become founder members of the U.K.P.A. almost twenty years later.

Pilots in the smaller ports were only partly organised; licenses were issued but no rota schemes and no recognised tariffs of fee collections were arranged. In the Wash for instance, pilots for Kings Lynn and Boston were licensed by Trinity House of Hull and occasionally they piloted vessel into the Humber estuary much to the chagrin of the Humber pilots.

There is a record of one unnamed Wash pilot who was active for at least 42 years. He went to sea aged 10 in 1823, obtained a license in his early 20's, retired at 56 but apparently thought better of it and continued for a further 18 years. When he died aged 87 in 1910, he left behind a notebook much as any pilot has kept from the time when pilots first could write. It shows that much of his work came from German and Danish vessels bringing timber from the Baltic, although he had regular trips with other vessels, often barques, brigs and snows from Papenburg (on the River Ems above Emden). One entry seems to make a note of an exceptionally large vessel April 28, 1873, *Bergen* of Bergen, Capt. Christiansen, 925 tons, length 249 ft. He owned his own cutters. *Julianna*, launched in 1854, had a mast 46ft long, main book 38ft, bowsprit 32 ft and gaff 26 ft.

The first entry in the book reads: 11th April 1837, *Ocean*, from Blankenese (on the Elbe near Hamburg) Capt. Hagen for Lynn. The last entry was *Gefle* of Gefle, Capt Waxin, Sutton Bridge to sea. By 1869 he had piloted 958 ships in and out of the Wash Deeps. He made the odd navigational note: 'If bound to Bruncaster with a neap tide low water you can bring the north part of the schold head to bear SWxS. Steare that course. Will have no less than three fathoms water.'

One note among many will bring a smile to not a few pilots' faces: "There is a conveyance to Boston from Wisbech passing through Long Sutton at twelve o'clock noon". I wonder if there was a hostelry nearby?

There was a Parliamentary Inquiry into pilotage in 1835, possibly the first to open up the subject in any depth. Its report covered all the major ports around the British coasts and the findings were that to make pilotage entirely optional would "hold out a boon to the foolhardy", and recommended that certain exceptions to compulsory pilotage be made for vessel in the short sea trades. The Commissioners further stated that the evidence before them demonstrated the need for a central body to control the acts of local authorities and proposed that Trinity House fill that need. No action was taken on the report. About this time the pilots of the east coast ports were badly hit by Parliamentary legislation giving preferential taxes to the Canadian trades. Timber from the Baltic abruptly dropped to the minimum. Pilots of the west coasts ports such as Liverpool and Bristol found their incomes rising: an example of the wild swings and variations of incomes due to political decisions.

A further Act in 1840 covered many aspects of pilotage and continued exemptions from compulsory pilotage to non-British vessels flying the flags of countries having so-called reciprocal treaties with Britain. Several decades later the Board of Trade was to use this provision against British pilots even to the extent of allowing complete falsehoods to be used about exemptions for British-flag vessels in continental ports.

Following the Merchant Navy Act of 1849 the Merchant Navy List of 1850 (dated to 20th December 1849), a Government publishing, listed every licensed pilot port by port, in the British Isles, including the Orkneys. Exceptions were those of Bristol and Liverpool where the masters of the (Bristol) Skiffs and the (Liverpool) cutters are listed but the pilots working from the craft remain unlisted. The comprehensive list of pilots was discontinued in following Merchant Navy Lists. In the book 107 ports are listed although small ports were included under major ports. Newcastle Trinity House issued 620 licences, more than half were for outports and coastal licences. At least 2,500 pilots are listed.

Before mid-century the administration of the Cinque Ports came under the magnifying lens of progress. A schooner of about 75 tons, found difficulty in taking a pilot on board in strong winds off the North Foreland, and sailed on to Gravesend. On arrival the master consulted with his agent and ordered that the pilotage fee be sent to the Cinque Ports office in Dover. Two days later the ship sailed for a northeast coast port, but in the meantime the Warden at Margate had asked the solicitor at Dover to send off a warrant for the arrest of the ship. The warrant followed the ship and was served at Hartlepool some ten days later and the ship detained there for two weeks, causing considerable and unnecessary distress to the master/owner.

Such situations led to complaints against the Dover organisation: the Court of Loadmanage was not moving with the times. There was little need for ships to shelter in the Downs waiting for a favourable wind; steam tugs were able to tow the sailing vessels to open waters and many in the shipping industry raised the cry that pilotage need not be so costly.

In 1853 an Act of Parliament dissolved the Court of Lodemanage as such; it became a Trinity House outport. One of the conditions was that the pilots could retain their licenses which were issued for the district from Dungeness to London Bridge and vice-versa. It was this condition that was to prove so disastrous for the Cinque Port pilots some 30 years later.

1862 *Kent newspaper report*:

Serious & Fatal Accident to the Deal Pilot Cutter

The *Princess* (No.3) Pilot Cutter left the Downs for her station at 7.30 on Wednesday evening last with a crew of 8 persons, consisting of the master, mate, cook, steward and four seaman; also 14 Deal Pilots viz., Messrs. John Potts, Thomas Birch, John Arnold, William Mackie, Daniel Goldsack, Joseph Hartley, Henry Millen, Robert Finnis,

George Moon, Henry Petty, James Gosley, A. Burton, John Pembroke and Frederick Warner.

Shortly after midnight, a strong wind with rain prevailed, and as they were in the act of reefing the sails, or had done so, they saw a ship approaching them. The cutter burnt the usual flare-ups, and the masthead light was also clearly visible. The ship, however, failed to notice these signals, when the order was given to shift the cutter's helm and get her before the wind; but before this order could be carried out into execution, it became evident to those on deck that the ship must strike them. The master then gave the alarm to

Sailing cutter off Dover. (Image © Cinque Ports/ Trinity House)

the pilots below, who had all turned in, and implored them to prepare for the catastrophe which afterwards befell them; but before anyone could reach the deck, the ship struck the cutter violently on the port bow, hooking some part of her on the fluke of the ship's bower anchor, which dragged the cutter through the water with velocity, carrying away masts, bow-sprit, in fact everything above deck. At the moment of the collision tremendous efforts were made by the pilots to spring on board the ship. Many succeeded in gaining the deck of the ship. Mr John Pembroke had succeeded in laying hold of some part of the ship, but before he could haul himself up a heavy sea struck the cutter and jammed him between that and the side of the ship, by which he was, no doubt, instantly killed.

The ship proved to be the *Stirlingshire*, from Trinidad, West Indies, she was afterwards took charge of by one of the pilots, Mr. John Potts.

There had always been a base for pilots at Gravesend, but it was not until the Merchant Shipping Act of 1854 that it was established by law, and the river pilots were given the opportunity of applying for a license for the Gravesend outward pilotage. When the "Choice" pilotage was permitted by Trinity House a couple of years later, the river pilots with the licenses now 'vice-versa' and having direct access to shipowners and agents, were able to collect almost all the "appropriations". They arranged to meet the vessels down Channel at Falmouth, Plymouth, Brixham, or off the Isle of Wight and sailed past the Dungeness and Dover cutters leaving the Cinque Ports pilots without work. The earnings of the latter were reduced by up to two thirds. At the 1888 Inquiry into pilotage, it was stated that there was bribery and corruption and that a few pilots had obtained more "choice" work than they could handle and farmed it out making considerable income in additions to their ordinary fees. Trinity House seemed to meet the situation with complete inaction.

The Merchant Shipping Act of 1854 collected all the pilotage laws then in force and re-enacted them into part V. In 1860 shipowners still affected by the freedom from liability of compulsory piloted vessels, again attacked the principle of compulsory pilotage at the meeting of the Parliamentary Select Committee into Shipping. The Committee recommended its abolition but Parliament took no action. In 1870 there were yet again attempts to abolish compulsory Pilotage: the Parliamentary Select Committee into Pilotage was established with terms of reference that were much the same as the previous committees. But this was the most comprehensive Inquiry ever. The minutes of evidence covered more than over 500 pages of close print on a 13"x 9" (35cm x 28cm) page and there were nearly 200 more pages for the appendix which contained much of the written evidence.

The witnesses were called from all sections of the shipping industry, port authorities and government departments. The Deputy Master of Trinity House, Charles McIver, managing director of the Cunard Line, and his commodore master, C.H.E. Judkins were called and gave evidence of the need for compulsory pilotage. Capt. W. Ballantine, senior master of the Allen Line (later the Canadian Pacific Steamship Co.) also asserted that pilotage should be compulsory. There was hardly a major port or trade which did not come into the proceedings, and the minutes of evidence provide a superb statement of pilotage and the vagaries of the pilotage systems for the 30 years 1855 to 1885. Through the Inquiry, many pilots gained an insight into the work of other districts and their mutual problems. It is thought that the pilots attending the sitting of the Select Committee were able to discuss the advantages of a national association of pilots, but nothing came of it at the time.

In this atmosphere a number of incidents, mostly in the Bristol Channel, occurred all unconnected and spread over a period of about ten years from 1871 to 1881. They created great unrest among pilots.

In 1880 the Liverpool pilot cutters were taken over by the Mersey Docks Board. Compensation was fairly reasonable but unevenly balanced – in 1870 there were 267 Liverpool pilots. Some pilots having substantial numbers of shares in the cutters were able to retire as early as 55 and live comfortably without other income. Others, with merely one or two shares, had to remain at work and there were many of the latter.

Towards the end of the 1850s the ports of Cardiff, Newport and Gloucester began a campaign to remove the superiority claimed by the Bristol Council in the matter of pilotage since the 16th century. Their efforts were rewarded in 1861 by the passing of an Act which gave them control over their own pilotage affairs. This had the effect of disturbing the pilotage income of the Bristol pilots and caused a number of them to move across the Bristol Channel to take licenses at Cardiff.

Tyne Pilots circa 1870. (Image © South Tyneside Archives)

Sunderland 1876

Stabbing of Sunderland's Pilot Ruler in 1876

Having been dismissed from the service for fraud i.e. claiming pilotage fees for which he had eared or was not entitled. Pilot William Davison idly swore to kill the Chairman and Secretary of the Pilotage Commission. The former, a shipowner, was away from the port ship, so Davison trailed the Secretary instead, but failed to catch him. Some time later he caught the Pilot Ruler, Fairley Downs, by chance at the pier head, and viciously stabbed him in the back without warning. Immediately turning the knife to his own breast, the would-be murderer exclaimed melodramatically and drunkenly, "Here is the heart of a man". Finishing the whisky in the bottle he smashed the bottle and slashed himself a dozen times before jumping into the river to finish it all – it was low water! He survived as did fairly Downs, but only just. Downs himself in fact on until 1911 and achieved local fame by speaking before the 1910 Parliamentary Inquiry into Pilotage. Davison died in gaol before the end of his ten-year jail sentence.

From mid-19th century the UK shipping industry was subject to severe swings in the British economy. The improvement in steam propulsion using larger vessels tended to reduce incomes and disrupt pilot working routines and rotas The larger ships reduced the number of vessels required for carrying cargoes and thereby reduced the work of the pilots. But the underlying cause of the pilots' apprehension was the clause in the 1812 Pilotage Act relating to the freedom of liability from vessels liability for vessels subject to compulsory pilotage: it was also the cause of about seven major Governmental inquiries into pilotage, and it can be said to be one of the several problems leading directly to the formation of the United Kingdom Pilots' Association.

PART TWO

PART TWO

The Origins of the United Kingdom Pilots' Association

IT WOULD BE reasonable to assume that the initiators of a national association for pilots would be found on the Thames, where pilots were more numerous, or perhaps on the Mersey, where the pilots were a more close-knit unit. In fact they emerged at Pill Creek in Somerset, a few miles down-stream from Bristol docks. It was the situation in the Bristol Channel, particularly at Bristol that brought together all the parties most likely to form a core of a national body; a series of events confronting the pilots there as a consequence of the change in the nature of maritime traffic and trade, with a growth of the South Wales ports.

In the 1870s Samuel Plimsoll, campaigning for increased safety for British ships and seamen, called together a number of interested parties: M.P.'s, shipowners and mariners. Known as the Plimsoll Committee, the secretary was Plimsoll's brother-in-law Roger Moore, a Bristol toilet-soap manufacturer. Discussion covered a wide field and many shipmasters were consulted; a load-line was one topic, the retention of compulsory pilotage another. Among the members of the Committee was Captain Bedford Pim,

QC M.P. for Gravesend, who had cut short an outstanding naval career to take up law at the age of 45 working from chambers in London, Bristol and Plymouth. As Gravesend's M.P. he came into contact with a great number of Thames pilots. No doubt he had talks with another member of the Committee, John Puleston, M.P. for Plymouth/Devonport, who had had a successful commercial career in Virginia, as a banker and as owner of a newspaper called *The Pilot*, and retained many useful associations in the American maritime sphere.

One of those consulted by Plimsoll's Committee was Captain George Cawley, an experienced shipmaster, and part owner of a steamship, who later left the sea to take a post ashore. A few months after being appointed pilots master at Cardiff, he was drawn into a serious dispute between the 84 pilots there and the port management.

A channel dredged through notorious banks, the Cefyn-y-wrack shoal, in the approaches to Cardiff docks, silted up. In March 1878 the pilot of the *Royal Minstrel*, John Howe, refused to take her to sea with a draft of 24 ft 8 inches. The dockmaster said that there was 25 ft of water over the shoal at the time. A month later, David Samuel, pilot of the *Prince Admadeo* also refused to take the ship to sea in similar circumstances. The charterer of both vessels complained that his ships had been neaped and thereby delayed three days. Both pilots were suspended. The Cardiff pilots were so infuriated that there were threats of a strike; Cawley resigned in disgust, warning the pilots against any action that would harm their cause, and advising them to contact Roger Moore with a view to gathering support from Samuel Plimsoll and his Committee.

Within a month Plimsoll had visited Cardiff, gone out with the pilots to the shoal and personally checked the sounding. A few weeks later, with John Puleston, he raised the matter in Parliament causing the Board of Trade to explain their actions. The questions posed by the Government Department embarrassed the Pilotage Board, but as no infraction of the law had occurred any further action was out of the question. Nevertheless there was enough of an outcry for a local inquiry to be set up in 1879 that established the need for new by-laws governing the composition of the Board. In spite of strong opposition a private act of Parliament was passed through Parliament in 1880 giving the pilots two seats on the board. What happened to Howe and Samuel is not recorded.

Across the water the 37 pilots at Bristol were also unhappy about the actions or inactions of their pilotage authority. With 37 apprentices and 74 Westernmen (time-served apprentices), any fall in shipping activity affected the whole village of Pill – a small community of watermen and pilots living around a creek of the River Avon about a mile from its confluence with the Severn. A change in the traditional working routine could mean a loss if income of disastrous proportions: they were now to be faced with "choice" (appropriate) pilotage.

The pilots did not work a "turn" or "rota" system; sailing in competition the first pilot to board an incoming vessel was normally given the pilots and would also have the outward pilotage. In November 1880, however, a firm of Bristol shipowners, the Great Western Shipping Company, with a very successful line across the North Atlantic, built several larger steam vessels to cope with the trade and resolved to have their own "choice" pilots to conduct them in and out of the port of Bristol. Altering the usual routines for taking on pilots, the masters were instructed to take only the pilots displaying the prearranged signal. In the meantime three pilots, Case, Ellis and Reed, were covertly selected and informed of the date and time of arrival of the ships. This arrangement meant that 34 pilots and their assistants, were deprived of a share of the income from the most lucrative vessels, without any infringement of rule or regulation.

In December the same year, one of the ('choice') pilots, Reed, on the way to sail his cutter from Pill Creek, walked into a crowd of some 50 women and boys and was tarred and feathered. Immediately after the New Year the Westernmen went on strike –

licensed pilots could not. Ellis and Case tried in vain to get boatmen at Ilfracombe, (some 30 miles down the coast) to take them to a couple of inward-bound ships. Returning to Pill they attempted to take their cutter into the river but were barred by a chain made fast to a bollard held taut across the Creek by a large number of women and boys on the other side. They were all being advised and encouraged by the owner/manager of the Waterloo Hotel, Captain Henry Langdon (who was also secretary of the Bristol Pilots' Association). The following day Ellis and Case again tried to take their craft for sea; this time they were stopped by a number of small craft, manned by Westernmen drawn across the Creek. The Haven Master of Bristol, Captain Parsons, R.N., a former commander of the R.N.R. base at Bristol, hurried down to Pill and demanded of the Westernmen as to what they were doing. The Westernmen, all naval reservists, called back, "You taught us to blockade the port"!

That night at a meeting in the Pill Parish rooms, all involved in the dispute were addressed by a solicitor, a town councillor and a couple of local dignitaries among whom was Roger Moore. In the same year, 1881, Roger Moore was elected to the Bristol City council and appointed to the Docks and Pilotage Committees. He had immediate experience of the friction between the pilots and Bristol Corporation officials.

About this time a fairly large steamer ran aground in the Avon not far from Pill; after a very short time she was re-floated without damage, but the pilot, Canby, was suspended for 12 months. Roger Moore, present at the proceedings and at a Board of Trade Inquiry in London, protested vigorously against the severity of the punishment. Canby, in fact, did not have his license returned to him for a further five years. The first twelve months of the Pilotage committee meetings gave Moore an unusually deep insight into the problems of the pilots and their negotiations with the Corporation. He was also to meet the work with Joseph Browne, a former Westernman, who was about to take up work as Collector of Pilotage dues for the pilots.

A little before the incidents at Bristol, George Cawley had returned to sea as master on the maiden voyage of *Clan Alpine,* the first ship of the then new company: Cayzer, Irvine Ltd. Although he was very popular with passengers, being known as the courteous commander, he left the sea for a second time in 1880 to set up offices as a marine consultant at 69 Queen Square, Bristol, which was to become the office of the United Kingdom Pilots' Association from 1884 to 1924.

One of Cawley's first clients was the De Bay Direct Acting Propeller Company, which fitted an experimental geared propeller to the *Cora Maria,* a working cargo vessel owned by Edward Capper (who was also charterer of the *Royal Minstrel* and *Prince Amadeo*). The De Bay system was in fact two propellers, each turning in an opposite direction, one on the main shaft and the other on a tube around the main shaft: the second to counteract of the transverse thrust of the other. Cawley even went so far as to take command of the ship for three voyages, and, in 1881, his sympathy for pilots was strengthened. After discharging cargo at the Geestemunde (Bremerhaven), the vessel made for sea. In a bitter December gale, the Bremen-bound *Cora Maria* was partially disabled by the "breaking of the gear which actuate the forward screw", her boats swept away and visibility severely reduced by snow and sleet squalls. Cawley had other difficulties for all the German light-vessels had been damaged, driven from their moorings or withdrawn; even the shore lights had been damaged. In these conditions, off the Weser, navigation was impossible. Fortunately a German pilot schooner, itself damaged, stood by for 48 hours until she could lead the *Cora Maria* to safety. Cawley never allowed himself to forget the incident.

All the circumstances likely to generate the need for a national pilots' association were now present; many potential members were in a good mood to join. In 1883 Joseph Chamberlain, President of the Board of Trade, a brilliant but erratic politician, was prevailed upon to take up a lead in promoting parliamentary action against the principle of compulsory pilotage. As much as anywhere, pilots in the Bristol Channel were at risk. The spokesman of the Swansea pilot, Captain David Tamlin, approached the Cardiff pilots who, in turn, were in touch with their counterparts across the water at Bristol.

At the suggestion of Roger Moore, Tamlin, with Edward Edwards of Cardiff, met representatives of the Bristol Pilots' Association, Craddy (chairman), Langdon and Joseph Browne at the Waterloo Hotel, Pill. Initially a Bristol Channel Pilots' Association was envisaged, but Moore prevailed upon those present to take a wider view and encompass pilots from other districts, perhaps forming a British Pilots' Association that would have more respectability and greater negotiating power at Parliamentary level. David Tamlin was especially enthusiastic and volunteered to sail his own cutter round the Irish Sea. Moore offered to make contact with other pilot services, notably through Bedford Pim at Gravesend. Plimsoll was about to retire from Parliament and introduced the pilots to John Puleston. There were favourable responses from all the major pilot districts around the British Coasts. In October 1883 a meeting of representatives from the largest ports was held at Bristol, and a decision to form a national body using the services of the Bristol Pilots' Association was confirmed. In January 1884 plans for an inaugural conference were prepared and the steering committee began looking for a leader impressive enough to keep the Association together, powerful enough to present the pilots' views at national level, yet independent enough to have an unbiased opinion of what pilot's needs were. Plimsoll was approached and refused, but suggested Captain George Cawley.

The Early Years

The Inaugural Conference was opened on 11th June 1884 in the Athenæum Hall, Bristol. Supported by a few remarks from Bedford Pim, the 30 delegates from a total of 18 UK ports were asked to approve the selection of George Cawley, Lt. R.N.R., as president. Observers from Spain and Denmark also attended. Roger Moore represented the American Pilots' Association.

Cawley then took the chair and spoke at length to the assembly, pointing out that a pilots' union had been mooted some 10 or 12 years earlier and received little support. It was the proposed Shipping Bill with clauses abolishing compulsory pilotage that was the catalyst bringing together pilots from all over the United Kingdom. The compulsory pilotage issue would be improved by a change in the new law relating to responsibility. He continued, "Today we know what has been accomplished by the pilots of Cardiff, Bristol and Swansea. The Cardiff Pilotage Board, formerly universally condemned, has been reconstituted; there are now two seats on the Board for pilots".

Henry Langdon, as Secretary, addressed those present on the aims of the United Kingdom Pilots' Association (he added "or whatever name is here decided upon"), explaining much of the work to be done. There were 3,168 pilots in the British Isles and in 1883 they piloted 168,418 vessels for an income of £427,532. The aim was to knit together all those pilots and to endeavour to operate in procuring redress of wrongs, repealing bad laws, and obtaining proper representation. It was proposed that where a member had been in a major accident with a vessel under his directions, he should be adjudged by a tribunal of which pilots were members.

The many aspects of compulsory pilotage were discussed. A pilot from Holyhead explained that in the 1840s, the Government called pilots to work there, but in 1864 a breakwater was built and the district made non-compulsory. 70 pilots were reduced to paupers, being thrown overboard with a loss of £160 per man per year. In recent years three ships have been lost with all hands when entering the port without a pilot: one of the three had avoided paying a pilotage fee of 16shillings and sixpence. E. Edwards said that Cardiff had worked fairly happily under non-compulsory regulations for more than 20 years, but recently a couple of ships had moved without pilots and their members were becoming worried.

Bedford Pim taking up a point raised by one of the Thames area pilots proposed a motion. "That this Conference of pilots wishes to condemn, in the strongest manner, the coercive conduct of Trinity House in demanding from their successful candidates, before issuing a licence, a document waiving their right to compensation in the event of the abolition of compulsory pilotage". This was passed unanimously.

There was a little discussion, but no arguments when the matter of subscriptions arose. It was decided that every member should pay 12 shillings per year. There were also different categories of membership but no indication of their subscriptions. The members agreed to set up a fund to provide annuities for aged and infirm pilots. For the first five years, one third of all subscriptions were to be set aside for the purpose. They also agreed that a voluntary death fund be formed, presumably for payments to relatives of pilots dying in service.

Towards the end of the Conference, which lasted two days, Cawley reminded the delegates, that although Chamberlain had withdrawn the section of the Shipping Bill so obnoxious to pilots, they had to be careful to maintain a watch that no further attack on compulsory pilotage should be made.

Cawley was elected President for the ensuing year, Moore vice-president, Henry Langdon, Secretary, Bedford Pim was elected legal advisor and at his suggestion, the Lord Mayor of London at the time was elected Hon. Treasurer. It is of interest to note that none of the principal officers was or ever had been a pilot.

The second Conference was held in London in 1885 with 50 delegates 20 more than attended the previous year and representing 28 ports. The new association was on firm ground and there was confidence among the members. In his opening speech Cawley reminded the Association that there was still agitation to abolish compulsory pilotage and said that the UKPA must take steps to get rid of this idea once and for all, perhaps with interactions at Parliamentary level. Bedford Pim returned from New York where he had been legal adviser and guest of honour at the inaugural conference of the American Pilots' Association (APA) in October 1884. Read a letter from the President, Captain H. Harbison, a New York pilot, expressing fraternal greetings and good wishes for the continued success of the UKPA. Pim then followed this with a speech that included a vitriolic attack on the Marine Department of the Board of Trade. This was supported by Admiral Gough M.P. The Department must have felt the bite of these attacks, as John Puleston was present with four other M.P.'s.

In his report as Secretary, Langdon gave the UKPA membership as being between 1,200 and 1,300 out of a possible 2,955 licensed pilots, explaining that many of their number were in receipt of earnings of less than £30 per annum. All the officers were re-elected with the exception of the Treasurer whose function seems to have been taken over by the Secretary. Two trustees were elected one of which one was Joseph Browne.

Not all pilots suffered from the depression of the 1880s. "Men might act both as outward and as inward pilot, taking a vessel out and then waiting on the station for an inward-bound ship and pilot her to Gravesend, or vice versa; but that system was found to be so unfavourable, especially to the cruising pilots, that in 1886 it was done away with; and now a pilot taking a vessel out, either by the North or the South Channel, is not allowed to bring one back."

It should be explained here, perhaps, how the present Thames district pilotage system works. The outward sea pilots are stationed at Gravesend, which is probably the largest pilot station in the world, the staff of river and sea pilots permanently stationed there numbering upwards of 300. The river pilots bring the vessels down from London to Gravesend, where, they hand them over to the sea pilots. These, if the vessel is bound north – that is, to the Baltic or North Sea ports – carry her by the North Channel as far as the

Sunk light, or Orfordness, on the Suffolk coast leave her, being put on shore by one of the pilot cutters that are always cruising on that station, in order to intercept ships coming from the north.

If the vessel be southward bound, she is taken away from the Thames by the South Channel, the pilot quitting her at the Downs at Dover, or at the Isle of Wight, whence he returns home by train. Formerly, there were four cutters constantly cruising between Dungeness and South Foreland, to meet the needs of the inward service, as at Orfordness; but two or three years ago they were replaced by two steamers. When a vessel comes up wanting a pilot she is supplied with one from the steamer on duty, which is kept fed with pilots by one of the old cutters, each pilot going off in rotation. Like the outward pilot, the inward pilot returns home by train.

The Chief Clerk to Trinity House, Mr. Keigwin, asked why the system by which the outward pilot could also take a vessel inward was done away with, replied:

"Well, as a matter of fact, because certain men took all the cream of the work. But I can best explain the thing by letting you into another peculiarity of the pilot system. There are among sea, as well as among river pilots, what are called 'choice' men, that is, men who are chosen by companies having a large number of vessels, such as the P and O, the Orient, and other lines, to do all their pilot work. These men have the pick of the service; they have their own regular boats, and whatever other work they can get in between in addition. Thus, one might take one of his own boats down to the Isle of Wight, Plymouth, etc., and then ship on board a vessel coming up, and so deprive one of the 'turn' men, as they are called, of a turn. Hence, in fairness to the 'turn' men, the system was done away with."

"And what will be the average income of a pilot?" he replied, "That is hard to say – they vary so considerably, As I have already said the 'choice' pilots take the pick of the work, and some of them enjoy a very handsome income. Look at this: it will show you what the pilots' incomes are better than I can tell you."

The document produced was the report of a committee of inquiry into the system above referred to, and now abolished. According to it, in take year 1886 two men employed by the P & O Company earned respectively £1,646 and £1,635. One of the two British India Company's pilots earned £1,570, and three others ('choice pilots') earned respectively £1,331, £1,159 and £1,032 less expenses. Out of the whole number of London pilots, 57 earned over £300, whilst of the Cinque Ports pilots (those plying off Dungeness) only one earned £400, the majority earning between £200 and £300. The following shows live earnings of the London pilots in a still better light: In the same year outward pilotage earnings between Gravesend and the sea, in both North and South Channels, and inward pilotage through the South Channels, amounted to about £70,217, being an average of £337 per man. Of this sum rather more than one-eighth, or £8,393, was earned by six men alone out of two hundred and sixteen.

In the same year, outward pilotage earnings between Gravesend and the sea, in both North & South Channels, and inward pilotage through the South Channels, amounted to about £70,217, being an average of £337 per pilot. Of this sum rather more than one-eighth, £8,393, was earned by six pilots alone out of 216.

Liverpool, the largest port in the U.K. after London, was the venue for the third conference. In 1886 it was in the throes of a severe depression, but its maritime system and connections were unsurpassed in efficiency if not economy. Cawley opened the Conference, not with a speech, but to announce that Bedford Pim,

21 CENTURIES OF MARINE PILOTAGE

now an Admiral, was seriously ill. He then informed members that prior to leaving for the Conference, he had learned that two Poole pilots had been suspended for six months for attending the previous

Bedford Pim plaque. (Image © Bristol Seafarers Centre)

year's conference without permission, even though their colleagues had undertaken to carry out their work in their absence. This left a bitter taste among those attending at Liverpool; obviously the penalties and the timing were intended to dampen the enthusiasm of pilots for the newly formed organisation.

Cawley's speech drew the attention of the members to the legal difficulties of pilots. A pilotage board was able to remove a pilot's licence and living without even a charge being made against him, yet the jurisdiction of a County Court was limited to £50. In another direction, Gloucester pilots had had their rates reduced without notice, a mere two weeks before the conference.

Complaints against Trinity House were raised regarding heavy penalties for trivial offences. If the pilots reduced their grievances to writing, they were suspended; if they endeavoured to ventilate their grievances in the columns of the public press, that was another unpardonable sin. Cawley and the other officers demanded a say in the management of the funds that the pilots were legally bound to contribute to pensions and welfare.

Falmouth pilot R. Andrew, explained that his service had requested an increase in their inadequate pensions, only to be told that Section 6 of the Merchant Shipping Act 1854 was not to provide pensions for pilots, but to meet Trinity House's expenses in aiding incapacitated pilots, their widow and orphans. Nevertheless by economical management the Corporation had been able to devote a sum equal to the whole contributions of the pilots in payments of pensions. The Elder Brethren pointed out that in seven years £1,875 had been paid by pilots from incomes and £1,960 used up in pensions leaving a deficit of £85. The Falmouth pilots drew attention to the Corporation's use of seven years as a statistic against which the pilots had been paying for something like 21 years.

John Puleston, M.P. sent his apologies to the conference, explaining that he was instead presenting a petition on the pilots' behalf to the President of the Board of Trade.

In the following year, 1887, at South Shields the UKPA Committee introduced two new officers, J.T. Board, solicitor, and A. Northmore Jones, barrister. The legal work was to be separate from the day-to-day work of the Association. Cawley's address carried criticism of T.H. Farrer, former permanent Secretary to the Board of Trade. He had been leading proposals for the abolition of compulsory pilotage and removal of restrictions on the issue of pilotage certificates. But the most important matter discussed was the Alien Pilotage Bill, introduced to Parliament by T. King, M.P. for Hull. It was intended to limit pilotage qualifications to UK citizens only, but in spite of support from 300 members of the House, the Bill failed. It was stated that Farrer was still influencing the Marine

Department of the Board of Trade. In the later discussions, choice pilotage on the Thames was criticised. The river pilots were said to have earned £800 to £1,400 annually, whilst those of Dover and Deal only £200 (£150 net).

David Tamlin (Swansea) proposed a special signal for pilot cutters in fog as several had been run down and sunk recently. Not everyone agreed with such a move and the matter was dropped. John Puleston spoke to the delegates and said that now the Alien Pilotage Bill had failed, the UKPA must press for a full Parliamentary Inquiry. He would introduce a deputation to the Minister responsible. In addition to Roger Moore, three additional Vice Presidents were appointed. They were Messrs Coates, (Belfast), Colquitt (Liverpool) and Pearce M.P. for Glasgow. It was agreed that the 1888 Conference would be held in Ireland in June, but as a Parliamentary Select Committee on Pilotage was about to begin work in May of the same year, the fifth Conference was delayed until October and the venue was returned to Bristol.

The principal topic at Bristol was the report of the Select Committee. As Cawley said in his opening speech, although the pilots did not get everything they hoped for, they were very successful in many aspects. Whilst they were disappointed that there was no recommendation to establish a central pilotage body, the Association still had much to do to ensure that all favourable recommendations were included in the Bill to go before the House. An important item was the provision for compensation for the superannuation of pilots retiring early where work was reduced by the action of the authorities. Referring to the situation in the Bristol Channel, Cawley pointed out that had there been general compulsory pilotage, many, of the 300 lives lost in the past ten years could have been saved.

In the ensuing debates, Bristol pilots explained that as the average age of their pilots was 54, their pension funds needed supplementing. They were in the process of promoting a

Parliamentary Bill to amend the local Act. Robert Blair said that the main problem in the Tyne was that 30 of the 161 pilots took two thirds of the gross pilotage income. Again this was due to the workings of the choice pilotage system.

The sixth Conference was held in London. The members were able to look back with some satisfaction at the development of the UKPA. It had been formed to protect the principle of compulsory pilotage, to ensure that pilots had proper representation on pilotage bodies, and to maintain a watch on the funds which pilots were expected to contribute to. During the first couple of years, the pilots, taking the best possible advice, realised that the best remedy for all their problems was to obtain a Parliamentary Bill devoted entirely to their affairs. They had petitioned the Board of Trade and followed it up with a deputation that then led to the Parliamentary Bill of 1889. The organisation had grown in stature: it was respected.

Pension Problems

At the inaugural conference a Pensions Fund had been set up specifically to provide some form of pension to pilots in those ports where there was no suitable pension scheme, the funds coming from one third of all subscriptions to the Association. By 1889 there was £900 in the fund, the income it provided had to be divided among almost 100 members; they received little more than £1 each! This left nothing in reserve and it was obvious that the fund would be in difficulties. Pensions for pilots would have to be a major feature in the objects of the Association in future.

The 1889 Pilotage Bill was about to pass through Parliament and each clause was debated with great thoroughness and enthusiasm. Alien pilotage and pilotage certificates were again points of irritation. Many pilots tried to have a clause inserted to make the towing of vessels without pilots illegal.

Thus the pattern of the work of the UKPA was set in the first five years. When the Merchant Shipping Act (Pilotage) 1889 came into force the members found that more than half of their wishes had been incorporated in its provisions. The moderate success provided a guide to their future actions. The new Act however was not without loopholes. In 1894 a Netherlands company, the Zeeland Shipping Co., successfully applied to the Hull Magistrates Court to obtain pilotage certificates for the officers of its vessels (non-UK registry). On appeal to the High Court, the Lord Chief Justice reversed the decision of the Magistrates. The Association had arranged for legal representation and paid the expenses of the appeal.

Problems in the Bristol Channel continued. Bristol pilots petitioned for a Parliamentary Bill to obtain representation on their pilotage board. The Bristol Council agreed to refrain from opposing a Bill, if the pilots agreed to a reduction in the area of the pilotage district. On the other side of the Channel, Cardiff pilots had been approached by the Barry Dock Company for assistance with a Bill to allow them to construct a dock there in 1885. When, in 1890, the docks were fully operational, the company formed its own pilotage district and appointed its own pilots. Cardiff pilots successfully prosecuted one of the latter, but there was an appeal, which although unsuccessful, brought about a later attempt to establish a separate pilotage district.

In the early 1890s Trinity House came in for strong criticism for its apathy in many respects of pilotage administration. It was said that their pilots were required to produce certificates from magistrates or clergymen that they were well affected to the "Sovereign and her Government", but a foreign subject could be handed a pilotage certificate at his will. It was also pointed out that the Corporation was well aware of the discreditable state of affairs regarding the choice pilotage situation and treated it as all other problems, with complete indifference. At Gravesend the choice pilots handled 2,810 vessels annually, all mostly deep laden, the rota pilots handled only 691 vessels, mostly in ballast.

In 1894 pilots in India from the Bombay and Bengal Marine, applied for affiliation to the Association. This was covered by making an amendment to rule No. 2, "Any person resident outside of the U.K. may be permitted to honorary membership on payment of 1 guinea: half to go to the Management Fund and the rest to the Annuity Fund".

1895–1900

1896

Orders in Council:
Thames Pilotage District. Evidence before the Select Committee

A notice distributed by the Trinity House, dated Dec 18 1888:

> "Sir, – I am directed to transmit to you herewith a print of the regulations made by this Corporation for regulating the *vice versa* system of pilotage, and approved by order of her Majesty in Council, of Feb.18 1854 slightly varied by Order in Council, dated Nov. l, 1862, In contravention of these regulations it has gradually become the practice (which has much increased of late) for London pilots, to leave their district for the purpose of taking inward pilotage work. This practice has been recently permitted (experimentally) upon a payment of a fee to the cruising pilots, but the experiment, has not resulted satisfactorily, and it appears to the Corporation desirable to discontinue the practice altogether. I am, therefore directed to acquaint you that on and after March 1 next the printed regulations above deferred to must be strictly adhered to, and in particular that no inward work is to be taken by London pilots or outward work by Cinque Port pilots, except under the circumstances and upon the terms set forth in the said regulations."

The Merchant Shipping Act of 1894 had facilities to amend sections covering pilotage in the form of Provisional Order Bills to be presented for examination by a Parliamentary Select Committee, one Bill for each pilotage district. Between 1890 and 1893 there were several such Bills; Liverpool, Humber, Newport, Bristol, Newcastle, Swansea, Clyde, all were opposed by the several organisations of their respective ports.

In 1896 A Provisional Order Bill for the Thames Districts pilotage came under the scrutiny of a Select Committee, the evidence came from a broad selection of the Shipping scene. One of the principal witnesses was Mr. James George Anderson, I am the senior partner in the firm of Anderson and Co., shipowners and ship insurers' brokers, London and joint managers with Messrs F. Green and Co. of the Orient Steam Navigation Company. I have been President of the Chamber of Shipping of the United Kingdom and chairman of the General Shipowners' Society, London, and am still a member of the General Shipowners' Society; also a member of the Committee of Lloyd's Register of British and Foreign Shipping. I have been an underwriting member of Lloyd's for the last 24 years, and I have served on two Departmental Committees of the Board of Trade. The Orient Line starts from Tilbury, and calls both inwards and outwards at Plymouth. Up to 1889 all our ships were piloted on the choice system.

Mr Walter Glynn. I am managing director of the firm of Frederick Leyland and Co. Liverpool. I own a large fleet of steamers, and trade chiefly from Liverpool, and am a member of the Mersey Docks and Harbour Board. I have been chairman of the pilotage committee, the present composition of which is eight shipowners or merchants, members of the Dock Board, two shipmasters, and three pilots.

Admiral Francis McClintock appeared as Chairman of Trinity House Pilotage Committee. And stated that he had been a member of the Pilotage Committee for four years and had no experience of commercial shipping.

Groups also represented were the 'Exempt' Pilots Association, Chamber of Shipping, a group of 70 compulsory river pilots and transport pilots of Dover. A general group of 244 pilots sent in a paper.

In the course of the proceedings concerns about Trinity House powers and the need for shipowners and pilots to be represented were voiced. Not all the pilots wanted representation on the Trinity House Pilotage Committee. The various ship owners were by no means in agreement as to how they wanted to Trinity House to act. The groups all appear to want to criticise the Elder Brethren of Trinity House, but were unable to agree what they wanted.

Mr. Anderson had specific complaints related to their choice pilots and the change in the system. Until 1889 the choice pilots had a vice-versa clause inserted in their licenses to pilot ships both ways. But the clause was withdrawn after being in operation for 35 years. He wanted his choice pilots to have the facility to pilot ships to Plymouth and whenever possible bring the next inward ship from Plymouth to the Thames. Mr. Anderson admitted that sometimes the outward pilotage was up to 36 hours. Under the new system the outward pilot had to return to London by train. He quoted the cost of pilotage in 1890 inward as £532,14s. 6d. and outwards, £570. A total of £1,102, 15s. 6d. In comparison he gave the Liverpool Pilotage paid as £279,9s. inward and £133,10s. outward i.e. total £412,19. In 1895 the Liverpool pilotage cost £1,784,18s. including the cutter money, one pilot received £275 and the other £780. And they have pilotage income from other ships. The £780 represented 32 turns.

Two choice pilots Messrs Rigden and Fostgate (Orient Line) choice pilots also pilot many other vessels when not required by the Line. But nobody else is employed if it can be helped? They are left quite free to attend to their own interests when not required by the Orient Line. There are no others payments.

A petition was read signed by 244 pilots in opposition to the Provisional Order, and which included the following:

> "We, the undersigned, beg most respectfully to submit that it was only intended to give such representation at certain outports where difficulties existed representation, and that it is not expedient that shipowners should have representation on the Pilotage Authority for the London district for the following persons:
>
> (1) That shipowners who employ pilots are not interested in test examination of masters and mates, and that no complaint has been made by them of such examinations.
> (2) That they did not subscribe to the funds provided by the pilots for themselves and families.
> (3) That the pilots are satisfied with the management of such funds by the existing authority, and are also satisfied with the examinations as now carried on.
> (4) That the shipowners representatives would not be competent to take part in the examination of either masters mates, or pilots, neither would they be interested in maintaining the funds referred to.
> (5) That the pilots are also of opinion that from the peculiarities of the London pilotage service, where a large proportion of the pilots do not contribute to nor receive any benefit front the fund, it would be manifestly unfair and contrary to the intention of the committee and the Pilotage Act of 1889 to place upon the authority representatives of either pilots or shipowners whose interests might be inimical to the preservation of the fund which the legislation referred to sought to protect.

(6) That the expense attending upon such elections would be a wasteful expenditure of the fund, that is already burdened to its fullest extent, in order to gratify, the desire of a limited few shipowners who have adduce no reasons valid, or otherwise, for their own representation, nor been desired by the pilots to interfere in matters which the undersigned submit concerns themselves only.

(7) That should pilots be elected it would be impossible for them to serve without considerable loss and expense in attending meetings while as a rule retired pilots would from age other causes be unable to serve.

There is no reference to the UKPA in any of the above reports.

In 1894 an Order in Council ordered that masters and mates with exemption certificates were required to contribute to the local pilotage funds as follows:

Ports at which contributions to Pilotage Funds by Masters and Mates have been sanctioned by Order in Council.

Ports	Date of Order	Fees for Certificates & Renewals	Contributions under Sec:582 P(9) of Merchant Shipping Act. 1894.
Cardiff	30 July 1890	£1.1.0 Renewal £1.1.0.	Sum not exceeding 5% of Pilotage
Bristol	30 July 1891	£2.12.0. Renewal £1.1.0.	5% Pilotage saved
Tyne	6 Feb 1892	Issue £2 Renewal 10/-	Sum not exceeding 5% of pilotage saved
Dublin	28 Jul 1893	Issue £3 Renewal £2	£1 not to exceed 5% of Pilotage saved

Ports	Date of Order	Fees for Certificates & Renewals	Contributions under Sec:582 P(9) of Merchant Shipping Act. 1894.
Cork	29 Jan 1894	Issue £6 Renewal £1	£1 (Masters only) not to exceed 5% of pilotage saved
Liverpool	28 Jun 1895	Issue £6.6.0. Renewal £3.3.0.	17 feet & upwards £3.3.0. Under 17 feet £2.2.0. not to exceed 5% of pilotage saved.
Newport (Mon)	3 Oct 1895	Issue £2.2.0. Renewal £1.1.0.	Sum not exceeding 5% of Pilotage saved
Belfast	15 May 1896	Issue £2 Renewal £2	5% of pilotage saved
Thames	26 Oct 1896	Issue £2 Renewal £1	Sum not exceeding 5% Pilotage saved

About the above Order in Council quite a few complaints arose, an example below

The LONDON DIRECT SHORT SEA TRADERS' ASSOCIATION

104 Leadenhall Street, E.C.
February 18th 1898.

Norman Hill esq.
Liverpool Steamship-owners Association

Dear Sir,
Pilotage Dues

As you are aware, vessels employed in the Home Trade and regular coasting Trade are exempt from compulsory pilotage unless they are carrying passengers, when the Masters or Mate, under B.C. 604 of the Merchant Shipping Act 1894, must either have a pilotage, certificate or a certificate issued by the Board of Trade, or employ a Pilot.

Under Sec. 699 of the Merchant Shipping Act 1894 the master or mote of any ship may apply for a pilot's certificate to the pilotage authority and if the pilotage authority refuses to issue it, he can, under sec.600 appeal to the Board of Trade against their decision and then obtain from the, a pilotage certificate.

The Home Trade Pilotage exemption is derived, as you know, from 6 Geo. 4 Chap. 125 and that exemption is continued under Sec. 003 of the Merchant Shipping Act 1894.

Under Sec. 7 of the Merchant Shipping Act (Pilotage) 1889 provision was made that in addition to the bye-law powers of a pilotage authority defined by the Merchant Shipping Act 1854, a Pilotage authority might, subject to the approval and confirmation of the Board of Trade, pass a bye-law requiring masters and mates who hold pilotage certificates, granted under that part of the Act, (which means granted under Sec. 999 or 600 of the Merchant Shipping Act 1894.) "to contribute to the pilotage fund of the "district an amount which should not exceed the proportion of the piloted dues which would have been payable in respect of his ship if he had not hold a pilotage certificate."

The certificates referred to under sec. 604 have hitherto not been applied for, Shipowners not realising the Risks attaching to the other certificates and it has been found more convenient to apply to the Local authority, but since the Act of 1889 was passed – and I – should add that sec. 7 has been embodied in sec. 582 of the Merchant Shipping Act 1894 para. 9 – several pilotage authorities, a list of which is annexed hereto, have applied to the Board of Trade for a bye-law requiring masters and mate, to contribute and, as is explained by the Board of Trade, these bye-laws have in the absence of opposition, been passed and contributions, are now demanded from the masters and mates in question.

Had the certificates been taken out under sec. 604 it is admitted – and a strong opinion from Sir Walter Phillimore has been obtained confirming this view of the law – that none of the contributions could have been enforced. The Pilotage authority of Cork Harbour is now applying for bye-law powers in the sense above indicated and the effect of that will be that the only shipowners to bear the contribution will be Home Trade shipowners. It is felt the time has arrived, when the legal status of the parties having been clearly ascertained, Shipowners must insist upon their rights and demand either exemption from the bye-law, if it is passed, or insist upon the Board of Trade issuing the Certificates which in effect will exempt them.

A second conference at the Board of Trade was held on the 16th inst. when the Harbour authorities assisted by a large number of members of Parliament attended before Sir Courtenay Boyle, and the Chairman and Secretary of the Cork Steam Packet Co. also attended on behalf of the Co. and Mr. Cattarns professionally represented the Clyde Co. and this Association.

The matter was very fully discussed and Sir Courtenay Boyle urged a compromise and at the same time said that he would find considerable difficulty in resisting a demand on the part of the Home Trade Owners that the Board of Trade in question should be issued to them, up to the present time no such certificates had been issued for the reason that no such certificates had been seriously applied for hitherto.

In the above circumstances my Committee feel that the rights privileges and interests of a large body of shipowners are in peril and they have thought it wise to lay the facts thus fully before your important Association in order that we should take united action and have the benefit of your advice and assistance. In the circumstances my Committee feel the proper course is to firmly resist any attempt on the part of a Pilotage authority to impose these additional charges upon shipowners and they think also that the rights attaching to the Home and Coasting Trades so dearly defined in the secs. above referred to should be jealously conserved. Looking at the very important principle at stake my Committee hope that your Association will render them such assistance in the matter as they may think most appropriate to the occasion. The two Companies concerned have hitherto borne all the expense. Mr. Cattarns has advised the Cork Co. to at once apply to the Board of Trade for a certificate under sec. 604, for an English Port. If this demand is refused it may be necessary to incur expense.

Sir Walter Phillimore and Mr. Scrutton have been consulted and both agree that the shipowners position is a strong one and Mr. Cattarns does not think the Board of Trade will seriously contest the point.

Steam Cutter circa 1903. (Image © Trinity House/Cinque Ports)

I remain,
Yours very faithfully,
(Signed) G.T.Smith.
Secy.

1901–1941

The following letter explains the complication and bewilderment among those who used the services of pilots; it also shows that the Trinity House Elder Brethren were confused as to the need to improved administration at the turn of the century.

THAMES PILOTAGE

TO THE EDITOR.
Lloyds List
SIR, – As I am connected with others in the Insurance of shipping of different nationalities, I wish to bring before the shipping community, and all interested therein, the utter absurdity of the recent alterations which the so-called Elder Brethren of the Trinity, House have made in the River Thames pilotage. When pilots pass their examinations they are granted a licence for 14 feet draught of water for a term of three years. After serving that time they are allowed to pass an examination again, and, if found qualified, are granted a full-draughted licence. Some of the sea pilots possess these licences for the North and South Channels and for the Isle of Wight, others have them for North and South Channels only, and others have full-draughted licences for South Channel and for 14 feet North Channel only. The new rules and regulations that have been brought into force within the last two months have practically deprived a 14-foot pilot of his livelihood. Owners. masters and agents have had the

privilege from time immemorial of employing their own pilots and signing a demand order for the same, which the pilots took to the Trinity House, where they paid a deposit of 10s. which was returnable within three months, and no draught of water specified. Now, according to the new rules, it is only the owner or his agent (no captain) who must sign the demand order and specify the draught of water. If under 12 feet the Trinity House will refuse to stamp or accept the order, for which the river pilot has now to pay 6d, instead of the 2s. 6d. he paid before. The sea pilot now pays 1s, instead of 10s, as formerly. These fees are not returnable to the pilots, and the Trinity House, as a result, are in hopes of making £500 a year. Just imagine the mercenary spirit of a body that styles itself the Honourable Corporation of the Trinity House! When you ask them what becomes of the 2s. 6d and 10s, that the pilots occasionally lost, they tell you it goes to that elastic fund known as the Pilot Fund, from which the pilot receives £1 per year for each year's service when he cannot work any longer. Now, here is a case in point showing the utter inability of these so-called Elder Brethren to deal with the Thames pilotage. On Oct. 1, this year, the steamship *Eidsiva*, 676 register, of Bergen, left London, drawing 10 feet 6 inches of water. She got to Gravesend, bound down the North Channel, and was supplied by the Trinity House with an unlicensed pilot for the Swin, or North Channel. Now what would have been the result if this ship had gone ashore and became a total wreck? The captain had not been in the Thames for the last six years. The result would have been his instant dismissal, and the insurance companies, after a lot of litigation, would have had to pay the insurance. Further comment on this matter is unnecessary.

Yours &.,

MARINE INSURANCE AGENT.

London, Nov. 10, 1903.

If previous reports of membership strengths are to be believed this was a time of falling membership and low attendances at conferences. If the venue was away from a major port or railway route, numbers at the conference dropped: Dover (1896), Deal (1904) and Harwich (1910) were poorly attended. The UKPA membership had fallen to between 650 at the time contrasting with claims ten years earlier when the numbers were said to be 1,200. The total number of pilots given in the annual returns of the Board of Trade was about 2,300: many of these were part-time pilots at very small ports.

Complaints against aliens obtaining pilotage certificates was a very strong card in the hands of the Association. The Foreign Office insisted that there were treaty arrangements between countries that made such arrangements inevitable; but whereas foreign masters could pilot their own vessels at each end of the voyage; British masters could not. In 1902 B.J. Foster (Hull) rose at the Plymouth Conference to announce that the holder of a pilotage certificate for the Humber was a commissioned officer in the German Navy who boasted that he would get promotion because of that qualification (during 1908 in fact there were at least 1,000 German masters in the British Mercantile Marine). The following year a proposition was passed that the Association should promote a bill abolishing pilotage certificates held by pilots other than British subjects. It was stated that alien pilotage had increased 200% under the 1889 Pilotage Act and that all members of the 1888 Select Committee on Pilotage who were not against alien pilotage, "had now seen the damage done and were entirely against the principle".

In Kings Lynn, at the instigation of foreign merchants, the local agents applied for certificates to be granted to foreign masters trading regularly to that port. After proceeding in the magistrate's courts such certificates were issued, but the pilots then complained that, after a time, the company had had the names of chartered vessels also entered on the certificates and asked the Association for assistance.

Legal matters concerning pilots were being handled by the Association's barrister and as the quirks of legal decisions arose, the cases were becoming ever more complex, In 1902 a Clyde pilot had to pay £1,071 damages even though the had not been found in any way negligent or to blame for an accident. The gist of the matter was that the ship owners had gone bankrupt and the costs had been set against the pilots! For many decades the pilots had assumed that the signing of the bond for £100 gave them protection from liability for damages: it was then found that for an unknown reason, this condition applied only to Trinity House pilots. In 1908 another Clyde pilot, J. McKinley, was accused of navigating a vessel in a dangerous manner. He was pilot of a steamer *Maracas* which was inward-bound for Glasgow and around the Cumbraes met H.M.S. *Harrier* outward-bound. The visibility was about 1½ miles and there was no collision, but the commander of the naval vessel made a complaint about the navigation of the merchant vessel.

Neither McKinley nor his legal advisors were worried about the outcome of the proceedings, however in court they were faced with mere written evidence from the *Harrier*'s commander – as the vessel was overseas he could not be cross-examined. The Sheriff, trying the case without assessors, said that it was a very clear case. As far as he could see is was not due to anything at the *Maracas* had done that averted a collision. His Lordship stated, "I should say that the risk having been placed there by the *Maracas*, it was only averted by the prompt action of those in charge of the *Harrier* who succeeded in preventing what might have been a very serious disaster". He found the case proved and fined McKinley £25 with £10 costs.

The incensed delegates to the Gravesend Conference six months later were unanimous in a demand for an appeal to a higher court at the expense of the Association. The appeal was dismissed, so the Association petitioned the King who passed it to his Scottish Secretary who merely passed it to the same High Court, not surprisingly with the same result. Cawley, at the London Conference 1909 said that he would try to appeal to His Majesty in person.

At Barrow in another case in 1902, a local official suspended a pilot for a very dubious infringement of the rules. The pilots took the matter to the County Court and proved that the official had no powers to suspend anyone. The official turned to Trinity House Pilotage authority, which, without further inquiry, agreed to suspend the pilot. The case was again taken to the High court and the Trinity House's action declared illegal. The problems are magnified when it is seen that the pilot was required to pay part of the court costs and his own expenses amounting to some £100. Cawley, in his speech of 1909, put the question: "Is it fair that when a pilot appeals against a decision against him, he is faced in the appeal court with a judge sitting with an assessor who is a member of the same body that has already adjudicated on the affair?".

In 1904 the Cunard Line had three choice pilots. They were to meet the liners in Liverpool Bay and conduct them into the Mersey for docking but after a sort stop at the Landing Stage to disembark passengers. But this was further extended to have the pilots take several ships to the cattle lairage stages on the Wirral side of the Mersey. There were two stages, Wallasey where most of the sheep were discharged and the Birkenhead stage where the cattle unloaded. The pilots then began to charge additional fees for the extra mooring and unmooring. The annoyed Cunard managers went to court to have the fees declared illegal. They lost!

Yet again on the Mersey in 1908, a pilot anchored his vessel in fog and remained at anchor until it had cleared. At the same time another vessel proceeded up the river and docked on the same tide. The owners of the first vessel complained that their ship had been delayed. After some discussion the Pilotage Committee suspended the pilot for twelve months. However the Mersey Docks Board overruled the decision and ordered the pilot to be dismissed from the service without considering the reasons for the Committee's decision and without hearing the pilot's point of view. To some extent the Liverpool Pilots' Association had brought embarrassment on themselves, for in 1889 they agreed to a certain level of representation on the Pilotage Committee without waiting for the Pilotage Act of 1889, which they believed would not pass through Parliament.

Cawley and Langdon each drew attention to the depletion of the Management Fund in providing legal advice in the many and widespread court proceedings against pilots and in obtaining assistance in Parliamentary matters.

In 1904 there was a serious stranding on the Australian coast. A P&O passenger steamship *Australia* making for Melbourne, stranded in the approach channel to Port Phillip, becoming a total loss although all passengers and most of the cargo saved. The weather was good and the coast line and navigation marks easily seen. It transpired that the pilot was affected by Bright's disease and his eyesight severely defective. This incident was widely reported in British administrations and the authorities brought in regulations requiring stricter sight-tests.

When it was obvious, in 1908, that all the members of the 1888 Select Committee were willing to assist the Association, Sir John Puleston arranged for a deputation from the UKPA to meet the president of the Board of Trade (Winston Churchill). Led by Commander Cawley and Michael Joyce M.P. (Limerick pilot), the Association Officers were introduced to Churchill and members of his staff. Churchill listened carefully to all the arguments placed before him. Given his ideas at the time (he was campaigning for the formation of MI5 to act against enemy agents), alien pilotage was a strong point in the Association's favour, as also were the court proceedings against McKinley. The success of the deputation was marked by Churchill signing the order for a Departmental Committee on Pilotage to begin work in 1909.

In 1909 the Cunard Company decided to provide a service embarking or disembarking passengers at Fishguard, the South

Wales terminal of the Great Western Railway, thus saving passengers from London the usual rail travel to and from Liverpool. They enquired from the Railway Company as to the port charges and at the same time the Railway Co,'s manager confirmed that there was no compulsory pilotage. The Cunard managers were advised that the Booth Line had been calling at Fishguard for over 16 months and no Trinity House pilot had tendered his services. The Cunard Marine Superintendent checked that there was no problem with the navigation of the port that rendered it either expedient or necessary to use the services of local pilots. The first ship to call at Fishguard was the *Mauritania,* at the end of August 1909 and for the following eight months a Cunard Liner called at the port every two weeks unless prevented by heavy weather. The procedure on each call was the same: the vessel was met in the bay off the entrance to the port by steam tenders to which the passengers and mails were transferred. The transfer time varied from 12 minutes to two hours according to the number of passengers and mails disembarked, but seldom more than one hour elapses between the time the vessel enters and leaves the bay.

At the beginning of September a Mr. James Thomas handed a letter to the master of the *Caronia* claiming that the port was within a compulsory pilotage district. The Railway Co. then explained that they knew nothing of this when first approached by Cunard. But that they were not aware that the appointment of a pilot by Trinity House would make pilotage compulsory in the port. It further appeared that a Mr. James Thomas, who had previously been in the employment of the Railway Company as a berthing master, had been appointed by Trinity House as a pilot for the district. It further transpired that Trinity House alleged that Fishguard was within the limit of the Out Port district of Milford Haven and that pilotage was and always had been compulsory on all vessels navigating within that district, Trinity House apparently admitted they had taken no steps towards providing pilots until Cunard vessels began to make use of the port. The Cunard directors

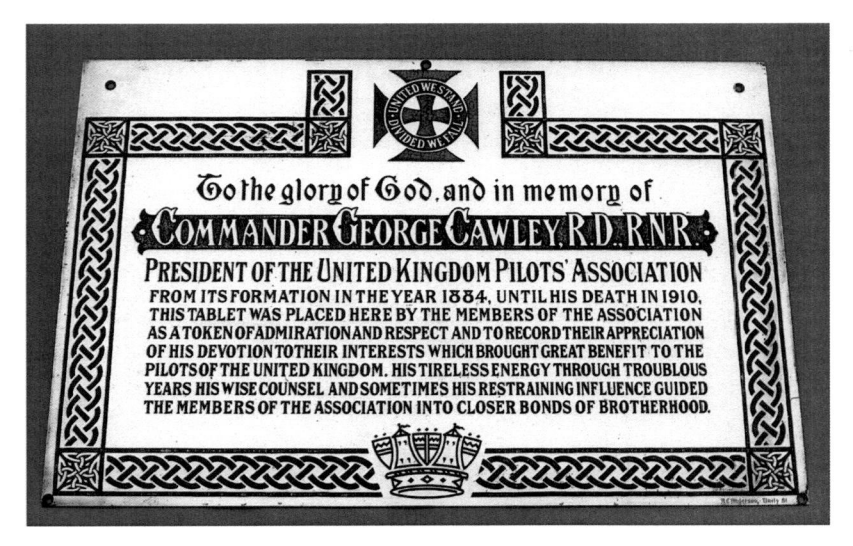

George Cawley, 1st President. (Image © Bristol Seafarers Centre)

left Trinity House to establish in law, if it was able, its power to compel the employment of its pilots.

This era was a time for changes in the officers of the UKPA. Sir John Pulestone was appointed Constable of Carnarvon Castle in 1892 and knighted at the same time; at his invitation the 1898 Conference was held in the Castle grounds. He died in 1908 and his valuable services were lost. It was fortunate that a fairly new member of the Association and also of the Executive Committee was available in the person of Michael Joyce, M.P. for Limerick (and ex-mayor of that town). He had been a pilot since 1878 and an M.P. for eight years. George Cawley, Commander R.N.R. (one of only two who were the first to be appointed to that rank up to that time) died in 1910, having just completed writing his annual conference address. Michael Joyce succeeded him as President.

The Counsel to the Association also died in 1908, and was succeeded by a Bristol solicitor, Sandford D. Cole. Cole was a very competent person, but did not always appreciate the 'inner spirit' of pilots that allowed them to form a united front. After Cawley's death he introduced a note of discord, tendering his resignation saying, "Commander Cawley had always maintained that no serving pilot (or even an ex-pilot) should become President of the UKPA". In justifying himself to the Executive committee he said to Michael Joyce, "You are an Irish Nationalist". This was repeated in open conference to cries of "shame". The matter must have been resolved fairly amicably for Cole was still Solicitor to the Association in 1913 when he resigned on becoming one of the Commissioners of Pilotage appointed under the provisions of the Pilotage Act 1913. Michael Joyce had entered Parliament in 1900 and was a member of the Marine Advisory Committee to the Board of Trade. In this capacity he was able to influence the composition of the Departmental Committee, of which one member was Sandford D.Cole.

The Departmental Committee was appointed to "Inquire and Report as to the Present State of the Law and its Administration with respect to Pilotage in the UK and as to what changes, if any are desirable". That was the title. There were 25 sittings from 15th November 1909 to 26th April 1910. For the first time in pilotage, organisation questionnaires were distributed to Pilotage Authorities, Pilotage Associations and Port authorities. Written evidence was requested from bodies outside the above organisations, providing a mass of paperwork. At the same time, wherever a pilotage district was in difficulties or where there were outstanding problems, witnesses were called before the Committee. In this respect Joyce gave evidence as to the state of pilotage on the Shannon and in the approaches. He was also able to bring in the subject of the Clyde pilot, McKinley, which, whilst the pilot was adversely affected, was a case entirely advantageous to pilots. From the work of the Committee arose the Pilotage act 1913, which encompassed much of what the pilots required: freedom from illegal pilotage; a restriction on the issue of pilotage certificates; better regulation of the rules generally and mandatory representation on Pilotage Committees.

Letter to the Secretary, Departmental Committee on Pilotage, Board of Trade, 1910

In the Tees Pilotage District in heavy weather the use of the small sailing boats is supplied by one steam tug, and when the tug is use a system of turns in rotation is adopted to regulate the working of the pilots on duty. There are certain pilots who are licensed for Hartlepool as well as the Tees. These are known as Hartlepool-Tees pilots. The Tees bylaws provide that the rules as to turns are not to prevent Hartlepool-Tees pilots from boarding ships when the Tees pilots cannot get off. In the case in question a Hartlepool-Tees pilot who happened to be out in his own boat boarded a ship in response to a signal and piloted the ship, but the payment was awarded by the pilot master to another pilot who was first on turn in the tug which had gone out. The Tees Pilot Commissioners upheld this decision, and the Hartlepool-Tees pilot was thus deprived of remuneration for the work he actually did, though it did not appear that he broke any regulation, nor was it clear on what ground the decision rested.

This Association would be pleased to furnish any details that might be desired in relation to the case, and begs to submit that the occurrence seems to afford evidence of need for improvement of some kind (possibly better co-ordination) in the working of the pilot service in the neighbourhood referred to.

Yours etc H. Langdon, Secretary UKPA

The report of the Committee disappointed many pilots and there were wild claims that they had been betrayed or let down by their friends. Indeed when the Bill was first published, pilots strongly criticised it, but when debated at the London Conference of 1911, their claims did not match their concerns. They had no real idea of what effect the proposed legislation was to have on the administration of pilotage.

In Parliament, the alien pilotage clause proved a sticky point at the last moment, but the Admiralty demanded the right to object to the issue of pilotage certificates to aliens. This was accepted as a compromise and the Bill passed both houses in 1912 to come into force in 1913.

At the 1912 UKPA Conference at Cardiff, during a parade of the Bristol sailing pilot cutters, a Cardiff cutter became marooned on mud-bank and the crew and its temporary passengers (wives and families) had to be rescued. On the previous day the Cardiff Pilots' Association had asked for advice in bringing in the use of steam cutters instead of sailing craft. Not all of the members were in agreement and at the Glasgow Conference of 1913 the UKPA was informed that some members had actively opposed the changeover to steam by objecting to the bye-laws that caused the Board of Trade to order an inquiry that would make things very expensive.

The secretary, Henry Langdon, who was then over eighty years old, retired after 28 years of service in 1912. It seems very strange that very little mention of him in the later years is found in the reports of the annual conferences. The new Secretary was Joseph Browne, one of the founders. Never a pilot, he was associate member No 1. It was Browne who introduced John Inskip to the Executive Committee and proposed him as successor to Sandford D. Cole, as the Association Solicitor in 1912; his appointment being confirmed by the 1913 Conference.

PART THREE

PART THREE

The Pilotage Act 1913 and After

THE IMPLEMENTATION OF the 1919 Pilotage Act was interrupted in many ports by the outbreak of war and there is no record of the activities of the Association for a couple of years. Many pilots entered the armed forces and several lost their lives on land and at sea. Those who remained in the pilotage services braved torpedoes and mines. Most received Mercantile Marine and War Medals, some were decorated for specific acts of bravery.

In 1917 the Liverpool Pilot cutter on station struck a mine at the Bar and even though another cutter was a mere mile away, only two persons survived. Twelve pilots and eight apprentices were killed along with 19 others (including the Examining Officer and Naval Personnel). In other districts, pilots were aboard vessels mined or torpedoed; many losing their lives.

The Admiralty took control of many pilotage districts, re-organizing the rota and working systems. In at least one instance this brought improvements in pay and conditions that carried on after the end of hostilities. At Manchester where the Admiralty

Sea Transport Division requisitioned half the pilot service to pilot vessels taken over by the Government Transport Service, re-arranged the rota system and instituted a "pooling of earnings". The Admiralty pilots seem to have been administered quite separately from the remainder of the pilots: no mention of such a separate service appears in the minutes of the Pilotage Committee, nor were there any references to accidents to any Government shipping. The remaining pilots were left to man the normal merchant shipping. Initially there was a fair income, but by 1917, they were in difficulties with ordinary shipping at very low ebb. A few pilots enlisted and went into the Pioneer Corps moving munitions and provisions over the French and Belgian waterways. The President, Michael Joyce was aboard a ferry between Holyhead and Dublin when the vessel was torpedoed.

Pilotage tariffs during the First World War, increased by an average of 75%, roughly in line with inflation. The Executive Committee met in London or Bristol quarterly throughout hostilities and in March 1918, an Extra-ordinary Conference was held in London to examine the work to be done when the War ended. The first post-war Annual Conference was held in 1919 at Hull, the venue originally planned for 1915. Michael Joyce told the assembly that the Executive had had several meetings with the Board of Trade and other Government Departments since March 1918. The subjects covered were the items liable to be affected by the introduction of the various pilotage orders. He was pleased to know that the Admiralty had suggested that henceforth the respective authorities should not grant pilotage certificates to any person not a British subject, but deplored the action of the Admiralty in withdrawing the regulation (a temporary war-time measure) of enforcing compulsory pilotage on all alien vessels in specified areas of the Bristol Channel.

There had been approaches to the UKPA to federate with other organizations but the Executive Committee considered it would not benefit the Association. They had also been asked to associate themselves with an International Seafarers Association. Several meetings were held in London, Paris and Genoa but the organization, in that form, did not survive. However the UKA in conjunction with the officers and seamen were co-operating in the Seafarers' Joint Council, a semi-official body first organized during the War to smooth out negotiations in matters of conditions, pay and manning levels. After the War the Seafarers Joint Council was instrumental in pressing for increased safety for all aspects of seafaring life, even to demanding more and better navigational aids. The Association's Solicitor, John Inskip, in conjunction with Michael Joyce, suggested that a Committee of Members of Parliament sympathetic to the pilots' cause be formed with a view to having assistance whenever legislation or matters affecting pilots was passing through Parliament. Inskip introduced the Officers of the UKPA to his brother, Thomas Inskip, KCMP, who agreed to assist. Thomas Inskip was to become Attorney General in several later governments and eventually a Cabinet Minister. This gave the pilots more confidence that they had friends in Government circles. A ten-member Committee was formed to continue discussions.

The introduction of new pilotage orders did not go smoothly. Inskip, in one of his reports as Secretary in the early twenties, said he had attended ten inquiries in one year. And in six years there were more than twenty inquiries, not all brought about by the same type of objection. In the Forth, the shipowners objected to the new 'pooling' arrangements, claiming that the pilots would become lazy, inefficient and incompetent. Cawley had warned, just before he died, that the Association had spent a large amount of its income on representing pilots and local associations in court and at inquiries. Now Joyce had to issue the same warning.

During the War the subscriptions had been raised from 1/- per month to 1/6*d.* and again in 1919 to 2/-. However the cost of correspondence, telephone calls, printing of agendas, minutes and expenses of travel were all putting the finances under continued pressure. A total of 24/- annually would not cover the amount required for long.

"*THE PILOT*", the Association's journal, appeared for the first time in 1920 and seems to have been instrumental in bringing about the 30% increase of membership from about 1,000 to almost 1,300 in 1921. It was certainly the most efficient way of increasing the pilots' awareness of the problems encountered by other pilots and indicating how difficulties could be avoided or averted by adopting better procedures.

This is a copy of the July issue of Volume 1 in 1921

THE PILOT.

37th ANNUAL CONFERENCE.

HOTEL ARRANGEMENTS AND ADVICE TO DELEGATES.

The Conference will open at 10 A.m. on Tuesday, June 21st, at the Midland Adelphi Hotel, Lime Street, Liverpool. Messrs. Arthur H. Evans and Lewis Jones are the Joint Honorary Conference Secretaries.

It is hoped that the business of the Conference will be completed on Thursday, the 23rd, and that as many delegates as possible will be able to stay for the river trip which has been arranged for *Friday*.

The following is a list of the hotels which have sent in their tariffs for bed and breakfast :—

Midland Adelphi Hotel, Lime Street: Single-bedded rooms, breakfast, a la carte...from 10*s*, 6*d*.
London and North-Western Hotel, Lime Street
Bed & Breakfast...12*s*. 6*d*.
Victoria Hotel, St. John's Lane

Bed & Breakfast..9s. 6d.
Compton Hotel, Church Street
Bed & Breakfast..10s. 0d.
Angel Hotel, Dale Street
Bed & Breakfast..11s. 0d.
Hotel St. George, Lime Street
Bed & Breakfast...from 12s. 6d.
Stork Hotel, Queen Square
Bed & Breakfast..9s. 8d.
Washington Hotel, Lime Street
Bed & Breakfast..9s. 0d.
Shaftesbury Hotel (Temperance)
Bed & Breakfast..9s. 6d.
Imperial Hotel, Lime Street
Bed & Breakfast..9s. 6d.
Bee Hotel, Queen Square
Bed & Breakfast..9s 6d.
Seacornbe Ferry Hotel, Seacombe, Cheshire
Bed & Breakfast..11s. 3d.
Woodside Hotel, Birkenhead
Bed & Breakfast..10s. 6d.
St. John's Temperance Hotel, St. John's Lane
Bed & Breakfast..9s. 6d.
Grove Hotel (Temperance), Grove Road, Wallasey
Bed & Breakfast..from 7s. 6d.

Delegates requiring accommodation may arrange same direct, or through;

Mr. Arthur H. Evans
14, Dale Street
Liverpool,

but it *is advisable that rooms should be booked early*, and that it should be clearly stated when the delegate will arrive, and how long he intends to stay. Delegates should also mention the Conference if they write direct to the hotels..

In the present condition of the railway service, it is impossible to make any announcement regarding trains, and delegates should make inquiries at their home ports.

The new state of Eire was in formation during 1921 and Michael Joyce would not be a member of the House of Commons for long. The Executive Committee discussed the matter before the 1922 Conference in London and a resolution was passed that another President should be sought, preferably a resident of the mainland of Britain and a member of the House of Commons. The proposed change of President caused considerable distress to all, not least to Michael Joyce himself. It was not going to be easy to replace one who had been a pilot and for two decades and an active M.P., and Joyce was also well liked and respected. As President he received £175 per annum plus expenses. Living in Ireland it would have been very expensive for him to attend the quarterly meetings, the occasional inquiries and conferences.

Ultimately the M.P. for Hull, Lieutenant-Commander Peter Kenworthy (Independent), who had previously been helpful in supporting the Humber pilots as member of the House of Commons Pilotage Committee, was asked to take the place of Joyce and agreed to do so when Joyce retired in 1923. Commander Kenworthy was paid £20 per annum, but received no expenses. In 1924 he underwent a serious operation and afterwards sent his resignation to the Association. Like Joyce he seldom missed an Executive Committee meeting, once slipping away from a crucial debate in the House of Commons, to attend a conference. Lord Apsely, M.P. for Southampton, and a person known for his sympathies with seafarers in general, succeeded him. He was to give invaluable assistance in the years to come and refused all fees. Commander Kenworthy attended the Swansea Conference in 1925 and supervised the election of his successor. Apsely was, in fact, overseas at the time and did not know of his election until he arrived home a few weeks later.

Joseph Browne, the last remaining member to have attended the Inaugural conference in 1884 took ill, and his duties had to be taken over by John Inskip. He resigned and Inskip became Secretary and Solicitor to the Association.

In the same year there was unrest again at Bristol, this time stemming from the introduction of steam pilot cutters, which was, as formerly at Cardiff, not to the agreement of all the pilots from Pill. New bylaws introduced by the Bristol Authority did not meet the pilots' demands; they objected and the Board of Trade ordered a local inquiry. The Bristol pilots told the Executive Committee of their intention to join a dockworker's union. The Bristol Pilots were warned that they could not remain members of the UKPA if they joined the Union on the grounds that the Association represented licensed pilots who were unable to strike. Any threat of a strike would undermine the Association's position in the matter.

At the Conference Inskip said that he had repeatedly asked for information from the Bristol Pilots' Association for use in the forthcoming Inquiry, but that they had ignored his requests. When the Bristol pilots' representatives arrived some-what late they gave several excuses: none of which had any real relevance. Finally it was said that the Bristol pilots thought that Inskip, being an Alderman of the City of Bristol, could not successfully argue their case against the Bristol Corporation which was the Authority and of which Inskip was a part. The Bristol membership lapsed during the following year although two or three pilots retained individual membership.

Immediately before the Conference, Sir Percy Noble, Chairman of the Chamber of Shipping made a speech that was virtually a diatribe against pilots and the responsible officials of the Board of Trade. The Conference gave both Kenworthy and Inskip the opportunity of reply without making a special case out of it. The pilots themselves were satisfied with the outcome for Noble had made quite a number of mistakes and factual errors in his speech and they were able to correct him.

During the immediate post-war years, many cases of maladministration of pilotage affairs came to light with Dundee offering the best example. Unusual precedents had been allowed to creep into the administration there. The pilots were in the peculiar position of being paid a weekly salary of £4 by the Authority, together with such further amounts as the Authority cared to distribute from the surplus earnings after they had met their own requirements. An important factor in the situation was a legal dispute between the Anchor Line and the Dundee Harbour Boards in which the pilotage funds had been used to defray the considerable costs that had little or nothing to do with pilots or pilotage. The amounts taken were to cover the cost of the court case. The Dundee authorities had been acting quite independently of any by-laws or regulations and helping themselves to substantial sums from the earnings of pilots at a time when pilots had been permitted to retain no more than £250 per annum. They even made a provision for an exempt ship to pay a lower rate for the services of a pilot, if and when employed, than that paid by a ship regularly employing a compulsory pilot. And in 1925, the Dundee Pilotage Authority did not even consult the pilots regarding a proposed alteration of the by-laws relating to pilotage. There were difficulties also at Aberdeen where the pilots had a peculiar arrangement whereby they shared their pilotage incomes equally with the boatmen – directly contrary to the Pilotage Act. The Association took up both cases – successfully.

In 1925 there were eight inquiries and local associations had been subsidised by £21 for each inquiry. At the end of the year the accounts showed a deficit balance of £686 that included arrears of £474. Calculated over a ten-year period, the Association's finances were in deficit of £212. They were beginning to make inroads into the accumulated funds; and the larger ports were, to a certain extent, subsidising the smaller ports.

At the 1925 Conference, Inskip impressed upon members that there were always to be two funds established in each district: a Pilot Fund for administration and a Pilot Benefit fund for disablement and retirement pensions. He took pains to explain and distinguish between the two types of funds that made it imperative and legally necessary to maintain them separate and distinct. But even after the examples above had been drawn to the attention of the membership, there were some services that were prepared to ignore the distinction.

Elsewhere, in spite of the relative efficiency of the 1913 Act, occasional loop-holes appeared. In the Thames districts, for instance, Danish Packet companies entered via the Middle Channels thereby avoiding any pilot wishing to offer his services. Trinity House stated that it was too expensive to maintain a cutter service in the Middle Channels. The companies paid the pilotage dues, thereby avoiding claims that they were deliberately flouting the custom of the port; but the monies were paid into the pilot funds and lost to the pilots. The situation was never really resolved.

Between 1928 and 1930, the Association was very active in working towards the standardisation of the helm orders. Until 1930, it was more the rule in countries on the eastern side of the Atlantic that the steering wheel was an extension of the helm and that the order "port" meant that the wheel and helm went to port, but the rudder and ship's head moved to starboard. The UK pilots were unusually unanimous in voting for making the rule that "port" meant the wheel, rudder and ship's head all moved to port. Not only that, they were in favour of abolishing the words "port" and "starboard" in favour of "left" and "right".

Reduction in Earnings and the Economic Depression

In 1929 the Bristol Pilots' Association lost an inquiry relating to their income. They were ill-prepared for their own defence and although Inskip and members of the Executive were present, there was little that could be done. Inskip explained his presence there as necessary due to the close connections between the Bristol Channel Pilots as a whole; the findings of the Inquiry could affect others nearby. Most of the members of the Bristol Channel Pilots' Association were members of the UKPA.

Towards the end of the 1920s, the cost of living against ever deepening depression was falling, the shipowners pressed for reductions in pilots' earning rates. Sir William Noble's speech of 1925 had had its effects after all. In 1929 the shipowners made a concerted attack on the Liverpool pilots. Until then the local inquiries had been 'round the table' affairs with no formal structure. At Liverpool the authority agreed with the pilots that a reduction of 10% was warranted. The Chamber of Shipping, however, brought in their own counsel who used formal procedures, leaving the UKPA somewhat short in its planning. The pilots lost the case and the previously agreed reduction was increased to 15%.

During the same Inquiry the shipowners managed to include another, yet more sinister, principle into the reckoning by having the pilots' earnings set against a point somewhere between the pay of the master and mate of the average vessel using the pilot.

Lord Apsley, the UKPA President, arranged for a deputation to attend the President of the Board of Trade to protest at the use of formal procedures at inquiries. The pilots, with members of the Parliamentary Committee, made known their strong case of injustice in the matter. The local, low-level inquiries had been more like conferences and were relatively inexpensive. Whenever there had been an objection to a by-law or dispute between the authorities, pilots or shipowners, the Board of Trade had found it easy to institute an inquiry. Now precedents had been set, the inquiries would be formal affairs and, with many counsel employed, thereby very expensive.

Between 1925 and 1930 there was a series of applications for reductions in pilotage rates or incomes, mostly demanding cuts of from 15 to 20%. The Association managed to hold most of the cuts to 10%. Inskip was invaluable in these matters and whilst he was Mayor of Bristol he was presented with £50 as a token of gratitude and in recognition of his expertise, for it was said he was the foremost expert on the law of Pilotage. And it was the problems arising from the legal aspects of pilotage that occupied much of the time the Executive Committee. The Association was also very pleased to congratulate their Secretary Inskip on being awarded a knighthood at the end of his Mayoralty.

Of course other, unusual problems arose, not least in matters of membership. Inskip (now Sir John) agreed with the Thames River Pilots' Association to pay two guineas to one of their members who unsuccessfully took a case to court. He later learned that the man concerned was not a member: in fact only 73 of the 125 pilots of that district were members. There was much discussion as the standing of lapsed members. If a lapsed member wanted to re-join, the rules stated that he had to pay all back subscription as if they were in arrears. This was unfair in some instances and inequitable. There were other actions too: in a couple of inquiries, the local pilots suddenly had 100% membership several months before the inquiries took place and in 1935 a rule was introduced and passed that before the Association assisted a local branch, there had to be a substantial membership at least three years before any assistance was granted.

The shipowners changed their direction of attack a little in 1935, turning to pilot cutters and boarding methods to reduce costs. They demanded that the Liverpool pilot station at Point Lynas be closed down and the cutter withdrawn. There was an Inquiry lasting seven days, four days in Liverpool and three in London. Six counsel were engaged, of which two were briefed by the Association. There was a principle involved and Sir John thought it worth the fight. The Liverpool pilots won the case. But the expenses paid by the Association were over £1,300; the Liverpool Pilots' Association returned £100 of this to the UKPA in appreciation of the support. The outcome was an approach to the Board of Trade asking for the costs, in future, to be borne by the losing parties.

In the same year, at Sunderland, the Authority there withdrew the steam cutter on the grounds that pilotage receipts were insufficient to cover the costs. However they continued to levy the pilots' earnings for cutter maintenance. The pilots then discovered that the moneys levied for the pilot funds were not, in fact being distributed to those funds in the correct proportions, and never beneficial to the Pilots Benefit fund. At Dundee the pilots were face with a pilotage order decreasing the cutter deduction from £250 per annum to £50. The Association was actively engaged in recovering the moneys in both instances.

History does repeat itself especially at Barrow-in-Furness. A pilot there was docking s.s. *Orion* in 1935, when, without warning, a dockmaster ordered the head-rope to be moved. The vessel sheered away from the lock wall and was damaged, for which the pilot was brought before the local Trinity House Commissioners and suspended. The evidence had been given in his absence and was later read over to him. When Sir John looked into the matter he found that one of the Trinity House Sub-Commissioners was a servant of the owners of the vessel. He wrote immediately to Trinity House, who, in turn, said they would restore the pilot's licence and re-open the proceedings.

Irregularities relating to the Pilotage Act also occurred at Swansea, where the pilots and shipowners had equal representation on the Pilotage Committee. The Harbour Board delegated their seat to the shipowners' representatives leaving the pilots outnumbered two to one.

In 1934 the Executive Committee attempted to formulate a policy that would cover all possible aspects of pilotage charges and their applications, not only in relation to pilots' incomes but also to their correct proportions to pilot funds and pilot benefit funds. After long deliberations the Committee produced a seven-point policy for discussion in the branches:

(1) Every vessel inward or outward entitled to use the services of a pilot, should contribute to the administrative expenses of the pilot service and maintenance of the cutter services.
(2) The cost of the cutter services should not be provided from the pilot rates proper.
(3) The cutter to be owned and run by the authorities; the pilots to confine themselves to pilotage duties.
(4) To cancel section 17(p) of the Pilotage Act 1913 relating to payments by shipowners to the pilot funds.
(5) The basis of pilotage dues should be altered to leave the pilots at each port with the same net earnings as before.
(6) The pilotage rates at each port to be left intact for the pilots, subject to his contributions to the pilot fund.
(7) That a Pilots' Benefit Fund be established at every port, and that this fund be submitted quinquennially to an actuary, and that the amounts certified as necessary for the fund, be contributed by the pilots and out of the pilot fund in equal shares.

After being circulated around the branches, 24 replies were received: 15 in full agreement, four wholly against and three agreed with everything except ownership of the cutters. Two made no definite decision, one of these was Gloucester, where they used the services of the Barry and Cardiff cutters. The seven points were eventually reduced to three: Nos.1, 2 & 7.

The Humber pilots disturbed not a few members in 1934 with a list of resolutions for the 1935 Conference:

(1) That the "*PILOT*" be issued regularly, quarterly.
(2) That the H.Q. of the Association be moved from Bristol.
(3) That the officers of General Secretary and solicitor be separated.
(4) That the question of pilots' representation on their respective authorities be considered as regards its usefulness or otherwise.
(5) That the attention of the Board of Trade be drawn to the danger that exists where the pilot-ladders are fixed to a rail or deck edge without adequate handrails being provided.

A sixth resolution was a suggestion for better representation of the branches on the Executive Committee, with improved geographical spread.

The venues for the Conferences continued to vary, and from 1926 at Southampton the presence of the ladies made things somewhat more pleasant occasions. This was at the request of Lady Apsley who, at that Conference, entertained the delegates and wives at the Apsley's home near Southampton. It was then that the Conference dinners became formal affairs with dinner jackets worn. There were complaints from some quarters that out-of-London conferences were too expensive, but this was not supported in debates. There was a tendency to provide better entertainment than previous conferences, which in moderate form is harmless. Cardiff managed to provide the occasional regatta during the conferences there, and in 1936 the BBC broadcast the opening speeches of the Cardiff Conference, and the singing of sea-shanties by the pilots.

In the late 1930s the Association of Dock & Harbour Authorities began work on a Parliamentary Bill to limit the liability of pilotage authorities. Nothing had been done to eliminate the risk to authorities in situations such as that at Dundee in 1925. Inskip was quite worried about suggestions that the pilotage authorities would try to limit their liabilities to £100 for every pilot under their respective jurisdictions. He thought it necessary to employ Parliamentary agents. Trinity House had the matter in hand as can be seen from the following extract from *Lloyds List*:

> As we report in another column the Pilotage Authorities (Limitation of Liability) Bill yesterday passed the report stage in the House of Lords. All the interests concerned—the shipowners, the pilotage authorities, and the pilots – having already expressed themselves as satisfied with the provisions of the Bill, it will now, as an agreed measure, become law during the present session. Pilotage authorities have for some time been desirous of obtaining the benefit of a limitation of their liability in certain circumstances. This the Bill will give them. Liability for damages is to be restricted to an amount of £100 multiplied by the number of pilots licensed by the pilotage authority for their district. This limitation will be applicable where, without the actual fault – or privity of the pilotage authority, "any loss or damage is caused to any vessel or vessels or to any goods, merchandise or other things whatsoever on board any vessel or vessels or to any other property or rights of any kind, whether on land or on water or whether fixed or moveable." This is the main provision of the Bill. Its other clauses are incidental, except that they will ensure that claims against an authority in one capacity are not enforced against funds held by it in another capacity. The limitation provided for is analogous to that enjoyed by shipowners under certain sections of the Merchant Shipping Acts. Wide though its terms appear to be in their scope, there would seem likely to be comparatively few occasions on which pilotage authorities may find it worth-while to invoke the protection given. A section of the Pilotage Act already provides that the licensing of pilots by pilotage authorities shall not involve them in liability for loss occasioned by any acts of the pilots. An authority is not

answerable for the personal negligence of a pilot, and the well-known decision of the House of Lords in the Dundee cane shows that, if an authority takes care that a proper system of pilotage is maintained and enforced, it is under no liability. In the Dundee case, which apparently alarmed pilotage authorities, the authority was judicially held to have been negligent – it had failed to enforce the attendance of pilots at a station where shipping had been led to expect that they would be found – and accordingly the authority would not have been entitled to relief had the Bill been in operation. Such protection as the proposed measure will afford will, however, be available. Having already passed through the House, the completed steps with reference to the bill will probably be formal.

Lloyds List 31st October 1936

The pilot services of the UK were proud to play a part in the Royal Naval Review at Spithead in 1937. Two cutters, the *Brook* (Isle of Wight) and *William M. Clarke* (Liverpool) were allocated splendid positions off Southsea. Lord Apsley and the Executive spent the day on the cutters with the finest views of the Review. There was even entertainment on the Liverpool cutter from Peter Dawson, the world-famous baritone, who entertained the pilots at the London Conference a few weeks later.

The Conference of 1938 on the Mersey brought more discussion about pilotage certificates. Liverpool pilots brought out an interesting point: they had 435 certificates in force in their district, with an average number of 29 vessels on each certificate. One certificate had 114 vessels entered thereon. Admittedly many of the vessels no longer existed, but they considered that more than 29 vessels on one certificate was ridiculous. At the time there was again talk of war, although it does not appear in the reports of Conference or minutes of the Executive Committee meetings.

Many members of the UKPA were commissioned officers in the Royal Naval Reserve and spent their leave and quite a bit of spare time attending courses at R.N.R. bases.

In 1939 the submarine H.M.S. *Thetis* left the Mersey conducted to sea by a Liverpool pilot Norman D. Wilcox. When the time came for him to disembark, he accepted an invitation to stay for the trials. On her first dive she struck the bed of Liverpool Bay at an angle of 45° and stuck firmly in that position. It was some time before the situation became known to the authorities, and in all 99 men, Norman Wilcox among them, died in front of the World's cine-cameras.

The last remaining founder member of the Association, Joseph Browne, died at the age of 89, a few weeks after attending the Liverpool Conference. Michael Joyce, at the age of 90, and shaken by the death of his old friend was unable to attend the 1939 Conference at Newcastle. He died at his home in Limerick in 1940. The Association had provided pensions to both since their retirement: £100 per annum for Joyce and £50 per annum for Browne, each paid from the annual income of the Association.

Splintering of Membership to TGWU

Lord Apsley died on active service in 1944, leaving Sir John Inskip as the sole person who could remember the Association as it was before the First World War.

For the first two years of the War, Inskip carried on almost single-handed. There were no E.C. meetings for almost two years, but its members were not idle. Mostly senior members of the districts, some were called into administrative matters and involved in the re-organisation of pilot services for war purposes. In the service of the UKPA they had to work as best as they could and often individually by letter or phone with Sir John. They had to consider the insurance of cutters during hostilities, employment of pilots (where there was lack of shipping) registration of apprentices to preclude calling up to the armed forces, the new compulsory pilotage order for war purposes, food rationing, clothing, and liability for fire-watch duties or Home Guard stand-by.

Many of the small ports on the south and east coast were badly affected, losing more than 60% of their normal shipping and traditional trades. The Wash, Goole, Shoreham, Poole, Plymouth, Ipswich, Dartmouth and the Medway pilots all asked for advice from the Secretary of the UKPA.

Membership figures in 1938/9 were said to be the highest ever, with nearly 1,200 on the register, but there was to be a change. In 1942 the Secretary told the Executive Committee that 25 members of the Manchester Pilots had not renewed their subscriptions and had apparently joined the Transport & General Workers Union (TGWU). The Branch Secretary was embarrassed and quite unable to explain the sudden loss of members. One reason could have been the closer contact between the pilots, tug crews, canal operating staff, and possibly even the dockworkers. Certainly the latter had had increase of more than 40% in incomes. The pilots could have been receiving less than a dockworker. The Admiralty taking a dozen pilots from the Manchester rota to work exclusively for Government requisitioned ships reduced the rota pilots' incomes by 50%.

A couple of months later, 112 Liverpool pilots led by a former member of the Executive Committee, W. Lewis Jones, resigned from the Association to join the TG.U. It was suggested that there was a motive for Lewis Jones in that he had not been able to obtain re-election to the Executive Committee for a number of years. The TGWU local Secretary had attended a couple of the Liverpool Pilots' Association meetings and addressed the members, apparently claiming they would obtain substantial increases in pilotage rates as members of the Union. The Union leaders also made statements, quite untrue, that Sir John Inskip had advised the Bristol Shipowners during a previous (1929) Inquiry. (The incident is mentioned above, p.50). The withdrawal of the Liverpool pilots was particularly galling for the members of the UKPA in view of the costly support given in defending the retention of the Point Lynas Pilot Station a few years earlier.

The appearance of the TGWU on the pilotage scene does not seem to have been entirely accidental. Every time there was an inquiry into local pilotage administration, the TGWU attended in an attempt to attract members. By the end of the War, Leith, Dundee and Blyth had also turned to the Union. In 1943 Inskip informed the Association that there was a concerted attack on them: he could find no reason for it. He was somewhat naive, for the approaches of the Union were, to some extent, geared to gaining control of the ports. There was also a certain amount of prestige in public and around the negotiating table if pilots were Union members.

In the 1943 Report, Inskip turned to the future, a central pilotage body was an ideal concept for pilotage administration. He cited as an example the multiplicity of authorities, a cumbersome system, around the Firth of Forth: Leith, Bo'ness, Methil, Grangemouth and Burnt Island. One authority could easily manage pilotage for the district and would probably be more efficient and cost-effective. A central pilotage authority could organise it.

Another idea proposed at this time, came from the Ministry of Transport: a single basis of adjusting pilots' earnings which would be applicable to all pilots whatever port or size, the Executive Committee agreed to study any proposals.

Because of the transfer of the major merchant and naval traffic to the northern ports, and particularly to the Clyde Estuary, a number of the Cinque Ports pilots were transferred there from 1941 until 1945.

From 1943 the Executive Committee met regularly every quarter, and in making plans for the future, a seven-point programme was resurrected, re-drawn and discussed at an informal Conference in the summer of 1944. Topics of most importance were the establishment of a standard rate for all pilots, better and more equitable funding for cutters and a central pilotage body. A short time after the conference it was learned that Lord Apsley had been killed in action. He had lost his seat at Southampton in the early thirties, but became a Member of Parliament for Bristol almost immediately. His death left the pilots without direct support in Parliament. The 1945 Conference in London was to be asked to consider a new President. There was another matter. Sir John Inskip said he would have to retire: he had been an officer of the UKPA for over thirty years and the work at that time was taking up too much of his time.

End of Hostilities

The planned Conference of 1945 had to be delayed, for a General Election was called at the same time. The results left the Conservatives in disarray. It was said at the Conference that the senior Labour Members of Parliament had insufficient time to represent the Association and the newer members were unwilling to take up the reins of a Conservative. The Association was still without a President and it was left to the 1946 Conference to make proposals.

In the debates in 1945 it was said that the subscriptions would have to be increased from 36 shillings per annum to £3. If proposals that some delegates were putting forward were to be taken up, such as the separation of the offices of Solicitor and General Secretary and a permanent office in London, the £3 would have to be increased to £4.

At the 1946 Conference, a call for suggestions for President of the UKPA, which had been in vain, suddenly bore fruit. The Barry delegate rose and suggested Admiral Lord Mountevans. He intimated that his Lordship had agreed to take the position and the following day was introduced to the assembled delegates and observers and elected. Ill health, however, forced him to resign after twelve months. It was two years before the Association could find another President, again from the Solent area, Sir Peter MacDonald,

M.P. for the Isle of Wight. He proved to be an excellent President, although with much reduced numbers. His Majesty's opposition in the Commons did not allow MacDonald to devote as much time to U.K.P.A. affairs as he would have liked. He was elected during the Conference of 1949.

That year brought not only a new President, but also a new post, that of Assistant Secretary. C. D. Griffiths, solicitor to the Bristol Pilots' Association, who originally came from a local government post in London to private practice in Bristol. This year also saw the first round-the-table meeting between the Association representatives and pilot members of the TGWU. This first meeting was arranged in January to form a united front at a meeting with the Chamber of Shipping in March, in an endeavour to find a formula for a general adjustment of rates (as had been envisaged in 1943).

In 1950, came a request, originally sent to Trinity House, from Danish pilots who suggested that a meeting of European pilots would be helpful. They thought mutual problems could be aired, and they for their part, wanted some clearance of the waters from pilots from other parts of Europe. It appeared that foreign pilots, who in effect, were conversant only with the district by memorising a chart, were conducting ships through Danish national waters. The request was left on the table for more enquiries. In the same year Swansea pilots did not renew their membership of the Association and joined the Union ports.

The UKPA supported the Humber pilots in the opposition, in 1950, to their Authority's interpretation of the by-law relating to choice pilotage, The Authority claimed they were able to appoint any pilot to a company even when he was unwilling to work as a choice pilot. The pilots withdrew their services on a technical point for a week, bringing about a public inquiry, which confirmed the pilots' stance that no pilot could be forced to become a choice pilot against his will. As a result of the findings of the Inquiry, no choice pilotage was taken up by the pilots and those who held such appointments resigned. The Association decided to take interest in the choice pilotage situation and circulated 48 of the 60 ports on their views: only 12 replied.

In 1949 and for the ensuing couple of years there were major strikes in the ports –the communists were attempting gain complete control of the work force. In one instance the Government used troops as a threat to striking dock workers by unloading a couple of ships in London's Royal Docks. In 1951 Jack Jones of the TW&GU with Lord Aldington, Chairman of the Port of London Authority, made an agreement that brought peace to the UK docks for a time.

The Future

In 1933 the Directors of the Cunard Line, when discussing the building of the *Queen Mary* the world's largest vessel, came to the conclusion that the future of North Atlantic passenger services would be aircraft.

It would be a second world war and two decades before that forecast would prove correct. The successful introduction of the jet engine for aircraft in 1953 signalled the beginning of the end of transatlantic passenger ferries. At that time Cunard had at last nine passenger vessels on the Atlantic with Canadian Pacific, Anchor Line, Furness Line and France and the Netherlands operating more than a dozen liners to North America meaning over 600 to 700 services per year for pilots at Liverpool and Southampton. Passenger services to India, the Far East, South America, South Africa and Australia provided treble that number of pilot services to the same ports plus the Thames.

Within a decade passenger services were decimated – the large passenger ships were being used for cruises. It was noticeable that numbers of pilots would become redundant. But it was not just the disappearance of passenger traffic that was affecting pilot service. The increase in Very Large Cargo Carriers (VLCC's) each carrying five or six times the previous amount of cargo caused a similar reduction in the pilot services required. The coming of the large container vessels had the same effect. The new Common Market rules also reduced the amount of cargo imported from distant lands and thus work for pilots.

Peace

Sir John Inskip resigned at the 1953 conference after 40 years as Solicitor and 30 as General Secretary. As expected C. D. Griffiths, a Bristol solicitor, took his place.

Gloucester pilots took unusual steps to protect their living when, in 1953, one of the pilots resigned from the service to take up work as master of a small tanker working in the district. He applied for a pilotage certificate, but the pilots refused to examine him, knowing there was no other body capable of carrying out the examination and that the ex-pilot could not be granted a certificate. The Association tried to persuade the shipowners involved to abandon the application, as it would seriously affect the extremely small earnings of the pilots. The following year there was one quarter when pilots had no distribution of earnings, there was not even enough to pay the apprentices' wages.

Two years later, Clyde pilots, without the Association's advice discussed a substantial increase in earnings, making considerable concessions to the Authority in doing so. When the report of an agreement was published, the Chamber of Shipping objected and at the subsequent Inquiry. For the pilots no further concessions remained and they lost over half of the proposed increase. As the Secretary remarked, "This is a salutary lesson for the members".

PART FOUR

PART FOUR

New Legislation

DURING THE EARLY part of the 1950s discussions towards a standard for pilots' earnings began to bear fruit. Led by Dan C. Tate of the Executive Committee, there was also talk of a scale being related to the size and nature of the ports. In 1956 the Ministry held informal talks with the pilots and shipowners, leading to an Inquiry, chaired by Sir Robert Letch, the report of which recommended that the earnings of pilots should be measured against the National Maritime Board Scales of Pay for Officers. To the "Letch Report" can be attributed the structure of pilots' earnings for the ensuing three decades. There was been much criticism of the findings, but, used as a basis for discussion it simplified negotiations during that time.

The previously war-ravaged nations of the shipping world had begun to thrive, as many countries reclaimed their former trading patterns. The pilots of the very busy major ports were enjoying full loads of work and earnings. But in 1955 the (45-strong) Manchester Pilots stopped work for almost 10 days, they wanted more pilots appointed. An un-foreseen expansion of trade brought congestion.

The vessels arriving were being moved along the waterway in short moves, almost like chess pieces. They resumed work only when the Canal Company agreed to appoint 9 pilots from the 25-strong Helmsmen's service. The delay in increasing the strength of the service would be mirrored by the problems encountered on the St. Lawrence Seaway a decade later: for another reason.

After the Seaway opened in 1959 the traffic slowly and steadily built up so that the Canadian pilot service, were under-staffed in 1966: in the Welland Canal salaried pilots were working under stress, the pilot rota depleted by sickness, and thereby producing even greater stress, a situation caused by lack of suitable qualified and experienced pilots. When the Seaway was opened most of the pilots recruited has been masters and/or officers Great Lakes ships. As the traffic increased the shipowners increased the pay of their officers and suitable pilot recruits were not easily available. For a time the pilots threatened to strike and the situation lasted for five or so years as more pilots became available and the traffic situation eased.

After the Second World War large numbers of pre-war cargo vessels and many war-time-built vessels and Liberty ships were released to the world to be purchased on a shoestring. They were generally operated by poorly funded shipowners and manned by inexperienced masters and crews. Pilot ladders on these ships could be found un-protected on open decks during loading or discharge of dirty, dusty and/or liquid cargoes, and ladders normally used for overside painting by crews were hung as pilot ladders. Many ladders originally in good condition were ill-maintained and badly-rigged over the ship's side, dangerous ladders are not easy to see from below even in daylight; the pilot in the launch was in peril and there were not a few fatal and serious injuries. Choice pilots were able to have the ladders correctly rigged, with good-sized rungs clean and not greasy, a painter aft for the use of the (rowing) pilot boat and a light illuminating the ladder area. As the pilot transfer craft became motorised the painter was not always demanded.

The pilot associations exchanging information were able in many instances to demand safe boarding conditions and apparatus and Government organisations began to discuss the safety aspects with shipowners. In 1963 the UKPA discussed the problems with other national pilot associations and the outcome was the European Maritime Pilots' Association, a body that was able to bring the matter before the European authorities. R.H. Farrands, of the Executive Committee, missed the inaugural meeting in 1963 but the UKPA became members almost immediately.

The 1960s brought a period of administrative and technical development.

In May 1965 the UKPA hosted the annual meeting of the European Maritime Pilots' Association. The Conference was held in the courtroom of HQS *Wellington*, London providing a suitable solemnity to the proceedings. Vice-President of the UKPA, Dan H. Tate, welcomed the delegates on behalf of the Association. The success of the conference was proved when the German pilot cutter *Kommodore Ruser* anchored in the River Thames opposite the conference and those present treated to a landing and taking off of pilots from seven nations using a French helicopter.

Those pilots whose charges were based on tonnage had problems. All ships were measured by two tonnages, gross and net, in 1969 another measure was introduced, the Delta mark. A ship showing a Delta mark near the load line marks paid only a standard charge for vessels under 500 tons. This meant that large vessels such as car or cattle carriers with a very large volume were charged only in 499 tons, the size of a small coaster, whereas the dimensions of the ship measured seven times that of the coaster. The best example can be seen when Danish pilots complained that large vessels with the Delta mark left port with the minimum draft possible and, as soon as clearing the port, ballasted to double the departure draft. When pilots complained to the port authorities they found that the authorities were also unhappy about the charges. The measure seems to have been withdrawn after about ten years.

Pilots a century earlier had had the same problems, the coming of steam with larger vessels and engines with higher speeds. But before the end of the 1960s container vessels of increasing size were appearing: high-sided and VLCC's moving in and out of (often unsuitable) ports. The vessels not only reduced the average number of ships entering and leaving port, thereby reducing the number pilots required but bringing ever more difficult boarding and disembarking situations, with pilots expected to climb 20 metre ladders. A walk along the deck and several ladders to the bridge could weary a pilot before taking charge of the vessel.

One development in this era, made many pilots happy, the 'pager' offered the opportunity to allow them to remain 'on call' on the golf course.

The "Letch" agreement was not without its flaws and one flaw, soon became apparent: fringe benefits. The Report made a list of ports and then suggested earnings level for each one (a *league table*) and proposed that the National Maritime Board Scales of Pay for ships' officers should be used in calculating any increase in pilots' earnings. The pilots' representatives generally accepted this. In 1960 the National Maritime Board laid down an increase of 20% to officers, which included 9% for work done at weekends, and extra leave for "Sundays at Sea". When the pilots' organisations applied for the same 20% they were met with a refusal on the grounds that pilots were not entitled to fringe benefits. In spite of the pilots' protests and a test-case Inquiry at Middlesbrough they did not obtain a successful end to the concept, and for some years the benefits were used to modify increases to pilots' earnings. Attempts to clear the points in the Letch Report were dropped when Sir Robert Letch, through illness was unable consider the matter. It appears that the representatives had been too easy in accepting a rigid agreement.

Redundancy had been a major point discussed at the 1959 Conference. Ardrossan was used as an illustration where pilots were at risk: the three pilots were dependent on one tanker visiting the port every ten days. If that traffic dropped, they would become redundant. As had occurred during the war, mergers with other, nearby pilot services, or transfer of pilots was suggested as an answer.

In the mid-1960s an Amsterdam pilot during legal proceedings for a divorce, was accused by his wife, of not declaring all his income. It transpired that the pilots were in a habit of asking for more tugs than necessary and receiving cash for the tugs not used. There was a lengthy court case in which the pilots and tug companies agreed to undisclosed fines.

At the 1960 Conference there was criticism of the Executive Committee by delegates from the Medway, Southampton and Preston. During the 1961 Conference the Medway representatives stood up and continued the criticism, using the words "a constant and faithful confidence in the shipowners" and accusing the Secretary of being far too friendly with them. Mr. Griffiths was on his feet immediately, retorting angrily; "Something is going on the Medway which I am not very happy about and genuinely dislike. It is not the first time I have heard Mr. Rhodes express dissatisfaction on behalf of the Medway pilots either with me in particular or the Association as a whole". He had offered to visit any port where there was dissatisfaction and do everything in his power to straighten things out, but had been completely ignored by the Medway. But the delegates from the Cinque Ports and the Preston pilots supported the words of the Medway pilot.

From 1960 onwards the Executive Committee turned its attention to pensions, collecting by means of a questionnaire distributed to the local Associations, details of the many and varied schemes around the UKPA ports. It was found that several ports had no official pension scheme and that the smaller ports were particularly badly off in this respect. Administration of a scheme for a mere few pilots was expensive.

In view of the problems related to fringe benefits, there was a ballot of the London District pilots in 1961. Of the 312 forms issued, 262 were returned, of which 233 were in favour of a three day stoppage. A firm guide for the Executive Committee. The discussions continued throughout the year, with threats of industrial action. At the 1962 Conference the question was put "Do the pilots want a general review of Letch?" The matter was left on the table for the next Conference. During the year the fringe benefits subject marred any possibility of an understanding between the shipowners and the pilots. Sir Robert Letch, by then retired, was asked for an opinion and although reluctant to comment, at the pilots' insistence he made his opinion known; that fringe benefits did not come within the scope of the Letch Report. Tim. O'Reilly of the T&GWU, was the only remaining member of the Inquiry. The pilots' organisations had a problem on their hands.

Remuneration and pensions also came to the fore and changes to the sizes of the vessels visiting the ports, the vast dimensions bringing manoeuvring difficulties and new boarding problems. The new engines and propulsion equipment, new rudder types and steering gear, and, the most important so-called improvements, the mechanical boarding and disembarking arrangements for pilots, containers vessels and larger ships featuring comparative low manning strengths.

In April 1962, a Southampton pilot appealed against the loss of his licence because he had refused to transfer to the Southampton station. It had been a convention that vacancies in that station were filled from the Isle of Wight station. With the support of the UKPA, the appeal was successful and the pilot regained his licence. In the same year the cutter in the western approaches to the Solent was withdrawn and a shore station introduced: the first of a number of such improvements.

NEW LEGISLATION

The Rochdale Committee reporting on the state of the docks industry in the early 1960s, recommended that pilots should be controlled by their respective port authorities. A Labour Government White Paper proposed that the ultimate aim was to place ports in public ownership and there were fears that this could lead to pilots becoming state employees. R,E. Sanders (later pilot superintendent at Harwich) countered this by proposing there should be a central pilotage authority. In 1967 the UKPA formed a joint working party on the matter with the TGWU pilots, setting out a plan for the constitution of a National Pilotage Authority. When the plan was laid before the Conference that year, a number of delegates became incensed about such plans and the acting Secretary (Dan Tate) had to rule all further discussion out of order.

Large Vessels and Pilot Hoists

The mid-1960s were a time of impending change. There was a proposal by IMCO to introduce new methods of tonnage measurement which were looked on with trepidation, in that they would affect pilotage charges. F. D. Amey, Chairman of the National Ports Council, queried the need for pilots on vessels trading regularly to a port. In his speech he coupled this with the potential of fast turn-round of container vessels. Ordinary vessels would take up to a week for a round voyage to continental ports, container vessels would be able to achieve the same voyage in 24 hours. With that experience in a shipmaster, a pilot was deemed unnecessary.

At about the same time the pilot hoist appeared on the scene. In 1967 Esso International (New York) Inc. ordered 16 pilot hoists for their larger vessels. It was stated that the hoist was the finest and most beneficial equipment then used for boarding. 81 ships had the MAJOR hoist fitted during its first year of manufacture. Whilst a definite advantage fitted in the larger vessel, there were design faults, operational blunders and misuse, which caused death and injury during the first decade of the use of hoists.

The introduction of VLCC's (initially 80,000 dwt) brought much discussion among pilots, shipowners and port authorities and towards the end of the 1960s plans were made for pilots to take part in courses and seminars at the Universities and Polytechnics.

1964

The International Organisation for Standardization (ISO) Pilot Ladders, drew up a recommendation (R799) by Technical Committee ISO/TC 8, Shipbuilding details, the Secretariat of which was held by the Netherlands Normalisatie-Instituut (NNI).

1965

At this time container vessels began to appear on the sea lanes. The first such vessels were converted tankers with large long open decks. By 1965 vessels designed and built as container carriers appeared. These were not only going to provide long term and dangerous features for pilots they later became a threat to the work of pilot. The vessels with high sides used long pilot ladders that were ill-designed for the work. The container vessels were able to carry ore cargo at a faster rate and carry more cargo than the post-war fast cargo liners. By 1970 it was obvious that the introduction of unit containers would reduce the need for pilots in many ports by 60%.

The safety regulations governing the deployment of pilot ladders were brought up to date and improved by the issue, by the Board of Trade, of the Merchant Shipping (pilot ladder) Rules 1965.

The Association suffered a hard blow in the Summer of 1967. The Secretary C. D. Griffiths, returning from holiday in Spain, died in an air crash. He had been Secretary for a decade and had had the opportunity of learning the unusual, complicated business of pilotage administration at first hand from Sir John Inskip. In addition he had been Secretary to the Bristol Pilots' Association. Up to this time the Secretary's work had been transferred smoothly through long service and forward planning. There was now a void with no-one of experience of pilotage affairs immediately at hand. The Senior Vice-President, Dan Tate, took over the office of Secretary for the time being and was promptly faced with a Conference.

On 3rd August 1967 Capt. J. Pearson, a Cinque Ports pilot lost his life when disembarking from m.v. *Afric*. The cause was set down as insecure ladder and lack of supervision of the disembarkation procedure.

At the 1967 Conference the Executive, through the Acting Secretary, pointed out that redundancy, due to the introduction of container vessels, was a growing problem which would affect pilots in the larger ports as well as in the smaller. A proposition that the principle of transfer between ports was an acceptable principle was discussed and passed. At this conference it was stated that the London Pilotage Committee (4 Elder Brethren, 2 Shipowners and 2 pilots) administer the 490 pilots of the London Districts.

In 1968 Mr. Edgar Eden was appointed General Secretary and Legal Advisor to the Association. A barrister, he had been Deputy Secretary of the Dock & Harbour Authorities Association. His previous contacts with the legal advisors and secretaries of the shipowners' and ports' organisations would be invaluable. At his first Conference in London on that year, Mr. Eden warned against any precipitate action on the part of the pilots. The question had been posed: how could pilots be independent and fee-earning self-employed individuals? If the pilots disturbed the balance of the Letch Report, there could be action from the shipowners who would love to overthrow Letch and make pilots salaried employees.

A joint UKPA/Marine Pilotage Branch working party co-operated with the General Council of British Shipping to form the Pilots' National Pension Fund using the Trinity House Pension

Fund as a basis. In October 1969 it was stated that the new Pension Fund would require a 15% contribution from all pilots and this would mean an adjustment in pilotage rates.

As at the end of the 1950s there was unrest about the application of the Letch Report; by the 1960s there were hints that the pilots' patience was evaporating.

Redundancy had been mentioned in the debates of the 1968 Conference, but many felt that lack of shipping was something that applied only to other ports. Looking back at the 1960s it is evident that there were many indications of the trouble in store for pilots during the following decade.

Pilots welcomed the introduction of a new form to report non-compliance of the Merchant Shipping (Pilot Ladders) Rules 1965. This form was to be filled (page 33 of EMPA Journal) illustration.

1970s

Entry as a fully-fledged member of the European Economic Community (EEC) was accompanied by a change in patterns of commerce. Cargoes were no longer permitted to be imported if similar commodities were available in Europe. There was pressure to allow pilotage certificates to be issued to non-UK citizens. Although pay, conditions and leave; the loss of trade due to recession; and the entry of the UK into the EEC were ever present constituents of the work of the UKPA, two important topics also arose in the 1970s: pilot unanimity and Parliamentary legislation.

Delays caused by differences between shipowners, pilots and Government Departments meant that at the 1970 Conference the delegates were ready to take strong action; pilots had not had an increase in earnings for two years, in spite of the annual increase in the cost of living of almost ten per cent. After discussions with the Marine Pilotage Branch (M.P.B.), it was agreed to arrange a meeting of all United Kingdom pilots to be held at a suitable venue as soon as practicable.

24 hour stoppage by all UK pilots

On 26th January 1971, after due notice being given to all sectors of the shipping industry, over 1,400 pilots met in Birmingham Town Hall.

Only two exceptions were agreed e.g. if a vessel on the Clyde was not launched that day there would be a delay of four weeks for another suitable tide. The show of pilot unanimity had little effect on shipping around our coasts, but it gave shipowners, port authorities and Government departments proof of unity of purpose among all pilots. For the next couple of months the pilots' representatives pursued a target of a 20% increase in pilotage incomes, but was not until May 1971 that a settlement was reached and even then the increase was only 16%.

The Pension Fund

The Pilots' National Pension Fund (PNPF) came into being in 1971. Not all pilots became members immediately, some delayed thinking their own schemes were superior. However, by the end of the decade 99% of the pilots were members of and contributors to the P.N.P.F.

At the 1978 Conference in Middlesboro Edgar Eden suggested that the P.N.P.F. was neither inflation-proof nor satisfactory so far as the older pilot was concerned. When the PNPF was established in 1971 the older pilot stood to benefit much less than the younger, but that was no excuse for the shipping industry in failing to make up the difference for the older pilots who had given the best years of their lives to that industry. The UKPA had reminded the Department of Trade (DoT) of the Government's obligation for fair treatment to pilots under a re-organised pilotage service in the better pensions for older pilots who have not had sufficient time to build up their pensions to a reasonable living standard. A paper was prepared for submission to the DoT to suggest ways and means to rectify the injustice.

The Secretary then announced the impending close of the port of Preston. (The port had been maintained by using hidden subsidies using finance from the local authority). The Association would need to protect the pilots from suffering financially or otherwise losing out.

Steering Committee

Recognising the difficulties under which pilot administration was operating, the Government formed a Steering Committee on Pilotage (SCOP) in 1973. All organisations concerned with or affected by pilotage legislation were represented on the Committee which was led by David Robinson, a shipowner. Every pilotage district was visited; the members meeting pilots, shipowners and port authorities. The final SCOP Report was not unacceptable to pilots. A Central Pilotage Board had been a recommendation (again the idea was ignored), the most contentious point was the proposal that a liberal attitude to the issue of pilotage certificates should be maintained. Changes in Government attitudes and indeed changes in Governments in the 1970s delayed action on many of the points raised in SCOP

It was not until 1977 that an Advisory Committee on Pilotage was established with the express task of promoting Parliamentary legislation. ACOP was smaller than SCOP but none-the-less made significant advances and many features of its Report were incorporated into the Merchant Shipping Act 1979.

The Merchant Shipping Act 1979 contained an innovation (although not a new concept to pilotage): a Pilotage Commission to offer the Secretary of State such advice as its members considered appropriate for the securing of safety of navigation in ports and around the coasts; ensuring sufficient pilotage services in such areas; with suitable equipment in connection with standards and qualifications; and looking into the arrangements for compulsory pilotage and the issue of pilotage certificates.

NEW LEGISLATION

A feature of a pilots' everyday work is the boarding and leaving of vessels under way at sea, an operation never without attendant dangers even on the calmest of days with vessels built, equipped and manned to the highest possible standards. In 1974 the car ferry *EAGLE*, operated by Southern Ferries, on her return from Lisbon to Southampton, ran into heavy weather suffering damage to her bridge equipment. She made for the nearest port, Falmouth. When attempting to board in bad weather conditions the Falmouth pilot, Captain L. K. Mitchell fell between the ship and cutter and lost his life. The UKPA obtained legal opinion that Mrs. Mitchell and her children had a reasonable case on liability with a good chance of obtaining substantial damages. Every attempt was made to secure an out-of-court settlement but without success. A writ was issued for proceedings in the High Court with the possibility of costs amounting to upwards of £5,000. Mrs. Mitchell could not afford such a sum but the Association offered to underwrite the costs. Southern Ferries tried all means of obstructing the action to the effect that the case was not heard until 1982. But it was successful and Mrs. Mitchell received substantial damages at least £5,000 with costs.

The UKPA was active in many spheres and it is worth recalling that the Association was an early member of the European Maritime Pilots' Association (EMPA). Due to a breakdown in communications EMPA was already in being when the UKPA was advised of an Inaugural Conference. Not so in the case of the International Maritime Pilots' Association (IMPA), talks for which began in the late 1960s and which came into being in 1971 with the active participation of the UKPA Secretary-General Edgar Eden.

During the 1970s there were many meetings at the joint working parties, seminars, conferences and pilot courses of the representatives of the U.K.P.A. and the Marine Pilotage Branch (M.P.B.) at which informal talks on the possibility of the two bodies being merged into one comprehensive association took place. In October 1977, a joint meeting of the respective organisations

discussed and clarified the proposed merger of the Marine Pilots Branch and the UKPA and issued the following statement:
"We fully believe that unity amongst pilots is not only desirable but essential if the wellbeing and interests of all United Kingdom pilots are to be protected and progressed. Therefore this interim report is presented in order that we may receive your confirmation that we are proceeding along the right lines, to solicit any fresh ideas, to invite constructive criticism and, hopefully, to receive your authority to continue our function until unity is achieved. We believe that it is essential that the present momentum is maintained."

Both pilot associations were working together and with EMPA their confidence in IMPA was justified when the organisation achieved status at IMCO (now IMO). However the structure of IMPA came under scrutiny: EMPA requested that one of their members be appointed a "co-ordinating officer" who would remain within the framework of EMPA but not as an intermediary between EMPA and IMPA, Capt. Dan Tate took up his function as promoting EMPA Pilot Hoists Recommendations to be submitted to the IMCO Conference in January 1973.

1973 Conference, London

At the 1973 Conference Frank Berry, vice-president and chairman of the Executive, spoke on the proposed Human Factors Study. Pat Shipley, from the Department of Occupational Psychology, Birkbeck College, and Geoff Crockford from the London School of Hygiene and Tropical Medicine outlined the proposal to delegates. The project was to be funded by Government and ports authorities.

About two years earlier Dr. M. Harrington of the T.U.C. Centenary Institute of Occupational Health undertook a mortality study of pilots in certain major British ports. The results showed a high incidence of coronaries amongst pilots aged 35-50, particularly since 1962. Further study of the problem, including an investigation of German pilots on the River Elbe and another major British port, seemed to indicate that the incidence of heart disease in pilots in this age category 35-50 approximately three times the national average. It is perhaps not unfair to assume that this abnormality may well be evident amongst pilots throughout Europe operating in comparable conditions.

Whilst the under-lying causes of these phenomena are not quite clear, its significance was emphasised when it is considered that all British pilots up to becoming licensed at about 30 years of age, have in the course of their career to satisfactorily pass at least three stringent medical examinations, and doubtless similar stipulations apply to pilots of other nationalities. It could be concluded then, that the health standard of pilots entering service is above the national average. We must not accept that heart disease is an unavoidable occupational hazard of a pilot's life.

Transportation vehicles for whatever media – road, rail, air or sea – are steadily being developed to an optimum size and operational speed consistent with present-day demand. Perhaps the greatest strides of all have been made in sea transportation, where ships of hitherto unconceived dimensions are entering and leaving ports with minimum physical tolerance and in almost all circumstances of weather. It is likely, as far as pilotage is concerned, that the work load on certain pilots was already, under some circumstances, beyond what should have been reasonably tolerated. The many and varied aspects of a pilot's life, such as stress, strain, anxiety and uncertainty, could have been exceeded beyond the norm for detrimental effects upon his life, and when coupled with the irregular hours, mostly night work, disrupted social activities. The core of the problem will most likely emanate from a detailed and specialised human factor study of maritime pilots at least as comprehensive as has been undertaken into civil aviation pilots.

Under the auspices of the Research Division of the National Ports Council (NPC) representatives from Birkbeck College, London School of Hygiene and Tropical Medicine, the UKPA, TGWU, Trinity House and the NPC met in March 1973 to consider the practicalities of a research proposal project for Human Factor Study on Maritime Pilots submitted by Pat Shipley, Lecturer in Engineering Psychology. A Human Factor Study was still very much in its formative stage, and its success would need the full co-operation and support of pilots generally, especially as conclusive results were only likely when a system of random selection was applied in the investigation. The aims of the project were agreed in principle without commitment to the project on the part of any attending the meeting, the two main aims of the project being:

(1) To assess pilotage activities for workload and stress problems, identifying the circumstances in which these may impair the safe judgment of the pilot;
(2) To give guidelines and recommendations for the alleviation of such problems as are found to exist.

If indeed it was accepted that a problem did exist, and the preliminary medical investigation seemed to point in that direction, an analysis of pilots' activities, selected at random, would be needed to more accurately quantify the matter. At this it must be emphasised that if more detailed investigation was to be undertaken, which could only be achieved with the full co-operation of pilots, medical information relating to individuals would remain strictly confidential between the researchers and the pilots concerned, and in the case of the study such pilots would be subject to certain instrumentation. Therefore further progress in this matter depended upon the views of the National Ports Council's Standing Committee on Research and of the pilots from the districts concerned. Should favour be expressed in proceeding, it was envisaged that a Steering Group would be formulated to monitor the project and provide the necessary forum for discussion between interested parties. Alas with lack of finance the concept was talked out.

1974

Work on the report of the UKPA and MPB on re-organisation of pilotage began and was completed in May 1894 but publication was delayed for another three months.

General Secretary, Edgar Eden, (as the Secretary-General of IMPA) announced that John Edmondson had been elected as Senior Vice-President of IMPA. In March John Tebay (Liverpool) represented the UKPA at the IMCO Safety of Navigation meeting in London.

1974 Annual Conference

Cardiff October: 72 Members attended, with about 5 others interested.

General Resolutions brought to light some anomalies of ports guaranteed working under the Letch conditions i.e. the port of Gloucester which had 11 pilots and had more than 25% of the 70 ports with Letch income rates – part of the problem was the large proportion of the trade was with smaller ships and thereby lowered the net registered tonnages (the NMB rates were tacked to tonnages of the visiting ships). A resolution was passed to rectify the situation.

The main topic was the 40 hour week which had been under discussion since 1972, regarding the report of SCOP published on 7th July (see p 109). A Special UKPA Conference on SCOP, in September had urged important amendments to the Report:

That compulsory pilotage should be introduced in every UK pilotage district. The practise of granting pilotage certificates to British or foreign subjects should be abolished this was said to be in common with the policy of other Common Market countries.

As suggested, a Central Pilotage Board would have a fairly effective voice in pilotage and the well-being of pilots and should be composed of at least 50% pilot representation.

The officers had meetings with the Chamber of Shipping to consider the values of a 44/40 hour week and the disparity between pilots' earnings and the sea-standard that had developed since the introduction of the Agreements in the Letch Agreement.

January 1977 the new IALA Buoyage system came into effect. In April the harmonization of the UK Buoyage commenced – the shapes, colours and markings of buoys etc were to be standardized. There had been numerous seminars, meetings and educational courses and at this time the International Association of Lighthouse Authorities (IALA) alternative system of international buoyage was displayed in the River Thames. The pilots almost in unison deprecated the value of buoys coloured entirely green.

The recent death of Captain Laurie Mitchell, Falmouth pilot, whilst trying to board the passenger ferry, *Eagle*, when she was in distress, brought attention to the need for an accident policy to protect the financial position of pilots' dependents.

From time immemorial, various attempts were made to reorganise pilotage by successive Governments. Mr Lloyd George, as President of the Board of Trade, referred to the pilotage service as a very dangerous service and very often led to loss of life. Sir Winston Churchill, as President of the Board of Trade, said that there was no doubt that Pilots had various real grievances which were increasing. Other Ministers of the Crown in successive Governments have also made similar pronouncements.

The Pilot is in charge of the most dangerous part of the voyage, and consequently it was believed that in the national interest the time has now come to remove these crowning injustices and urgently proceed with reorganisation in the light of the above UKPA comments.

If any impartial evidence is needed to support the true facts, the following extracts from Lord Simon of Glaisdale in a judgment of the House of Lords (McMillan v. Crouch, July 1972) must surely be the most revealing statement ever made:

"Experience has shown that it is not enough to trust to the benevolence or sagacity or even the self-interest of shipowners. Experience has shown that it is not safe to assume, as was argued for the respondent, that a master would not take any action that might hazard his ship. If these things provided sufficient safeguard, tribunals of admiralty would happily lose much of their work, and large portions of the Merchant Shipping Act 1894 could be eliminated from the statute book.

The need for particular statutory provision regulating pilotage arises because, by a cruel irony, as ships approach land the proximity of a haven from natural elements may actually increase the hazards. Sea lanes converge; and to the perils of wind and water there is now added a new – perhaps even greater – danger, constituted by human fallibility".

Mr Tom Morgan, delegate to EMPA, said that at the Annual General Meeting in May, the Southern Irish Pilots had applied for membership of EMPA and were accepted. Norway attended as an observer and, once their separate pilot bodies have all joined one organisation in Norway, they anticipated applying for membership.

The subscription (in Belgian France) to EMPA was being increased for 1975 on the following basis:

Organisations with up to 100 members – basic sum of 20,000 BF plus 25,000 BF.

Organisations with 101-500 members – basic sum of 20,000 BF plus 25,000 BF.

Organisations with 501 and over – basic sum of 20,000 BF plus 35,000 BF.

This means that the UK would pay about £450 in subscriptions to EMPA in 1975.

At this time EMPA member associations were urged to impress on their respective governments the need to regulate Deep Sea Pilotage properly to prevent the many abuses and unlawful practices in many local districts. In a safety campaign during 1974, 363 complaint forms were received and a list of defective ships was prepared to send to IMCO. Another campaign was to be held in 1975.

1975 Human Factors Study

The finance for the Study was raised from the Department of Industry, the National Ports Council, the Shipowners through the Pilotage authorities and from the Pilots' organisation themselves. The Study commenced 1st October '75.

Reasons for research:

(1) The dissatisfaction expressed by pilots with their conditions of work, and, in particular
(2) Their concern for the safe guidance of large vessels (which continue to increase in size). Accident statistics show a greater likelihood of incidents with larger vessels in pilotage waters.
(3) Recent medical evidence suggestive of a comparatively high incidence of heart disease in pilots from a particular British pilotage district, which may be related to work stress; a finding duplicated with a similar group in Germany, handling large
(4) Vessels in congested areas.

Aims of Research:

(1) To assess pilotage activities for workload and stress problems;
(2) To provide (and assist in the implementation of) recommendations for the alleviation of such problems as are found to exist.

(3) Longer-term improvement of pilots' satisfaction with employment conditions and with their maintenance of good health
(4) To contribute to the safer handling of vessels in ports and other confined waterways.

Outline of Research:

(i) Familiarisation with the nature of the work and conditions of pilotage in a cross-section of pilotage districts, involving discussions, the collection of opinions and the analysis of records.
(ii) The selection of pilotage districts and personnel to form a basis for sampling for systematic medical investigations and workload field studies.
(iii) The conducting of these systematic studies under various conditions.
(iv) The simulation of certain pilotage activities (time and facilities permitting) to test hypotheses generated in previous stages.
(v) The analysis of findings, formulation of recommendations, report-writing and discussion.
(vi) The implementation and follow-up of recommendations.

Programme:

The plan was for the work to fall into three over-lapping phases:
Phase 1, Background study work at base and in pilotage stations, collecting records, opinions, etc. Psychological scaling and other similar instruments were used. Six pilotage areas to be visited; (about 15% of the total population of pilots to be seen).

Phase 2a, Medical screening and shipborne workload studies involving London pilots and physiological monitoring. Estimates of task and environmental load made, on "difficult" and "less difficult" trips. A parallel diary study and questionnaire study was thought possible.

Phase 2b, Supplementary screening and workload study using other pilotage districts), if requested and added expenditure found.

Phase 3, Data analysis, integration; report preparation. Possible follow-up work if requested. (Outside time-scale and budget).

One facet of the Study was that some pilots were not only accompanied by a researcher but also were required to wear meters measuring blood–pressure, pulse rate and body-temperature. On the Manchester Ship Canal one pilot being monitored was asked " When we passed that ship a few minutes ago your blood -pressure rose with a mere slight change of pulse rate. But then a short time after the passing manoeuvre was over your, blood-pressure, pulse-rate and temperature all increased markedly. What would cause that?" The answer was simple. ' We were passing the golf course when I remembered the bloody awful mess I made of a putt at the second tee, yesterday!"

1976 Annual Conference London

The President the Rt. Hon. James Callaghan in his opening speech quoted a letter:

> to the Secretary of Trade, The Rt. Hon. Peter Shore M.P.
> "As you may know I am President of the UKPA, on honorary office I have held for some 12 years. It was in that capacity that I led a deputation in 1973 to the then Minister concerned to discuss reorganisation of pilotage. As a direct result of

that deputation, the DoT set up the Steering Committee of Pilotage (SCOP) the first Committee on Pilotage fully representative of all the interests concerned.

I am now writing to you to press for a Pilotage Bill to be included in our legislative programme as soon as possible. This would be the first pilotage legislation since 1913 and all those concerned are agreed that reorganisation of the pilotage service is long overdue, and is necessary in the interests of safety and the maintenance of efficiency in the vastly different conditions obtaining since the last Act was passed some 62 years ago.

As you know, the SCOP Report was signed unanimously and provided the Recommendations are taken as a package deal, the Bill should not be unduly contentious, and could be taken upstairs and not on the Floor of the House. For example, I know that the United Kingdom Pilots' Association have two objections concerned with the granting of pilotage certificates, and nationality questions (UKPA letter to you dated 16 September 1974), but I believe that these matters could be settled by certain safeguards which I understand have already been under discussion. I do not of course know whether you have received other objections, but as it is clear that the good will exists to get a Bill on the Statute Book, such objections could probably be ironed out.

In this context the request in your Foreword to the Report in September 1974 for comments "if possible within two months of publication" was taken that the Department viewed the matter as one of urgency. But a year has since elapsed and the pilots and others are now asking when legislation is likely to be drawn up.

I am aware that a policy statement is contemplated with reference to various steps that could usefully be taken in advance of new legislation. Whilst I welcome this as evidence that we are not standing still, I think it is also implicitly accepted that such immediate steps cannot in themselves be a substitute for a comprehensive Bill.

The unanimous signing of the SCOP Recommendations was the result of a great deal of hard work and compromise on all sides, and I would, therefore, be very glad indeed for any help you can give in getting legislation drafted with a view to its inclusion in the parliamentary timetable at an early date."

From: The Rt. Hon. Peter Shore, M.P. to The Rt. Hon James Callaghan M.P.

Thank you for your letter of 21 October about the need for new legislation on pilotage.

I share your view on the importance of this but there seems little prospect of finding Parliamentary time to introduce a new Bill this Session. However, I am anxious to clear the ground so that advantage can be taken of any opportunity to present a new Bill which may arise. This is why we have been consulting the interested parties on a Government policy statement which I hope will be made public early in the new Session.

I fully understand that the delay in introducing legislation to implement the unanimous recommendations of the Steering Committee on Pilotage has caused disappointment. I very much hope, however, that the impetus for reorganisation stimulated by the SCOP report will not be lost and that the organisations represented on the Committee will continue to lend their support to the recommendations as a whole despite misgivings on one or two points. This is important both to facilitate any desirable changes which can be made under the existing law and in the interests of securing a non-contentious measure which will be easier to introduce and to pass through both Houses.

Of course, I fully accept your point that apolicy statement is in no way a substitute for a Bill and that the scope for introducing helpful changes under the 1913 Act is limited.

I hope that, despite disappointment, the forthcoming annual meeting of the United Kingdom Pilots' Association will accept my assurance that I regard new legislation on pilotage as an important matter and that it will be introduced as soon as opportunity offers. Meanwhile, the policy statement will, I believe, represent a helpful step forward.

1975

The Letch Report recommended levels and the actual number of pilots in the Districts (per the DoT returns for 1974) were as follows:

Actual No of Letch Recommended

	Pilots	Level
Aberdeeen	9	£4963
Barrow	5	£4838
Belfast	18	£5386
Blyth	8	£4763
Bristol	33	£6058
Clyde	45	£7174
Dundee	44	£4607
Falmouth	4	£6058
Goole	30	£5386
Forth	52	£5546
Hartlepool	12	£4607
Humber	144	£6579
Ipswich	11	£4763
Liverpool	173	£6397

	Pilots	Level
London (other than Cinque Ports & North Channel)	255	£7302
London (Cinque Channel)	212	£7971
Londonderry	8	£4287
Manchester	80	£6329
Newcastle	48	£6192
Southampton	64	£7210

Advisory Committee on Pilotage (ACOP)

With pressure on the parliamentary timetable making it impossible to introduce legislation on pilotage in the current Session, it was decided however, very conscious of the concern felt by most of the pilotage interests, that the implementation of the recommendations of the Report of the Steering Committee on Pilotage was not to be further delayed. Accordingly, the Secretary of State has appointed an Advisory Committee on pilotage with the following terms of reference:

> To advise the Secretary of State for Trade regarding changes in all aspects of pilotage arrangements in the United Kingdom which can and should be made in advance of new legislation; in particular, to progress the reorganisation of local pilotage authorities on the general lines endorsed in the Government's policy statement of December 1975; and to work for early agreement on the content of future pilotage legislation.

The Advisory Committee, chaired by Dr. Denis Rebbeck, C.B.E., consisted of:
  Mr. Frank Berry, Humber pilot.

Mr. George W. Brimyard, Port Services Director, MDHB
Mr. Geoffrey Clayton, Chairman, Gloucester Pilotage Authority.
Mr. Fred A. Everard, C.B.E., Chairman, F. T. Everard & Sons Ltd.
Mr. Harry Frith, Manchester pilot.
Mr. George C. Howison, Clyde pilot.
Mr. George A. B. King, Managing Director, BP Tankers Ltd.
Capt. Peter A. Leighton, Director of Marine Services, PLA
Mr. Daniel I. McMillan, River Thames pilot.
Capt. Peter Mason, Elder Brother, Trinity House, London.
Mr. David M. Robinson, C.B.E., Director, Stag Line Ltd.
Mr. John B. Williams, Port Director, Cardiff, British Transport Docks Board.
The Secretary of the Committee was Mr. Stuart Hampson of the DoT with other officials of the Department attending meetings as necessary.

1976

89th Conference Middlesboro

This followed the IMPA Conference the previous day Falmouth pilots reported they had applied to the Trade Secretary (DoT) for permission to have their pilot boats with bright orange hulls. Formal permission was needed: the Pilotage Act of 1912 requires that all pilot craft have black hulls. Orange colour for visual contact and recognition contributed much towards the safety in port approaches.

The Port of Preston was about to cease operation as a port. The officers of the UKPA were careful to ascertain the protection that all the pilots' social and professional needs were carefully protected.

1977

At the Ninetieth Conference in London in November, Edgar Eden reported the major development for a year which has been full of activity. The major issue has been pilotage legislation.

> "It is only in the last four years that the Government set up two Committees – SCOP and ACOP – to examine the arrangements for marine pilotage in the UK with a view to preparing new legislation. Pilots will have read the SCOP Report of 1974, the Government Policy Statement of 1975 and latterly, the ACOP Report of 1977."

The latter set the wheels in motion for the amendment of the Pilotage Act, 1913. The year is remembered by those most closely connected with pilotage reorganisation as the year of "hard labour" – endless meetings, endless discussions, endless drafting of papers – and for what purpose?

We learn from the Government in their Policy Statement of 1975 that the principal aims of reorganisation of pilotage are safety in changing conditions, improved organisation of the system and fair treatment of the pilots themselves. Safety in changing conditions is not in question since successive Government Committees including SCOP have had nothing but admiration for the pilots for the high standard of service they give to shipping throughout the year in all weather conditions and often at great risk to themselves.

Pilotage Commission

A Pilotage Commission will be set up with pilots as Pilotage Commissioners. But what of the resolutions from successive UKPA Conferences and Special Conferences calling for 50% pilot representation on the Commission. Pilots are asked to agree to changes in pilotage organisation without any assurance that the pilot representation on the Commission would be at least the largest single representation on the lines of the present composition of ACOP.

The Commission will have appeal functions on pilotage dues, thereby streamlining the procedure for increasing pilotage dues without recourse to byelaws and will also deal with pilotage certificates, to ensure that the numbers of pilotage certificates granted do not impinge on the viability of individual pilotage districts. Such functions as research into manpower requirements, collation of statistics, responsibility for the pension fund and other advisory functions could prove helpful to the overall improvement of the present system. But a national "Contingency Fund" and a national "Pilot Boat Fund" are essential functions of any pilotage reorganisation and provisions for the setting up of these two funds are of paramount importance to pilots for any meaningful improvement in the present system. The Commission is expected to be the catalyst to local pilotage reorganisation, particularly in districts where the structure of Pilotage Authorities leaves much to be desired. Enshrined in the various Government reports is the extension of compulsory pilotage "as a general principle" and this should be clearly indicated in any new legislation. Provision for licensed pilots to act as assistants to other licensed pilots on ships, will clarify the position of pilots presently acting as Assistant Licensed Pilots, provided of course that it is not extended to persons other than licensed pilots.

In exchange for the above improvements in the present system, pilots are asked to concede pilotage certificates to EEC nationals on a carefully monitored system, with provision – as outlined in para 14 of Annex B of the ACOP Report – for compensating pilots in that (I quote) "reserve powers would also be taken for the Secretary of State to make regulations by Statutory Instrument, providing for payment of compensation to any pilot who suffers loss or diminution of earnings attributable to any provision of the Act – including the issue of pilotage certificates; such compensation would normally be paid by ships using the district through pilotage dues or contributions by certificate holders".

The General Council of British Shipping (GCBS) have accepted in para 10 of their notes of 11th July, 1977, the establishment of a central fund to compensate pilots in this respect and have also indicated the shipowners' willingness "to discuss details of this with the pilots' organisations in advance of the legislation reaching the statute book".

A third principal aim of the Government is fair treatment of the pilots themselves. Great effort has already been put into long, protracted negotiations with the GCBS on restructuring of earnings, methods of reviewing earnings, and pensions, as some of the major issues involved in the fair treatment of pilots.

The GCBS are proposing a new arrangement for the Letch Scheme Districts with not more than six levels of earnings. In return for the above, the GCBS are asking for an in depth productivity deal by requiring pilots to give up their present right to earn 10% above their mean Letch earnings, within the Letch tolerations,

(a) to participate in studies to review their workload and establish "accurate" proper numbers of pilots "throughout the country"; in short, participate in a productivity exercise giving (to quote GCBS's para 15 of their paper) "an acceptable level of efficiency under reorganisation from the point of view of shipowners",
(b) to give up all income derived from pilotage within the district which is presently excluded from their current recommended level of earnings and also give up future income derived from pilotage work in newly extended limits of districts under reorganisation,
(c) to accommodate, subject to safeguards, the possible effects of pilotage certificates on the District,

(d) to undergo an assessment of their different responsibilities on the basis of agreed yardsticks before being slotted into new categories.

Districts outside Letch will have "the same rational approach" applied to them to determine their future recommended earnings.

On the important subject of pensions, the GCBS acknowledge the real concern of older pilots and pensioners about their "restricted entitlements or rather small pensions" and have said that they are "in principle anxious that means should be found as quickly as possible to provide satisfactory pension arrangements for pilots".

On the PNPF being re-established as a Section 226 Scheme for the self-employed, the GCBS would not seek to benefit from rates reduction, would be willing to explore how to make up the difference between 15% gross and net relevant earnings, would be willing to participate in joint examination of the problem. On the topping-up scheme, the GCBS are receptive to the idea and are willing to participate fully in further studies involving professional advisers. On-going meetings with tax experts and actuaries are being held with the object of producing an acceptable solution to the pension problems. The situation, on the eve of another national meeting with the GCBS on 23rd November, 1977, has yet to be crystallised and must await the outcome of the discussions on reorganisation at this year's Annual Conference

The officers had meetings with the Chamber of Shipping to consider the values of a 44/40 hour week and the disparity between pilots' earnings and the sea-standard that had developed since the introduction of the Agreements in the Letch Agreement.

In April 1977 the Harmonization of the UK Buoyage commenced – the shapes colours and markings of buoys etc were to be standardized. There had been numerous seminars, meetings and educational courses and at this time the I.A.L.A. alternative system of international buoyage displayed in the River Thames.

The pilots almost in unison deprecated the value of buoys coloured entirely green.

1978

The Association

Edgar Eden addressed the Conference "The UKPA must deal with a host of pilotage matters, both at national and local levels. I draw your attention to the Executive reports which have appeared in the last three of the four issues of *THE PILOT* for 1977 where brief mention is made of some of the matters handled by the Association. If delegates wish to raise any particular matter under the debate of my report, I would welcome it.

There are, however, two national matters which deserve special attention. The first concerns Pilot Boat Surveys. Meetings at the DoT considered how best to progress the Department's commitment for the survey of pilot vessels, responsibility for which was accepted in the Government Policy Statement of 1975. A Working Party under the Chairmanship of the Deputy Chief Surveyor of the DoT has been set up to review the practical requirements of pilot boats.

The second concerns the application of the Health and Safety at Work Act, 1974, to marine pilotage in health and safety matters. A meeting with the DoT when a Health & Safety Executive representative explained the administration of the Act. The point was made that the Health and Safety at Work Act did not apply to vessels navigating in territorial waters and, consequently, it provided no protection for and imposed no duties on pilots if they were boarding or landing in this area which was outside Great Britain. When ships were loading or unloading in any dock the Dock Regulations applied in conjunction with the Health and Safety at Work Act. The Health and Safety Executive expressed the view that legislation covering pilotage must in practice be the main means for ensuring the health and safety of marine pilots.

The Officers of the Association

The work of the Association continues to place a heavy burden on members of the Executive. Reorganisation of pilotage in particular has taken the "lion's share" of the meetings held in London, and this is reflected in the accounts for the year. Special mention must be made of the Members of the Executive on ACOP – Frank Berry, Dan McMillan and George Howison – who have had to bear the brunt of the main work on reorganisation of pilotage. To them, and all other members of the Executive, we extend our thanks and appreciation. We are also indebted to the Local Secretaries of UKPA Districts who continue to perform a most valuable service to the Association.

The Members of the Association congratulated Chairman Frank Berry, who in the New Year's Honours was awarded the O.B.E. for services to Pilotage.

Delegates were then made aware of the resignation from the Executive of John Edmondson: his departure from the Executive Committee was a tremendous loss, not only to the Executive, but also to the membership as a whole. His clear and concise presentation of facts based on his well-found grasp of the intricacies of pilotage will be sadly missed. As a representative of the UKPA on Government and other committees he has done much to improve the stature of the Association. He has proved to be an asset on any Committee on which he was involved. We offer him our sincere thanks for his unstinting work over the many years he has served the Association on the Executive.

The Editor of our journal continues to project the image: we have had requests for copies of *THE PILOT* from a US Government Department and from other parts of the world. All with good measure of savings.

The Pilotage Commission was expected to be the catalyst to local pilotage re-organisation, particularly in district where the structure of Pilotage Authorities leaves much to be desired.

Enshrined in the various Government reports in the extension of compulsory pilotage "as a general principle" and this should be clearly indicated in any new legislation.

In exchange for improvements in the present system, pilots were asked to concede pilotage certificates to EEC nationals on a carefully monitored system, with provision for compensating pilots by the Secretary of State making provision for compensation pilots who suffer the loss of earnings attributable to the issue of pilotage certificates.

1979

Margaret Thatcher became Prime Minister and industrial turbulence was about to be transformed and increased earnings more difficult to attain.

1979

Merchant Shipping Act

The important provision of this legislation was to change the authority for pilotage administration to local organisations i.e. commercial concerns operating port facilities and to be known as Competent Harbour Authority. The latter would authorise suitable persons to act a pilots, and, if not employed, to be engaged by contract with the CHAs.

At the 1979 Conference, the members agreed to hold their 1980 Conference at Liverpool, with the aim of holding one or two joint sessions of the two organisations, thereby bringing into the open the subject of unity. At that Conference, held in Liverpool Town Hall, there were quite a few direct and pointed remarks from both bodies all given and taken with the best of good humour. There was disappointment among members of the Association that unity was

NEW LEGISLATION

not achieved on the spot. But when they dispersed there seemed no doubt that unity would soon be achieved.

The 16 pilots conducting ships in and out of Great Yarmouth were in attendance when on Friday 15th June 1979 they were visited by the Duke of Edinburgh, the Master of Trinity House to open the new Pilot Station at Mission Bay. The new building comprised a Duty Pilot Office, an administration office and conference waiting room for the pilots, accommodation for the Pilot boat crews and a small workshop.

SCOP secretariat was appointed an announced as agreed in November.

The Chairman was named as Dr. Dennis Rebbeck, formerly the Chairman of the Advisory Committee on Pilotage. In January the names of the Pilotage Commission were released as:

G.W. Brimyard, B.J. Evans
G.S.C. Clarabut, H. Frith
K. Cooper, Capt. P.F. Mason
J.P. Davidson. N.C. Walker
Capt. A.F. Dickson

Ordinary Members were paid £1,2000 each annually free of tax. There was considerable discussion concerning the possible merging of the UKPA and MPB. Harry Frith stated that as the TGWU had links with the International Transport Federation they had been unwilling to cut links with the TGWU, which meant a connection with the international scene. But as the ITF was primarily interested in seafarers' welfare he recognised that as the International Pilots' Association now had a place at the IMCO meetings, pilots were better served with that arrangement and the MPB thought the two bodies should merge as soon as possible. There was now the need to take action. It was hoped that the joint Conference in Liverpool in October 1980 would be the best time to confirm the merger.

The Secretary pointed out the contracts arising from the 1979 Merchant Shipping Act and the Finance Act 1980 would affect the pilots' pensions, the National Agreement on the Earnings of the Pilots including pensions and the Pilotage Commission. There were many points of reform: the pilots would have to achieve a greater collective responsibility towards the public for the safety of the environment, the safety of life and the safety of shipping.

	DISTRICTS
£12,708	LONDON (INTEGRATED), ISLE OF WIGHT, CLYDE, FORTH, HUMBER, LIVERPOOL, MILFORD HAVEN, TEES.
£11,463	MANCHESTER, SOUTH EAST WALES.
£10,218	BELFAST, BRISTOL, FALMOUTH, PORT TALBOT, SWANSEA, TYNE.
£8,973	BARROW AND FLEETWOOD AMALGAMATED), DUNDEE, GLOUCESTER, GOOLE, IPSWICH, • KINGS LYNN, PRESTON, *SHOREHAM, TRENT, ♦YARMOUTH AND SOUTHWOLD.
£7,729	ABERDEEN, BLYTH, *BOSTON AND SPALDING, HARTLEPOOL, LONDONDERRY, PLYMOUTH, ♦ POOLE, SEAHAM, SUNDERLAND.

Recommended Earnings on Annual Review of Rates Basis
♦ Non-Letch Scheme Districts with five or more licensed pilots.

It is emphasised that these are the recommended net earnings for the proper numbers of pilots in the districts concerned. Before they can become operative in any particular district, studies will have to be made by the Pilotage Authority to establish an equitable and appropriate workload as the basis of an accurate proper number of pilots under the revised conditions created by reorganisation.

The establishment of the Pilotage Commissioners was to facilitate the necessary review of workloads and proper numbers of pilots throughout the country for the various districts as they are established or re-established under reorganisation and the parties to this Agreement urge that individual Authorities and the Commission should tackle this review as a matter of high priority.

The establishment of equitable workloads to the satisfaction of the Pilotage Commission was an assurance of fair treatment of pilots in different districts and of an acceptable level of efficiency under reorganisation so far as shipowners were concerned.

Pending the completion of this review in any particular district, the recommended earnings of pilots continued to be determined under the provisions of the 1957 Letch Agreement which in due course was superseded by this Agreement. It was anticipated that in most cases the new recommended earnings would be introduced without any initial increase in pilotage rates. If an increase in rates should be necessary in any particular district it would be accepted in one step provided it did not add more than 5% to the rates and charges from which pilots› earnings were derived in the district. If the full implementation of the new recommended earnings in a district should require an increase greater, then unless there were agreements between the parties to the contrary through the exercise of a degree of flexibility, it was to be phased in with no increase in excess of 5% being applied for the purpose in any one year.

The 1980s

This was a period when the pilotage acts were almost ready to go before the Houses of Parliament. But the Prime Minister had a habit of moving junior ministers from their departments after two years so that the minister responsible would leave before the legislation entered parliament. Several occasions it was seen that the minister delayed action and avoid making a decision.

From late 1982 the Humber pilots, already busy with extra work, brought larger and unusual import traffic carrying coal to several sites along the Trent and Ouse building coal stocks to combat coal strikes in 1983/4. There were many strikes and most failed completely. There would be no major industrial action affecting the whole of the UK.

In 1976 the 12 pilots at Great Yarmouth were covering the work of 25 pilots with only 12 pilots and thought that the traffic would continue for another ten years. The rate of work was far too heavy to carry on for long and the ship-owners objected to the earnings generated for the pilots and another four pilots were taken on.

The UKPA had already agreed to a free flow of pilots from one district to another.

Three transferred from the Thames and one from Sunderland although they were all over 40 and did not merge easily into the wages regime, but were accepted per the UKPA policy. Then, in 1980, a sudden and unanticipated edict from the Norwegian Government which virtually stopped the passenger trade to the oil rigs in the area. One third of the one of a port's trade ceased overnight. One year undermanned, next year they were over-manned. They began to look for transfers for the three pilots over 40: their former districts refused to accept them back (due to the age limit of 40). The UKPA policy of free flow of transferees did not have a happy effect in all cases.

1981 April:
Fourth International Symposium on Vessel Traffic Services Bremen

At the fourth international symposium on VTS systems held in Bremen in April, a meeting of some 22 licensed European pilots attending the seminar was called by Captain Albert de Vries, the then President of E.M.P.A., to enable the pilots to support as a unanimous body Captain Zweidorff's paper "Vessel Traffic Services – a Pilot's view". I am pleased to say that the United Kingdom pilots' delegates have now alerted their colleagues to the fact that pilots must become involved in that part of vessel traffic services which is directly involved with the practical movement of vessels. The United Kingdom pilots hope to have a paper accepted for the fifth international symposium on vessel traffic services planned for Marseilles in 1984.

The Deep Sea Pilots' Association were finally accepted into membership of the UKPA (as Europilots).

The Association of Licensed British Deep Sea Pilots

Deep Sea Pilotage exists outside of the areas controlled by port or river pilots. Records show that the origins of licensed Deep Sea Pilots in the United Kingdom can be traced back to 1581. At that time the Hull Trinity House was granted, by charter of Queen Elizabeth the First "the authority to licence mariners to take charge of vessels sailing the seas". Over four centuries later the Trinity Houses of Hull, London and Newcastle are still responsible for examining and licensing Deep Sea Pilots.

During the Second World War many navigational marks and aids were removed from around the coasts of Northern Europe. Vessels, both military and commercial, were still required to transit the waters, often under cover of darkness. Special skills were needed by the pilots who assisted with this navigation through the banks, shoals and minefields in those days before radar and other electronic navigational aids. After the cessation of hostilities the demand for these Channel or North Sea pilots was still apparent. George Hammond Shipping of Dover took over the management of the British Pilots, acting as agents for them. In 1950 a number of the pilots set up their own agency under the administration of Captain Hutchinson.

This agency evolved to become Deep Sea and Coastal Pilots. Sixty years later these two agencies that supply Trinity House licensed pilots from the United Kingdom are still in competition with each other

During the early 1970s the pilots of both agencies were unsettled due in part to issues regarding working practises and employment. Many of these practises arose as a result of the pilots then (and now) being self-employed paid only for the work they do and there were instances of refusing to take the first job offered to wait for a better paid job. Rules and regulations being drafted, putting pressure on pilots, with planned changes to working areas (without input from the pilots) affecting the licensing areas and livelihood of the North Sea pilots. Then it was possible for a North Sea pilot to obtain a license to act within the Baltic Sea.

A meeting of British Deep Sea Pilots was held in 1973, when the formation of an association was agreed. The objectives set out by EUROPILOTS (named in 1974) remain current today:

a) to promote the professional interests and well-being of Deep Sea Pilots.
b) to speak on behalf of Deep Sea Pilots and express their views and opinions.
c) to receive representations and to attend to any business in the best interest of Deep Sea Pilots.

EUROPILOTS needed to be heard within both Britain and Europe at the highest possible level. The way forward was for an application to be aligned with the UKMPA. Over the ensuing years and into the early 1980s the membership of the association peaked at around 60 pilots. Applications were made on a frequent basis to join UKMPA, which would allow EUROPILOTS access to the fledgling organisations of EMPA, and IMPA. Unfortunately the applications were repeatedly turned down, the main stumbling blocks were the lack of an official association rule book and that the Trinity Houses issued their Deep Sea Pilots with a certificate not a licence. It was thought at the time that there was opposition from some UKMPA members who had been moonlighting as North Sea Pilots, a perk that would be removed if the licensed Pilots could achieve recognition.

Helicopter boarding. (Image © Europilots)

Why Deep Sea Pilots? A question are best answered with a statement about experience. All British Deep Sea Pilots are master mariners with a minimum of 5 years command experience prior to commencing their pilotage career. Carriage of a licensed Deep Sea Pilot ensures that the vessel has on board, a dedicated professional navigator fully conversant with all aspects of the area to be transited. A Deep Sea Pilot can help to alleviate these problems and enable doubling up of the bridge watch without introducing problems with fatigue or rest-hour regulations. Summing up, a Deep Sea Pilot, on the bridge, reduces individual errors of judgement and helps to prevent the build-up of 'error chains' commonly referred to in accident reports. Most shipmasters are appreciative of the assistance rendered by a Deep Sea Pilot, they value having someone on board they can converse with who fully understands the problems encountered in these days of ever increasing regulation and the threat of criminalisation. One pleasing aspect is the high number of masters who request the services of the same Pilot on subsequent voyages: the best indication possible of a job well done. Although most of the jobs undertaken by Deep Sea Pilots tend to be on board the larger, deeper or quicker merchant vessels in the Southern North Sea there are exceptions. During the 1st Iraq war the steady stream of US military vessels which mobilised from NW Europe to the Gulf employed British Deep Sea Pilots for the transit of the Dover Straits. More recently the experience and versatility of Deep Sea Pilots has seen them on board guard vessels deployed to protect underwater cables and intercontinental pipelines.

All EUROPILOTS members are eligible for membership of the UKMPA. Given the initially aims and aspirations of the original founding members it is disappointing that not all Deep Sea Pilots take up the available membership. Since affiliation into UKMPA was agreed in 1981 there have been Deep Sea Pilots who have represented UKMPA both on their own technical and training committees and also at meetings of the United Kingdom Safety of Navigation Committee. Currently EUROPILOTS member Kevin Vallance is the UKMPA participant member of the EMPA e-Navigation working group. Recently Tony Jameson stood down after many years representing the Association on the UKHO – Hydrographic Office chart user council.

Each year the EUROPILOTS elected Chairman (currently Chris Hughes) attends the EMPA annual conference, making up the largest single annual expenditure of the association. However the membership feels it is important to be represented and take a part in the development of European Pilotage brotherhood.

Over the years there have been various initiatives and investigations into the carriage of Deep Sea Pilots in particular through the Dover Straits. Mandatory carriage of Deep Sea Pilots is not an aim or objective of EUROPILOTS. Currently IMO recommendation 486 dating back to 1981 is in force. There have been attempts originating from 1991 to revise and strengthen the recommendation to align it with the situation in the Baltic and at other locations worldwide. Due to its non-mandatory status Deep Sea Pilotage is highly affected by market forces. During the current economic situation the competitiveness of the different agencies in Europe is driving down the rates being charged, having a detrimental effect on the earnings of the Pilots. Whilst researching this article one consistent comment of the retired members was the feeling of frustration that EUROPILOTS had failed in one of its original stated aims, that of one British Agency with standard tariffs. Unlikely under the present European administration.

1982

The annual conferences of the UKPA and Marine Pilotage Branch of the TGWU were held in September: both voted by substantial margins to combine under a single body to be known as the UKPA. The revisions needed to enable the UKPA and the Marine Pilots Branch to merge were discussed at length.

With the Deep Sea Pilots' Association "Europilots", also members of the UKPA, almost all UK pilots are expected to be represented by the one body.

1983

On 1st January 1983 pilotage rates nationally were increased by 5.5% in line with the merchant navy officers. The 1983 Pilotage

Act consolidated the existing pilotage laws and prepared the way for a comprehensive Act to make major structural alterations to pilot administration in the near future.

In October a delegation from the Joint Executive met the minister to discuss three central and difficult problems in pilotage. The first concerned compensation for early voluntary retirement. The second was more complicated in that it was to resolve the pilotage in the London Districts; the ministers wanted to take into account the pilotage Commission recommendations for that district before dealing with other districts a delay that affected the remainder of the UK for over four years. The ministers involved were also very concerned especially when London district was under the eye of Parliament, Prime Minister Margaret Thatcher and the press. The third problem was the possible long term solution to pilotage i.e. widespread reappraisal of the pilotage service. The Pilotage Commission was seen to have taken the lead by raising the problem with the previous minister, however due to the London District situation the reappraisal was left inactive.

The West Coast ports had been badly hit by changes in trade. Over 30 pilots from Sharpness. Liverpool and Manchester were working as pilots overseas: West Africa, Libya, Red Sea, Persian Gulf and Pacific Islands. A number of pilots from Liverpool and Manchester transferred to Milford Haven Southampton, Thames, Ipswich and Humber.

There is little evidence of the difference between pilot earnings according to district or even between the major ports as per the tables following:

1984 December

Parliamentary Green Paper published. The Executive Committee believed that the Green Paper was cobbled together by civil servants in attempts to solve the problems arising in the administration of pilotage that appeared following the 1983 Act.

Pilotage as a profession would be destroyed and the status of self-employed fee-earning pilots become that of a port employee. The new bill abolishing existing Pilotage Authorities transferred their functions to Competent Harbour Authorities (CHA's) having the sole duty and responsibility for provision of pilotage within their harbour limits. They were to authorise only the number of pilots they considered appropriate and employ the future pilots unless both the C.H.A. and the pilots agreed to a form of self-employment through a contract with the C.H.A. This feature proved to be problematic, almost a decade later.

The pilots surplus to a port's requirements would have the option of seeking a transfer to an undermanned pilotage district during the "shake-down period" or, if that was not possible or desirable, accepting severance from pilotage. The terms of which would a lump sum of approximately a year's salary to be raised from pilotage dues and person enhanced from out of the Pilots National Pensions Fund's surplus.

The Pilotage Commission

This had been in existence since November 1979 and had undertaken a great deal of work in the past year reviewing and visiting a number of districts and advising the Government on byelaws for their reorganisation. It was again unfortunate to have to report that the Government had yet to fully endorse or implement a good deal of this advice and thus pilots found themselves in an administrative no-man's land awaiting such decisions affecting their respective districts allowing them a reorganisation plan for the future.

It appeared, however, that there was also a problem with funding of pilot boat services. The current recommended Government policy that would probably be established was on the "user only shall pay" principle, with the anticipated large number of ships, currently using pilots, changing to movement under control of pilotage certificate holders and many other ships, the size and type yet to be decided, becoming "excepted" from pilotage control altogether. The revenue available for maintaining boat services must inevitably drop. There were indications that pilotage authorities planned to reduce their operating areas and even close down pilotage stations in order to operate within their reduced income, a situation that could hardly improve the safety of navigation which was the sole intention of the 1979 Merchant Shipping Act.

The Technical Committee continued their work throughout the year on a range of subjects, taking into consideration the views of the European and international technical committees of their respective pilots' associations.

1986

A New Pilotage Act

Edgar Eden resigned 31st January after 17 years as General Secretary taking the secretary Penny Mobley to form the secretariat for IMPA.

Clive Wilkin, chairman, spoke to the delegates: "this year, however eventful with the passage of the Pilotage Bill, the Association has been involved in several local requests for information and help and we have been able to call on the TGWU Legal Department for advice".

In the case of the Humber, Goole and Trent, the pilots there withdrew their services to shipping on 9th October to hold a meeting to discuss amalgamation of the three Services, Humber, Goole and Trent, and the appropriate income levels. This withdrawal of the services from shipping was brought about by deadlock in negotiations with ABP. The meeting was attended by approximately 200 members with pilot observers from Manchester, Liverpool, Southampton and South East Wales.

A stoppage for the pilots to discuss the future pilotage arrangements and working systems was unusual, and set out a stressed situation that would last for five years.

Most ports were then in some form of negotiation with their local CHAs and members kept the Association informed the progress made in their Districts. Most obvious is that, notwithstanding, the object of the Green Paper and the Pilotage Bill was presented on the premise to cut the cost of pilotage administration considered by the ship owners and Government to be unnecessarily high. There was never any talk throughout the passage of the Bill to cut Pilots' earnings, only the number of pilots. The Section Committee were, therefore, entitled to think that, with some adjustments, pilotage earnings would remain similar to the recommended level of the Letch earnings suitably adjusted over time, however that was not so. In the majority of cases reported to the Association CHA's attempted to down-grade the profession both in earnings and status. I can only hope that this is a sparring period we are going through, otherwise there must surely be serious trouble ahead for us all.

UKPA(M)

Secretary of State's communication of 23 May 1986 on a Pilots' Compensation Scheme

My right hon. Friend, the then Secretary of State for Transport, confirmed on 24 March, in answer to a question from my hon. Friend the Member for Bristol, East (Mr Sayeed), that the Government intend to bring forward as soon as possible legislative proposals for the reform of pilotage administration. Those proposals will include provision for a compensation scheme, to be funded by the industry, for those licensed pilots whose services are not required by the harbour authorities once they have taken over responsibility for pilotage.

Although attempts to obtain agreement among the parties concerned on the terms of compensation payments have previously been unsuccessful, it was considered right to make one further attempt, and at my right hon. Friend's request Mr James Davidson, the chairman of the Pilotage Commission, held discussions with representatives of the pilots, the shipowners and the harbour authorities about the terms of a compensation and finked early retirement scheme. He has also held discussions with the Pilots' National Pension Fund whose board of management has agreed to make available £15 million from the fund's surplus towards the cost of early retirement.

Mr Davidson has now reported that he has been able to secure the agreement in principle of the *United Kingdom Pilots' Association (Marine)* and of the British Ports Association to terms which he has drawn up, however, the General Council of British Shipping has not been prepared to agree them. Under the terms proposed by Mr Davidson, any pilots over the age of 50 whose services were not required would receive a lump sum payment equivalent to one year's recommended level of earnings set for 1984 for his district under the former Letch agreement, increased by RPI until the scheme takes effect. Payments in districts not formerly covered by the Letch agreement would be related to the equivalent earnings for 1984 subject to the same increases. For pilots over the age of 60, the sum would be reduced by one-fifth for each year by which the pilot exceeded the age of 60. I understand that the rules of capital gains tax will apply to the lump sum payments.

As regards pension arrangements. Mr Davidson has reported that although the board of management of the PNPF had taken no decision as to the precise benefits to be applied to individuals, they had prepared a scheme under which surplus pilots aged 55 and over would be able to retire with an immediate pension determined on the basis that:

1) the abatement factor on the pensions of those retiring early applied under the normal PNPF rules would be removed;
2) credits of ½ per year to cover the years to age 60 and for those due to retire at 65 or over, double credits to age 65 would be added;
3) pre-membership service credits of ½ per cent per month would be added in respect of expected service from age 60 to 65 (with maximum of 30 per cent);
4) the maximum additional credits under 2) and 3) above would be 15/60 per man and the Inland Revenue limit on the size of the pension would of course apply.

Any pilots aged between 50 and 55 who are surplus to requirements would receive similar benefits save that the abatement factor referred to in 1) above of 1/: per cent per month would apply. Mr Davidson has advised me that in his view the sum allocated by the PNPF would be adequate to meet the early retirement on this basis of such pilots as are surplus when the new legislation takes effect, and also any further surplus over the ensuing three years.

I know that some may regard the lump sum and pension terms set out above as generous, and it is indeed unusual for such payments to be made to people who are classified as self-employed. However, in view of the fundamental change which our proposed legislation will cause to the circumstances and expectations of many pilots, I accept that there is an obligation to ensure that they are fairly treated, and it is my intention that the statutory scheme to be introduced in association with the new legislation will provide for compensation on the basis which the representatives of the pilots and of the harbour authorities have now agreed.

I am grateful to Mr Davidson for his efforts in bringing forward these proposals.

An Extraordinary Conference by the UKPA (Marine) held in Transport House, London on 28th May considered the developments leading from the Government's Green Paper on Pilotage of December 1984. Dissatisfaction was expressed on progress of the pilots' requirements for an orderly reform of the industry. The Section Committee proposal, overwhelmingly endorsed, was that discussions should commence at the earliest possible time with the British Ports Association to lay down the framework for the industrial agreements which will apply, should the new regime come into force.

The Conference was also concerned that there should be no compulsory redundancies as a result of the negotiations that were due to take place. Serious anxiety was expressed about the safety of navigation in certain, specifically the Thames Estuary, where under certain conditions the current port proposals may leave large areas unguarded thus courting environmental disaster.

The pilots, albeit reluctantly, were prepared to support the proposed legislation provided it could be modified with satisfactory safeguards for the profession. Unfortunately, right from the beginning, the then Chairman of the British Ports Association, Mr A. G. Robinson, in a letter dated the 13th December 1984 (the very day of publication of the Green paper) made it quite clear in a letter to all M.P.s who could possibly have a constituency interest in port affairs warning them of the pilots' attitude to the proposed changes. This letter reduced the status of pilots to some form of interpreter between the Master and the VHF port control. This alarming attitude, coupled with the proposed radical changes in the legislation, resulted in the Section Committee receiving instructions to merge the UKPA and the MPB into one organisation under the umbrella of the Transport & General Workers' Union (TGWU).

During 1985, talks were held with senior officers of the TGWU and, notwithstanding the fact that previous attempts to unite the two parties under the UKPA had failed, the TGWU were prepared to accept the pilots into the Union on most acceptable terms. It will be recalled that, at the 1985 Conference, delegates were asked to vote and pass new rule changes permitting the machinery to be set up to hold a ballot allowing all UKPA members to vote as to whether the UKPA should merge with the MPB. In order that there should be no doubt as to the members' wishes, an 80% of votes cast would be required for the merger to take place. In the event, the UKPA accountant, Mr Guy Myers, was employed to count the vote and recorded a poll of 80.04% in favour. The merger duly took place in late 1984.

During the interim period the UKPA was obliged to vacate their office in Peel Street as the building had been purchased by the Spanish Embassy. Fortunately, with the good offices of the Honourable Company of Master Mariners, the UKPA was accommodated on board HQS *Wellington* for a period of 3 months until the changeover of the UKPA to the UKPA (Marine) was completed. Office accommodation for the new organisation was then in the TGWU Head Office in Smith Square. The General Secretary and Legal Adviser, Edgar Eden, who had been with the Association for over 17 years, retired on 31st December and Miss Penny Mobley, who had so admirably filled the gap left by the death of Yvonne

Lord Strathcona /E.Eden. (Image © UKMPA)

Blake, terminated her contract in the early part of the year. Both however, remained connected with pilots, administering the IMPA offices in London from HQS *Wellington* and the successors to those positions continue to do so.

UKPA(M)

The newly founded UKPA (Marine) came into being six weeks after the ballot count, on the 31st January 1986, under the stewardship of Mr John Connolly, the National Secretary of Dock Workers and Inland Waterways. The office of the UKPA (M) was currently run on a day-to-day basis by the new Secretary and Administrator, Miss Phillipa Julian. The Association executive began working on the question of reducing the number of pilots overall; the change permitted by the 1987 Act allowed pilots to take over shore positions.

1987

The Pilotage Act 1987

The most eventful Year in the History of British Pilotage would eventually become a severe disappointment – the effect of its provisions having repercussions that were never foreseen.

Annual Conference London

The first conference after the introduction of the 1987 Pilotage Act. The following resolution passed by the assembly: that the use of a strong national organisation with the TGWU is essential to co-ordinate, maintain, and enhance the pilotage profession, mandates the Section Committee to do all in their power to assist local pilots in furtherance of that objective.

Long debates took place on (1) Compensation, (2) Lump Sum Payment, (3) Guidelines for Future Employment of Pilots.

PNPF

Harry Frith (Manchester) of the Section Committee opposed a resolution that the membership was considering issuing an instruction to PNPF. To ask for a categoric statement is insulting. Fears that £15 million would be used up at an early stage was unfounded, £15 million was locked away. If further funds were needed they would be found. Slump in Stock Market will not alter the surplus in the Fund. The Actuary is more interested in dividend fluctuation than day to day share values.

Points from debate included: London could be last settlement – many men to go. Where would extra money come from if £15 million exhausted. What is the 'early' Early Scheme that was being talked about in the hall? Harry Frith answered – it is to be the basic scheme made available to proven surplus pilots before the appointed day. Such men would have to be identified by the existing Pilotage Authority and agreed to by its successor, CHA's: four authorities have applied for Early-Early Scheme: they are Liverpool, Clyde, Bristol and Manchester.

There was debate about the severance scheme being used up. However, Messrs. PNPF Committee members Frith, Connolly and Vaughan gave repeated assurances that there would be sufficient funds to cover all severance requirements. PNPF would look very closely at applications for the Early-Early Scheme.

Compensation is a national scheme. 1984 should be used as a benchmark, and indexed by RPI to calculate "year's pay".

Anybody declared surplus under the age of 50 (could be that number at Liverpool) is not covered. Guidelines for future employment are not an agreement but a 'final document'. Arbitration panel would be an independent Chairman and a representative from ports and pilots. Any member of the Section

Committee would be acceptable and may be changed from time to time. Re the position of a pilot who is released by a port that does not have a surplus – all costs will be met by the port from whence the transferee comes. Ports are reluctant to agree any extension to three months between appointed the day and the time when a surplus pilot is paid. Pilots are confident that paragraph 9 of the "Transfer Arrangements for Pilots" paper will cover this difficulty.

The role of the TGWU was explained. There is a difference between a contract of service "between an employer and an employee, when there is no Union involvement, and a "collective agreement" which will be between Union and CHA's – it will be made clear that collective agreements will continue to have TGWU – UKPA(M) involvement. Asked what will happen if there is no agreement with CHA before the appointed day J. Connolly said arbitration would have been reached before that.

There were reports from districts pertaining to Reorganisation: Humber, Isle of Wight, Tees, Forth, Swansea, London, Liverpool, Manchester, Great Yarmouth, Fowey, Falmouth, Penzance, Plymouth, Londonderry, Sunderland and Shoreham.

UKPA(M) Insurance

Group Accident Insurance – Premium increased to £16 per quarter. Claims had risen from 17 in 1985/6 to 80 in 1986/7.

Legal Expenses Scheme – two new cases in '87; many others continuing. Employer responsibilities had not yet arisen, but expected fairly soon with change of status.

Group Permanent Health 13 new claims this year, costing an extra £85,000 per annum. Weekly benefit is £115. No change in benefit or premium (£21 per quarter) was in prospect.

Treasurer's Report

Subscriptions needed to be increased to £30 per quarter; £28.35 net of political levy.

Treasurer had budgeted for £3,500 surplus in year to November 1988.

There were 50 British Deep Sea Pilots' licences – they seem to be doing well and unaffected by the new Pilotage Act.

Pilotage Commission was reduced from ten to five and despite objections from UKPA(M), the DfT insisted that there should be only one pilot – I. Evans, at the time, the only Pilot Commissioner.

Pilots' National Committee on Pensions. The large committee (20 members) expected to continue until appointed day when, if it was to continue, it would be reduced to the same number and geographical division as the Section Committee (8 members).

Chairman's Annual Report

1987 must be the most eventful year in the history of British pilotage. I am indeed grateful to the Section Committee for the help and hard work they have put in during this difficult year and particularly grateful to all the back-up facilities that membership of the TGWU has given to the pilots.

Immediately after conference last year, we engaged the services on a full time basis of Charles Barker, Watney and Powell, a firm of parliamentary consultants, to keep a watching brief and to advise the Association on how to achieve maximum input while the Pilotage Bill was passing through Parliament. They also advised us on which Members of the House of Lords and House of Commons we should approach. They also ensured that all amendments reached the influential members who were concerned and taking an active part with the Pilotage Bill. On their advice, to ensure that our amendments were legally acceptable, we engaged the services of the Parliamentary Draughtsman, Sharp, Pritchard & Company.

Members recalled that the Section Committee decided to hold a special Delegates' Conference on May 15th when a detailed summary was given to 96 pilots of the events which took place during the passage of the Bill. The Section Committee was reduced from sixteen to a more economic eight matching the future numerical strength of pilots' services.

The Queen's Speech on 11th November, the White Paper on Marine Pilotage Legislation Proposals and the Pilotage Bill published on the 13th November 1986, set in motion the parliamentary procedures with the Pilotage Bill starting its passage through Parliament in the House of Lords. (It is interesting to note that the Pilotage Bill did not follow the normal procedure for the House of Lords but was debated in the Moses Room by a reduced number of Lords representing each party and cross benches.) The Association is indeed fortunate to have our Honorary President, Lord Strathcona to support us through the whole of the 27½ hours of debate, where over 100 amendments were submitted on our behalf. Lord Underhill, Labour peer, argued the pilots' case admirably and took a great interest in our affairs on behalf of the Opposition.

The Bill passed to the House of Commons on the 12th March and the Association is indeed indebted to Malcolm Thornton MP, ex-Liverpool pilot, for the eloquent way in which the Pilots' case was put before Parliament. The Committee Stage and the Third Reading and Report took place on the 4th April where the Pilots tabled a further 16 amendments. All told, the debate in the House of Commons took eight hours making a total of some 35½ hours of debate in both Houses. On this occasion the Pilots were supported by most of the MPs a clear indication of the lobbying effect of individual pilots on their Members of Parliament up and down the country. However, notwithstanding this support, when Malcolm Thornton pressed for a Division, Members of Parliament appeared from all directions and the pilots lost 82 to 121 and the Bill was passed back to the Lords for them to agree the Commons

Amendments on the 7th May and on the 15th May became The Pilotage Act 1987. All the efforts and the cost involved in an attempt to modify this legislation were justified and the bill with better legislation for pilots than when it was presented.

Guidelines for the Future Employment of Pilots by pilotage authorities

At the time of writing the Conference report the final guidelines were not available. However, this document dealt with transfer arrangements, earnings, pensions, compensation, the resolution of disputes and arrangements for pilots awaiting transfer.

In1987, however eventful, with the passage of the Pilotage Bill, the Association had been involved in several local requests for information and help and the Association had to call on the TGWU Legal Department for advice. Significantly, in the case of the Humber, Goole and Trent, the pilots there withdrew their services to shipping on 9th October to hold a meeting to discuss amalgamation of the three Services, Humber, Goole and Trent, and the appropriate income levels. That withdrawal of services from shipping was brought about by deadlock in negotiations with ABP.

The meeting was attended by approximately 200 members with Pilot Observers from Manchester, Liverpool, Southampton and South East Wales.

It would seem that most ports were then in some form of negotiation with their local CHAs and local members kept the Association informed of progress made in their Districts. Most obvious was that, notwithstanding, the object of the Green Paper and the Pilotage Bill was presented on the premise to cut the cost of pilotage administration, considered by the ship owners and Government to be unnecessarily high. There was never any talk throughout the passage of the Bill to cut Pilots' earnings, only the number of pilots. We were, therefore, entitled to think that, with some adjustments, pilotage earnings would remain similar to the recommended level of the Letch earnings suitably dynamised. This was not so. In the majority of cases reported to the Association, CHAs attempted to down-grade the profession both in earnings and status. There seemed serious trouble ahead for us all.

Group Personal Accident Insurance Scheme

The quarterly premium was increased to £16.50 at the start of October following payment of two further claims for permanent total disablement. The first payment of £45,000 was to Mr Edward Levine (London-Sea Pilots North) who sustained multiple injuries when his car was crushed by a lorry in December 1985. The second claim arose from an entirely unexpected quarter and involved William R M MacFarlane of Liverpool. In June of last year Mr MacFarlane was on holiday in Scotland when he damaged he left leg while manhandling his car trailer – it was however only in May that the serious consequences of this accident for the member's career became clear. As he could no longer climb pilot ladders, Mr MacFarlane lost his pilot's licence in July and subsequently received settlement for £45,000 for his disability.

The number of accidents reported to date increased from 17 to 20 – no less than 80% of these accidents were job related and 50% involved boarding and landing or comparable situations when accessing vessels or wharves. As half of all the reported accidents concerned members over 55 years of age, we might be tempted to conclude that experience is not always a substitute for agility or perhaps simply that older members are more aware of the need to report accidents – either way, it is to Douglas M Wilton, a 63 year old Cardiff pilot, that congratulations should go for his presence of mind and physical fitness. At 7.45am on 9th October, Mr Wilton arrived at Dowds Wharf on the River Usk to take the mv *Ballygarvey* to sea at 8am. As he put his foot on the boarding ladder, it seemed to turn and he was dropped between the ship and the quay into the flood tide. He managed to grab one of the support columns of the jetty, but no one aboard the vessel seemed to be aware of his plight and his shouts for help could not be heard due to the noise of a mobile crane working on the dock above him. After 20 minutes in the water he managed to spot and make his way to a steel ladder and pull himself on to the wharf whereupon the crane driver saw him and sent for an ambulance. Fortunately, Mr Wilton was able to resume pilotage duty four weeks later.

The majority of accidents whilst boarding or aboard ship did of course give rise to painful physical injuries such as sprained ankles, bruised knees, twisted backs and jarred necks but the members involved all appear to have made good recoveries. During the earlier part of the year, the Association was particularly concerned for Mr G. Hegarty of Londonderry who fractured his kneecap in three places due to falling on a rock and was therefore extremely pleased to learn from him that he had been able to resume pilotage duty after a 5 month absence. More recently we have been advised of a further accident involving another South East Wales Pilot, E J Glover, who sustained a broken finger and a broken wrist due to the collapse of a temporary gangway within Newport Docks and we understand Mr Glover is not likely to be fit for pilotage duty for several months.

On the subject of Legal Expenses Insurance, the DAS Family Legal Policy remained available to Association members on preferential terms – the cost of £34 per year was increased to £40, representing a 50% discount on the normal premium of £80.

Group Permanent Health Insurance Scheme

Another area which is not the legal responsibility of the employer – namely, the provision of income during long term disablement, the Association's Group Permanent Health Insurance Scheme provided this facility. A facility was much needed and a further 13 new claims became due for payment during the last year. We calculate these new claims would cost underwriters almost £85,000 per year in addition to all the claims from earlier years which are still in course of payment. Apart from the two accident victims already mentioned, all of these new claims arose from illness with a preponderance – some 45% – involving hypertension, depression and anxiety neurosis. Other sources of disablement include various types of arthritis, heart and liver conditions and one victim of multiple sclerosis. The geographical distribution of claimants was widespread – from Aberdeen in the North to the Isle of Wight in the South, but London Sea Pilots South were particularly badly affected with no less than five new claimants in 1987 year all suffering from different illnesses. The outlook for the following 12 months appear very similar with a known further five potential new claimants in various Districts.

The standard level of weekly benefit under the Scheme was fixed at £115.50 per week at the beginning of 1986. Taken in conjunction with early retirement pension as is usually the case, recent experience seemed to confirm that the current benefit level was about right for the majority of members and no change recommended. On this basis, the standard quarterly premium remained unaltered at £21 per member.

1988

This was the first year when regulation action came under the 1987 Pilotage Act. 317 pilots retired, of which 250 had enhanced pension benefits for early retirement.

Total pensions (UKMPA membership in January 1986, 1,300) there were 807 at the end of the year, 53% employed, 47% self-employed. Negotiations began on reducing the number of London Pilots from 109 to 36: London 36 pilots and 3 temporary pilots. On 1st October approximately 823 pilots remained in the profession, with 167 pilots not being authorised and consequently being entitled to the Lump Sum and Linked Enhanced Early Pension scheme.

The 'Early' Early Retirement Scheme launched at the beginning of 1988 released sixty-five pilots from Liverpool, Manchester and the Clyde, easing the situation at those ports. But this also meant that the UKMPA had lost 65 members.

There was praise for the former Chairman of the UKMPA, Paul Hames, on his appointment as Pilot Manager of the Spurn (Humber) pilots.

1989

The Pilots' National Committee for Pensions. The PNCP, had become heavy with 17 members and three Pilot Trustees of the Pilots National Pensions Fund (PNPF) with the Secretary Jan Lemon who was also the Secretary of the PNPF. Such a large Committee was expensive to run. Members were chosen from a large number of ports but the reduction in pilot numbers needed to be reflected in the size of the PNCP. The new committee would be formed by members elected from larger areas comprising more ports. The PNPF had then been divided into employed pilots and self-employed pilots: the proportions being 445 to 335. The employed pilots were either on a straight salary or a salary consisting of basis plus bonuses. The Chairman was usually invited to make a report to the annual UKPA(M) Conferences presenting a unique opportunity to explain what had been achieved or attempted by the PNPF during the year. This committee now represented the members.

Pilot Training

Members of the Section Committee noted a general concern regarding future recruitment. Pilotage had become dated, and the stranglehold of the 1913 Pilotage Act had inhibited modernisation of pilot services. Accordingly the Government set up the Steering Committee On Pilotage – SCOP. (See appendix A.)

Their recommendations were published in June 1974. One of their prime recommendations was that there should be a central pilotage authority, which would be responsible for every aspect of pilotage, including the training of future pilots. However, the SCOP recommendations, although unanimous, were never implemented, and a further committee was set up – Advisory Committee on Pilotage (ACOP) – recommending the establishment of the Pilotage Commission, which in turn set up, amongst other things, a committee to look into the training of future pilots, and circulated all pilotage authorities for their views. The majority of the papers returned indicated that the basic qualification for entry into a pilot service should be a Master's Foreign-going Certificate (MFG). Following the further reduction in the British Merchant Navy, from 1,378 vessels over 500 GRT in 1978 to less than 500 vessels in 1987 (and falling), pilot services in the future were going to be hard pressed to find British officers who hold foreign-going masters certificates.

At the 1989 Conference, the subscriptions were raised to £40 quarterly. Resolutions proposed by the Chairman of Europilots, representing 45 members, with the aim of reducing the Trinity House pilots working as Deep Sea Pilots – as a spare time activity. There was mention of moves to set up a single licensing authority under the jurisdiction of the DoT for issuing Deep Sea pilot certificate.

This was a settling down period for UK pilots under the new port-orientated regimes: the Section Committee assessing the new terms and conditions. 288 pilots left the service on early retirement including 74 on medical severance. 841 pilots remain members on the UKPA (M), 441 as employees of the ports and 400 as self-employed pilots. A small number of authorized pilots are members of other organisations. Six Liverpool pilots transferred to Southampton.

CHANGE IN PILOT NUMBERS
As at May 1989

EMPLOYED STATUS

	1987	1989		1987	1989
Aberdeen	9	9	Plymouth	3	3
Belfast	12	12	Portsmouth	New	3
Berwick	2	1	Ramsgate	New	3
Bridgewater	1	1	Seaham	3	3
Clyde	26	13	Shoreham	8	7
Coleraine	3	3	Southampton	40	31
Crouch	6	2	Sullom Voe	11	8
Dover	New	4	Sunderland	5	6
Falmouth	6	6	Swansea inc Port Talbot	11	9
Harwich new	3	8			
Heysham	4	2	S-E Wales	29	20
Inverness	2	2	Gt. Yarmouth	11	6
Kings Lynn	9	9			
Liverpool	130	55			
London					
North	193	32			
Medway	31	29			
River	52	37			
South	64	26			
West	61	28			
Lowestoft	3	3			
Milford H	17	13			
Montrose	4	2			
Peterhead	3	3			
	640	441			

SELF-EMPLOYED

	1987	1989
Blyth	3	1
Boston	2	12
Bristol	24	12
Brixham	1	1
Dundee	9	8
Europilots	43	44
Forth	9	41
Lond/erry	5	4
Fowey	7	4
Gloucester	1	1
Penzance	1	1
Holyhead	1	1
Lancaster	1	1
Manch/r	60	33
Mostyn	2	3
Poole	7	4
Spurn (Humber, Goole & Trent)	177	164
Tees & Hartlepool	53	44
Teignmouth	2	3
Tyne	27	12
Weymouth	1	1
Whitehaven	7	3
	491	400

The UKPA (M) had the continued asset of excellent back-up and facilities from the Transport & General Workers Union. There was discussion as to the proposal of VTS officers being accepted as members of the UKPA(M). The Conference voted against – VTS officers could in any case become full members of the TGWU. Dundee took possession of their new pilot craft: a semi-rigid boat.

The legal advisors reported that 75 claims on the Personal Health Insurance policy, with ensuing pressures of administration with regard to loss of voice, eyesight and hearing and to 'Pickwickian' illness. Claims have amounted to £2.25m. The Private Health Insurance had been a catastrophic loss to the insurance company with further claims due.

There was a problem of the DAS Legal expenses and a new policy which covered the members and their families needed to be found. At Lincoln Crown Court a pilot won £90,000 for injury in 1980.

The July issue of THE PILOT changed to a new format. The old A5 format with glossy paper became A4 format with a matt paper appearing more attractive.

The Pilotage Commission was liquidated September 1990 (see letter by David M Robinson (appendix B)

Conference 1991

Pensions

Harry Frith Chairman of the PNCP gave an excellent report of the surplus and how it was apportioned. The main uses were:

To allow for 5% future indexing (1992)	£4.5m
To allow for 10% graded increase (1991)	£5.7m
To achieve 4% increasing instead 3% p.a.	£13.0m
To bring self-employed members in line	£3.3m
To fund national service to 65 for 60 NRAs	£0.6m

To fund ill-health retirees	£0.25m
To fund commutation rate from 9% 10%	£2.1m
To fund early retirement scheme	£1.09m
Reserved for future increases	£4.05m

For these added benefits the Ports were granted a 2% reduction in contributions.

The Pilot Trustees failed on only two counts. They were unable to achieve increase in the granting of service cred and could not get agreement for year: year service. Discussion took place on the future the Fund, during which it was stated that the average pensionable earnings in 1988 were up by £5,500 in comparison with 1987. At December 1989 the average pension paid was £8,360 and the average widows' pension was £2,960. 310 pilots had retired on the early retirement scheme, 232 being surplus to requirements and 78 on medical grounds. Harry Frith thought that the Ports were by no means opposed to a continuing early retirement scheme, but that it was still a subject for negotiation.

1992

The UKMPA hosted the EMPA Conference in Liverpool 21/24 May

London Conference

Difficulties with the authorities and future problems with the Pension Fund still had to be solved. The Liability of Pilots and the ability of the CHA's to vary Agreements was the main discussion topic; the amount of legal advice needed over the past year. Arbitration had been necessary in Aberdeen, Liverpool and the Clyde. The arbitration agreement at Aberdeen had not been implemented, and the Clyde had an on-going problem. The end of the fourth year since the 1988 implementation of the Pilotage Act brought several legal battles with CHAs who were trying to vary their original agreements. It was very difficult to stop any CHA changing their Pilotage Directions except where such action would create a safety problem. The Government deemed it not to be their problem under the 1987 Pilotage Act.

The Holyhead Pilot, a single port pilot, had a responsibility for pilotage written into his contract which made him liable if any ship elected not to use him as a pilot.

Pensions

An Association of Competent Harbour Authorities was set up to represent the ports on the PNPF. The Section Committee would study the new Association's constitution. The ports would like the PNPF to founder and use the funds to run their own pensions. The SE Wales pilots had unhappy memories of running their old pension fund and the subsequent lost pension years. The Section Committee had deemed it prudent to tell the Fund's Actuary of the declining number in the Fund and the inability of newly employed pilots to join the Fund. Pilot numbers would continue to decline to between 690 and a possible low of 500 in 10 years. The PNPF may be a self-employed pilot fund as the current employed pilots returned. The PPF is a 'Mature Fund' i.e. where the ratio of pensioners to pilots is high and will obviously get higher. It did not mean that the Fund was under threat, or that there were insufficient funds to offset its liabilities. The actuary's advice was to change the 70% investment in shares and 30% in bonds to holding 60% in shares and 40% in bonds. This action would take up to 5 years for the investments to be realigned. The Actuary had not been informed in 1990 that serving pilot numbers would drop by a third in a decade.

1993

The UKPA(M)'s legal efforts had made exceptional demands on the members. The result of arbitration was on the whole in Aberdeen pilots' favour, but it had involved a long hard and expensive battle with the hostile CHA. Two ports, Falmouth and King's Lynn, had been asked to look at self-employment and the UKPA(M) had engaged their solicitors to draw up suitable contracts with an emphasis on the pilots' terms, and were to be presented to the respective ports. Liverpool was considering a self-employed option as possibly in the longer term the Medway would also achieve.

The situation of pilots working in VTS and of VTS officers as part time pilots was vigorously discussed and the question of reduction of membership fees arose. The question of insurance for this 'outside' work and the liabilities was discussed. This position emphasised the independent position of a pilot and reinforced his unique position in the port with relation to the other employees. It would be helpful to outline some of the judge's comments. Numerous court cases reinforced the limited liability position of the pilot. Simply stated, it meant that the pilot when aboard and having conduct of the vessel is the servant of the owner/master, and thus it is they who carry his liability above the amount specified in the 1987 Act (£1,000).

In the latest case the judge found that because the pilot can be servant of one constituency only, i.e. the ship owner/ master he cannot therefore, in law, be the servant of his port authority, and thus they in turn cannot have vicarious liability for him. It should further be noted that CHAs under their statutory duties do not undertake pilotage, but only comply with the requirements of the law, that is they authorise and make pilots available. Thus no contract is entered into between the port and a ship requesting the services of a pilot. The judgement quoted from previous cases and certain paragraphs are of interest to pilots.

"In their Lordships' opinion these Acts of Parliament did not alter the original status of a pilot, which is, in effect, that he must be regarded as an independent professional man in discharging his skilled duties. If it had been intended to alter this old and familiar status, it is to be supposed that the Legislature would have done it more explicitly. What it has done is more consistent with a different and limited purpose, namely to secure a proper selection, a proper supply, a proper supervision, and a proper remuneration of men to whose skill life and property is committed, whether the ship owner likes it or not. For this purpose they become servants of the Government. For the purposes of navigating ships they remain what they were, and the duty which the State or Government owes to a ship owner, exercised, it is true, by various authorities, is to provide a qualified man in the terms of the Statutes, but not to take the conduct or management of the ship. It is not said that they have failed in this duty of providing a qualified man."

Lord Loreburn

(Fowles v. Eastern & Australian Steamship Company [1916] 2AC 556). From this judgement it can be seen that a CHA had a responsibility in law to provide, where pilotage was compulsory, a well-qualified pilot.

A CHA could not put out its pilotage services to tender, and have those positions filled by new recruits who could not fulfil the criteria laid down by Lord Loreburn. It is clear to the UKPA(M) that unless a 'new' pilot has been trained to the same level as 'new' pilots in the past, then there are ample grounds for the district pilots and UKPA(M) to take steps to prevent such a situation arising. In view of the above legal statement the management of the ABP were quite mendacious.

1994

Continuing Safety concerns

This year two European pilots lost their lives during transfers. The continuing non-compliance with SOLAS V/17, the difficulties of transfer on those ships with constructional features such as fixed longitudinal fenders and the deaths of the pilots whilst transferring, convinced the Nautical Institute to give prominence in "Seaways" to pilot ladder safety campaigns and to the September EMPA campaign in particular and to encourage a submission of pilot transfer related incidents or the Monthly MARS report. The Technical Developments Committee (TDC) submitted an article *Pilot Transfer*, published in "Seaways" August issue.

The Royal Institute of Naval Architects Conference in Southampton was themed on "Surveillance, Pilot and Rescue Craft for the 21st Century". The TDC presentation stressed the need for standardisation of equipment on pilot boats, of both the familiarity with and the ease of availability of rescue and retrieval equipment. Much interest was shown on the UKMPA(M)'s Marine Pilot Safety video which led to its further sale abroad. In this respect the TDC also took every opportunity of exchanging information with the Royal National Lifeboat Institution.

At this year's Annual Conference a motion was passed that the UKPA(M) should resign from IMPA because the members felt that IMPA needed more control over its own finances.

The UKPA(M) as one of the consultees to the DfT's circulated draft, *Statutory Instrument*, was able to comment on technical aspects of the proposed amendments. Of particular concern to pilots was the ambiguity of a 1987 regulation re the joint use of pilot ladders with accommodation ladders, with the incorrect placing of the phrase "as far as practicable" in the sentence. The Department accordingly amended 7(2)a to read:

"Where an accommodation ladder is provided for the purpose of reg 5(2) it shall be so sited that, where used in conjunction with a pilot ladder for embarking or disembarking pilots, officials and other persons, the lower end of the accommodation ladder rests firmly against the side of the ship and leading aft and, as far as is practicable, within the mid-ship half section and clear of all discharges".

The UKMPA was able to comment on other proposed amendments relating to accommodation ladders and in particular the security of lower platforms, of outward opening shipside doors and of ensuring that the pilot hoist shall "operate against" the ship's side as against "be placed as close as practicable to". At the request of the UKMPA the Department retained reg. 9(7)(a)(vi) requiring the fitting of an emergency stop-switch on a pilot boat.

After presenting a paper on "Safety on Deck of today's pilot boat" at the Royal Institute of Naval Architects Conference on "Surveillance, Pilot and Rescue Craft for the 21st Century", the Technical Developments Committee organised a video covering the safety of pilots when boarding that was very well accepted and had wide-spread sales abroad.

A motion at the Conference instructed the Executive Committee to withdraw from membership of IMPA. A few months later a number of pilots realising that IMPA, having a seat on the relevant IMO committees, formed the British Marine Pilot's Association to maintain links with IMPA requested temporary membership of IMPA, later granted in May 1995.

The charge for the journal THE PILOT was announced as £6 per annum

The Chairman of the UKMPA, Geoff Topp, outlined the work his predecessor, the recently resigned Paul Hames, had done for the Association and thanked him on behalf of the pilots for all he had achieved.

The failure to obtain legal redress at Mostyn was frustrating and the pilots involved lost their authorisations. To ease the financial loss the UKPA(M) had obtained, for the Mostyn pilots, unabated pensions from the PNPF from the residual Early Retirement Scheme.

1996

SEA EMPRESS

An incident at Milford Haven occurred that would have a significant effect on pilotage administration. A pilot taking a ship out of port, was expected to bring another vessel transferring from one ship to the other off the entrance to the Harbour. Unfortunately the inward bound vessel, a Russian tanker, approached far too near the entrance while waiting for the pilot. The master was not familiar with the port. As the pilot arrived on the bridge there were language difficulties and the tanker was too close to the shore before the pilot could obtain control, it grounded and subsequently was lost and the oil-damage devastated the coasts for miles away.

The pilot, a salaried employee, had been directed by the Harbour authority to bring the inward bound ship into the harbour. The use of one pilot for the two vessels in rota dispensed with another pilot thereby reducing the port fees. The authority found the pilot to blame and tried to punish him – however courts and the Government removed any blame from the pilot. (see the Legal summary by Barry Youde)

SOLAS /17 featured the need for special arrangements for ships with unusual construction features. The non-compliance with SOLAS V/17 was brought to the attention of the several associations. Not only foreign flag vessels but also it was found that Ministry of Defence (i.e. naval) vessels did not fully comply with SOLAS /17 regulations.

It was noted that employed/unemployed status brought complications to legal and income tax affairs – VAT ??

It was noted that the Seasafe All-Weather Ltd. was advertising their coat as being recommended by the Nautical Institute. The firm was asked to clarify their statement. The Committee reported that some SeaSafe coats were still not proving to be waterproof. And that, in general the jackets were difficult to keep clean. The Chairman prepared a check list for the better care and maintenance by the pilots of the SeaSafe Jacket. After consultation with British Millerain, the manufacturer of the Hydrophyllic material then being used, the Chairman included specific cleaning advice.

1997

SEA EMPRESS Incident

Due to the serious deficiencies in the way that pilotage was organised by the Milford Haven Port Authority, the Marine Accident Investigation Board found that the MHPA pilotage organisation was inadequately managed with questionable standards of training. They recommended to the DfT that important parts of the Pilotage Act 1987 needed review.

One of the problems is that, of the former 94 pilotage authorities, 70 remained representing a varied group of business corporations, concerns that hoping to make a profitable business from all aspects of port and harbour activities. And to attempt to make a profit from the safety in and around the ports is in itself a dangerous proceeding.

1998

In July the review of the Pilotage Act 1987 was published, consisting of 150 pages comprising 5,000 words. A meeting of all concerned was held by the DETR – CHA's port authorities, Chamber of Shipping, tug owners, pilots, Nautical Institute. Andrew Burr of the Dept. spoke for an hour using slides. It was explained that there was no prospect of a further Shipping Bill. When the concerns of the several parties were stated, Mr Burr agreed to meet the pilots at future date. But in the event he attended the UKPA(M) Conference at Middlesbrough in November. He stated that the reasons for the review were the Labour Government was very concerned over standards of port safety: a matter of public interest and especially over the statuary powers granted to CHA's and the absence of accountability for the stewardship of the public interest within the 1987 Act. There was a question and answer session

The Nautical Institute held a seminar to discuss the Review a week later in which several interests presented papers the proceedings being chaired by Peter Russell, President of the Nautical Institute (London pilot).

Yet more regulations and Merchant Shipping notices appeared to control and inform pilots and others of the need for improvement in the provision of pilot ladders, their correct positioning and improve standards of manufacture of the ladders and allied equipment: the new instrument removing some provisions in the existing legislation in excess of SOLAS requirements. But non-compliance with the regulations of merchant vessels due to hull design is a particular area of concern. In a particular the Technical & Training Committee had discussions with the Ministry of Defence re the pilot ladder arrangements on HMS *Penzance* class of mine-hunter. The Committee visited the vessel and founded improvements but the arrangements were still non-compliance.

2000

The First Decade of the 21st Century

This period had a series of problems for the Section committee, but also the members were becoming involved with a growing number of organisations and several government departments: Maritime and Coastguard service (`), Department of Trade (DfT), Advisory Committee on Protection of the Sea (ACPOS), UK Major Ports Group, Associated British Ports (ABP), Nautical Institute (NI), Chamber of Shipping (COS) among several others including the International and European Pilots' Associations, Transport & General Workers Union (TGWU). The SC members not only had to attend meetings but coordinate their attendances between rota duties as pilots in their respective ports additional to numbers of ports in the UK and Europe.

There was increasing concern among the members of the wish of the CHA's to increase the number of pilotage exemption certificates more available. This also was worrying in that shipowners wanted to reduce the standards of training and allow multiple vessels named on the certificates.

Pilot Ladders

The safety concerns of the UKPA(M) over the previous 60 years had not moderated. The efforts re arrangements for boarding and disembarking by IMPA, EMPA and the UKMPA in spite of the many improvements sought, proposed and tried there were no end to the number of new problems arising. It seemed that new ship-owners, using more minor countries as flags of convenience, continued to ignore the regulations promulgated in the World's maritime press. And even UK Government Departments were still being pressed to take measures to ensure safety.

Vessel Traffic Services

A few experts in this decade, looking at trials of electronic apparatus, the so-called pilot boxes, proposed that pilotage was possible by personnel in the Vessel Traffic Services. At the same time several electronic devices for a pilot to carry on the ship. One of the devices was to be used with a laptop computer. One of the problems arising with laptops appeared when the laptop was positioned on a secure flat surface inside the navigation bridge. In an incident in Moreton Bay, Queensland, Australia, (the approaches to Brisbane): the pilot, making a critical turn had to walk several metres to consult the laptop and during the few seconds the turn was delayed and the ship grounded. Where is the pilot expected to place the laptop ready for use?

The Effect of the 1987 Pilotage Act

The true effect of the provisions of the Pilotage Act 1987 became evident by the Millennium arrived. The wording of the Act ensured that UK Government departments no longer had an obligation to take action where there was a dispute between Pilots and the former pilotage committees. The retiring chairman of the Pilotage Commission foresaw the problems that were to appear. (see Appendix B) The provision, operation and management of pilot services was left entirely in the hands of the Competent Harbour Authorities (CHA's), that is companies both public and private. The CHA was to delineate the pilotage, recruit, train and direct pilots according to the needs of the harbour and provide challenges for the pilots.

This was to involve specifically the Humber pilots. They had had a very successful half century and, apart from the complicated Thames approaches, were the largest pilot group in the UK. They had benefitted from the change in trade after the formation of the EEC and in fact had recruited pilots from other, mainly western ports. There had been a couple of industrial disputes with several authorities around their district. However they were not happy with the provisions of the 1987 Pilotage Act which ordered a new structure of UK pilotage administration.

These effects stand out starkly when they arose in the Humber Pilotage District. For centuries there had been three separate pilotage districts, the Ouse, Trent and the Humber estuary. The CHA wanted to merge the districts and remove the need for a pilot changeover off Hull and thus reduce pilotage costs. As part of the 1989 re-organisation the Humber Pilots had formed a cooperative: Spurn Pilots Limited, obtaining a contract to provide pilots for the Humber rivers.

In order to discuss the changes the Humber pilots stopped work to hold a general meeting at which about 200 attended those from Liverpool, Manchester and Southampton and South Wales and several other ports. This did not make any improvement of the relations with CHA. A decade, later Spurn Pilots Ltd were informed by the Authority that in future they were to become employees. The SPL protested, the pilots threatened to stop work.

A short time later the Port Authority announced that they would not renew the contracts with SPL after 1st January 2002. Spurn pilots would be required to apply for work as employed pilots.

The Port Authority then recruited ships officers and masters who were then expected to learn pilotage around the estuary and along the Ouse and Trent. A few pilots did apply to return to the CHA service and were able to supply services for the larger vessels. This, however, did not provide sufficient training; not the usual experience of being on the bridge and observing an experienced pilot handle ships' movements. This now highlighted the flaws in the Pilotage Act and the subsequent review. The MCA and the DfT ignored any possible investigation as to the legality of the CHA regulation. In fact this led to a number of incidents arising from faulty pilotage, costly to the ships and the insurance underwriters. The Authority paid much of the damage expenses, thereby covering the embarrassment in having a port without a full corps of experienced and trained pilots: this also bending the regulations.

A considerable amount of legal action proceedings lasting almost three year failed to alter the Authority's stance, partly due to the scurrilous action by the so-called independent civil servants discussing the situation with other port services and shipping and 138 pilots were out of a job; the UKMPA lost over 100 members (15 pilots re-applied, some pilots were able to retire early and others were able to transfer to other districts. This was serious blow for all UK pilots in general, but disastrous for the then Humber pilots.

In January 2012 the Humber CHA advertised for more pilots – there was no limit to number of the pilots required. Seems they were constrained to use a very wide net. There was a considerable amount of mendacity on the part of the APB managers regarding the safety of shipping in the Humber.

The First Decade of the Millennium with the UKMPA

The Technical and Training Committee were involved with other organisations; the chairman was also involved with EMPA and IMPA. These duties were not reducing.

As the number of maritime organisations increased pilots needed to enter the realms of electronics and technology, environment and commerce. Committee Members were constrained to attend meetings at often in convenient dates, times and venues, in their own off-duty times.

2001

113th Conference Southampton

The name of the Association was changed from UKPA(M) to UKMPA, thereby falling into line with other pilotage associations

World-wide and removing an awkward, cumbersome bracketed appendage.

As UKPA pilots were concerned about the finances and management of IMPA, the conference in 1994 had voted to discontinue membership if IMPA. At the time the decision to leave IMPA was highly controversial and in fact some pilots formed the BMPA to main contact with the international body.

This year the UKMPA re-joined the IMPA – after an absence almost seven years. For over two decades many pilots were unconcerned with pilots being represented by non-pilots of the TGWU which had a seat at the IMO Committees. But the ITF was primarily striving to improve the working conditions, pay and socials rights of seafarers. The strength of IMPA was its recognition by the IMO and its seat on the IMO committees. It had been argued, without foundation, that pilots did not need to be part of IMPA because association with the ITF granted attendance at IMO. The importance of the presence of pilots the IMO meetings was underlined in the Spring when a proposal to require masters to provide detailed passage plans from berth to berth including times at reporting points, under keel clearances, speeds in reaches, wheel over positions etc. was raised under *Any Other Business* at the end of a session!

The intervention of pilots pointing out the total impracticality of such plans resulted in the proposal being postponed but the pilots present were subjected to considerable hostility. For some reason the coherent and informed professional arguments by pilots who were aware of the real situation facing the shipmaster seems to cause deep resentment and our attendance at such forums is therefore more important than at any time. Pilots became victims of their own success in as much as the thousands of pilotage acts every day go unnoticed because pilots are highly qualified and skilled professionals. On the rare occasions that an act of pilotage does go wrong, the environmental sensitivity and the escalating costs meant that the role of the pilot was subject to increasing scrutiny.

Extraordinary Meeting 7th December 2001

This was held in the Hull Guildhall for all pilots who were not working. In fact, with to the off-duty Humber pilots, almost 250 pilots, including representatives from the Netherlands Germany and Italy, filled the hall to overflowing.

The deputy Mayor welcomed the assembly and expressed the hope that the discussions could resolve the dispute between HPL and APB and ensure the on-going prosperity and safety for Kingston-upon-Hull. The UKMPA chairman Norman McKinney pointed out that the Pilotage Act of 1987 introduced a poor piece of legislation in the mistaken belief that costs to shipowners would be reduced. But it also transferred responsibility for pilotage to the CHA's who became prosecutor, judge, jury and executioner over pilotage matters without accountability.

The assembly were convinced that the ABP failed to support the Port Marine Safety code and the Government department responsible were powerless to interfere.

2002

Following the increase of subscriptions there were queries of what they were actually paying for. Chairman Joe Wilson explained:

UKMPA	32%
Insurance	30%
TGWU	30%
IMPA	8%
EMPA	5%
ETCS	2%

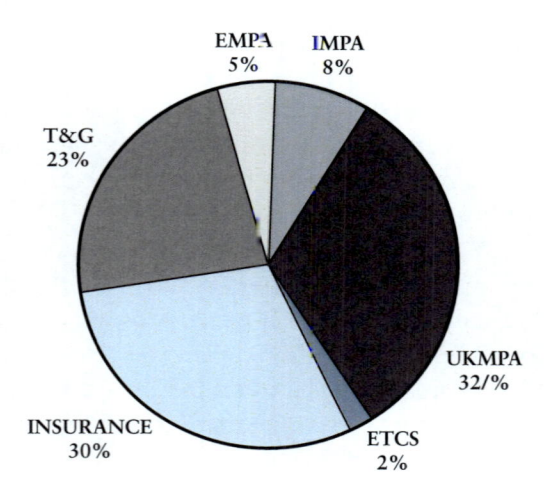

Pie chart:
- EMPA 5%
- IMPA 8%
- T&G 23%
- UKMPA 32/%
- ETCS 2%
- INSURANCE 30%

** Insurance with Navigators & General £100,000 cover
* Education & Training towards a common standard for EU pilots

UKMPA: Representation costs a lot but without a national organisation our voices would be drowned by the vested interests of ship owners, ports and others who see pilots as an expense to be cut. The volumes of papers collated and sent out to local secretaries by reveal the full extent of the representation provided by Norman McKinney, Section Committee and other members who support the various sub-committees etc. What is easily forgotten is that all those members who are actively involved with the UKMPA are attending meetings, compiling reports (editing magazines!) in their spare time. Why? Because those members believe passionately in the importance of ensuring that pilots and pilotage maintain the admirable safety record of UK piloting and that their professional expertise is not undermined. Can a price be laid on that?

INSURANCES: The joint policies of Navigators and General and DAS provide very comprehensive cover for pilots. Some employed pilots have questioned whether this is necessary when they are covered by their HA's group policy. In certain cases this could be true but there are occasions when there may be a conflict of interest between a pilot and his HA and this has been proven in the past. Section Committee have frequently reviewed insurance quotations but none came close to providing the cover offered by Navigators & General. N&G have also confirmed that the cover provided to UKPMA pilots far exceeds that offered through NUMAST. When one considers that professional insurance is becoming almost impossible to obtain (a window cleaner recently had his renewal quote leap from £900 to £9000!) our policies represent exceptional value.

T&G: brings many benefits, not least free legal advice on employment matters. With solicitors charging around £100 per hour and barristers around £250 the benefits are obvious. The T&G had been fully funding representation for HPL members during the on-going tribunal hearings.

IMPA and EMPA: Representation at IMO and within the EU for the price of a restaurant meal! No need to say any more really.

ETCS: What's this? Expenses towards the Committee's Socialising? Whilst they fully deserve it, ETCS actually stands for Education, Training & Certification Standard. This is similar to the BPIT remit for the UK. The EU is known to be keen to introduce a common standard for EU pilots and EMPA is working to produce a set of standards which will be presented to the EU commission. It was hoped that this initiative will prevent non-pilots from dictating the future of pilots without their participation.

2003

The ruling of the employment tribunal dismissed the claim by the HPL that they had been illegally and unfairly treated by the ABP and the repercussions of the Humber dispute became apparent. Although the UKMPA (and the TGWU) the admirably supported the Humber Pilots, it was also apparent that the outcome had proved very costly for the UKPA and the PNPF too. Without the services of the TGWU it would have been impossible for the HPL to take their dispute this far.

2004

Insurance

The N & G Insurance Co. withdrew their cover for sickness and accident insurance after five years. Paul Haysom was able to arrange a replacement policy with the Royal & Sun Alliance to cover members during 2005. A change in the rules by the Financial Services Authority meant that the UKMPA could no longer provide a 'group' policy but a similar policy with extended provision had been taken on which offered a discount on premiums, but in future each individual would be named. For this reason and also for the convenience of submitting the premium for tax relief it was decided to separate the premiums from the general subscription.

The new policy covered a member from the commencement of the pilotage act until the completion and also provided cover against pollution accidents. Members were able to choose their preference from two cover options available for £250,000 and £500,000. It was found that employed pilots were not covered by the Harbour Authority's insurance. With the growing 'blame culture' and the validity of the £1,000 limitation of liability under the Pilotage Act might be subject to a legal challenge, the Section Committee were satisfied that additional cover was essential for all pilots.

117th Conference Eastbourne

After short debate the delegates, by a narrow majority, voted a closure of the Pilots' National Committee for Pensions, a very successful forum that had worked well over the past three decades. The disappointed chairman of the PNCP, Mike Kitchen and Dan MacMillan, pensioners' delegate, stated that they intended to press for another body that would take up the work of the Committee, possibly linked more directly with the TGWU.

The UKMPA President, Lord Tony Berkeley, in his opening address remarked that the lack of interest in shipping by MP's meant no ports strategy from the Government. And by holding up development of ports, the UK could be left as a feeder outpost for the rest of Europe

The MCA which were expected to monitor the individual ports' compliance with the Port & Marine Safety Committee (PMSC), appeared to have been 'got-at' and were unenthusiastic in making a thorough investigation into the honesty effectiveness, safety and competence of the port administrations . Again, the MCA admitted that they could not investigate and take action whenever an offence against the use of pilotage exemption certificates: it is a matter for the CHA. The CHA say that they were not required to monitor the incorrect use.

The Section Committee (with EMPA) was working on the campaign to support the "Opposition to Competition" laws about to be introduced in the European Parliament, by MEPs, and all parties were to be lobbied. Eventually the "Competition" clause in the European Directory was abandoned.

For the first half of the year the UKMPA dealt with the renewal of contracts in the self-employed districts of Poole, Gloucester and Dundee and in the employed districts of the Tyne and SE Wales and various employment matters in Belfast involving a ballot for industrial action over TWGU recognition.

The Treasurer reported that at 30th Sept. the membership stood at 493 from 47 districts, this figure represented reduction of 8 over 2003. Neath district had withdrawn from membership. Dundee had reduced from 5 to 3 but the other two pilots had transferred to Perth thus creating a new District. The other 6 pilots were from ports where pilots had retired and were not replaced.

Barry Youde, barrister, presented delegates on several legal options available to HPL members against APB and David Fortnum confirmed that HPL members were taking the first steps to launch a legal challenge.

LEGAL: Mark Foden, of Blake Lapthorn Linnell (BLL) solicitors detailed the work undertaken on behalf of pilots during 2005. This included reviewing contracts for both employed and self-employed pilots, unfair dismissal and with the London pilots advising on the proposed new arrangement for Local Navigation Certificates for Thames watermen.

Limitation of Liability

Section 22(1) of the 1987 Pilotage Act had provided valuable protection for pilots and had thus kept the number of claims against them low. This legal protection was now being challenged and Mark was of the opinion that it was only a matter of time before a test case claim was made against an individual pilot. This section of the Act just covers civil liability for negligence but not criminal misconduct which is covered under Section 21.

In the case of a negligence claim against a pilot although 22(1) provides a maximum personal financial liability of £1000 the pilot would also be likely to have his authorisation suspended or removed and he would then be responsible for his own legal defence costs in fighting the suspension and potentially the costs of the claimant. The limitation also only applied when a pilot was undertaking his duties as a pilot. It did NOT apply to criminal cases brought following an incident under the other Acts such as the Water Resources Act or if manslaughter charges are brought following a fatality in which a pilot may be implicated. It was for this reason that Mark was of the opinion that pilots needed to ensure they had adequate insurance.

The N&G Insurance altered in that the £50,000 cover was removed and the premiums for £100,000 were increased. In the event the delegates voted to seek a cheaper alternative. Don Cockrill reminded all members that the Chamber of Shipping questioned the need for Pilotage Exemption Certificate standards and the ports generally were not willing to specify training and standards for pilots. There were also moves towards VTSB (shore-based) pilotage. The concept was being reincarnated using the heading "Navigational Assistance".

South East Wales pilot Kristian Pederson had been dismissed for "gross misconduct. The TWGU lawyer had provided all the relevant facts to support Kristian and the case had been referred to a full hearing. In considering the recent cases involving the Humber, Belfast and South East Wales it was seen that the cases were all inter-related.

2005

118th Conference at Maidstone (jointly London/Medway) November

The Conference was busy in that the following acronyms appear in the report PNPC, MFR, MNPA, IMPA, TWGU, MCA, DfT, BLL, PMSC, GLA, H&SE, MAIB, NRA, DESMERLDA, IALA, P&I, VTS, IMO, CHIRP, NMAST.

This bewildering number displays a fair idea as to the spread of the work interests covered by the Section Committee members.

The membership in September 2004 stood at 493 from 47 districts a reduction of 8 over 2003. Neath (South Wales) had withdrawn from membership

Qualifications for Pilots

The UKMPA was involved in the European project for setting standards for maritime pilots along the lines of STCW95 – ETCS (Education, Training, certification & Standards for maritime pilots). This is a project linked to EMPA and a possible European Directive. The DfT had to instruct the MCA to adopt the ETCS as the recognised "National Occupational Standards" for pilots in the Ports and Maritime Safety Committees. ETCS required a "Competent Pilotage Authority". The MCA in discussions with the CHAs decided that the CHAs did not want this complication and withdrew from the discussions. This meant that the ETCS will need to be "imposed" on the UK ports industry.

CHA's

It appeared that investment (private equity) companies, when they take over port plc's, are able to gain control over pilots and pilotage without accountability. This is highly disturbing to allow a distant company decide the standard of safety not only for pilots but also the shipping in the area.

The Section Committee were studying at Belfast, Dundee, Orkneys and Wisbech were there were contractual issues to be sorted. It was becoming evident that under the 1987 Pilotage Act the DfT and MCA together with the CHA's, who are all subject to commercial pressures, ignored safety practices and appeared willing to take chances. The pilots' organisations needed to monitor the compliance with safety procedures. The operations of the VTS's continue to be at the forefront of shore-based pilotage.

2007

The Conference was put back from November to May in order to make attendance more attractive for delegates and their wives. Peter Wylie was congratulated for the arranging the more central venue for a well-supported and successful conference. Membership was stated to be 492 pilots from 46 districts.

The speakers were Michael Grey of *Lloyd's List* and presentations from Stephen Meyer (Chief Investigator MAIB), James Weedon (Head of Ports division Dft) Geoff Stokes (Port Liaison Policy Leader MCA) and Kevin Austen (HPL pilot and solicitor, Barlow Lyle & Gilbert).

Another speaker was Andy Kirkham of the International Group of P&I Clubs, who had a very hard task to explain the use of the term "pilot error" to the assembly who let him know that they were by no means happy with the wording. However those present left with a far greater understanding of the work and the P&I Clubs. Andy Kirkham also agreed that the aims of the UKMPA and the P&I Clubs were the same, acknowledging that high standards in pilotage reduce incidents and therefore claims.

Maritime & Coastal Agency (MCA)

The MCA and the DfT wanted national occupational standards (NOS) but the ports authorities were reluctant to accept the concept. Two Section Committee members were working with the DFT & MCA on the several safety projects; the ports became obliged to have comprehensive Formal Risk Assessment in place. The ports were reluctant to accept that the Pilot Exemption Certificate PEC holders should have a level of competency equivalent to that of a pilot for the same ship, especially working with tugs. But incidents had been reported during port manoeuvres when using PEC personnel that needed examining although the relevant Departments were reluctant to take on such measures.

The Humber dispute and after

HPL members requested the Barrie Youde pass on their gratitude to all those from the UKMPA who had generously contributed towards the case. Chairman Joe Wilson paid tribute to Barrie Youde for his tireless dedication in supporting the HPL members which had resulted in such a positive outcome.

The result
The case of Pilot Colin Brammer (on behalf of 88 members of Humber Pilots Ltd). The claim was in the matter of misfeasance in public office, following the de-authorisation of the claimants en masse 25th January 2002. The case was settled prior to entering court. There was an agreement satisfactory to all concerned but the details were not made public.

2008

121st Conference on board HQS Wellington

39 Pilots attended from 15 districts: the membership was 493 from 45 districts. The TGWU and the union AMICUS were preparing to amalgamate into UNITE.

Concerns had been expressed that employed pilots were subsidising the self-employed pilots with their premiums. In reality the insurances were currently being required by more employed pilots than self-employed pilots and underwriters confirmed that, as a result of employment legislation, the policy was more relevant to employed pilots.

Clyde Dispute
Clyde pilots were in dispute with Peel Holdings. A Perth pilot, (UKMPA member) had applied to train on the Clyde during the

dispute and was expelled from the UKMPA. He took the UKMPA to an employment tribunal where UNITE provided representation for the UKMPA. The case was dropped by the applicant just prior to the hearing but the process revealed that there was no expulsion clause in the UKMPA rules and a rule change to cover this was later agreed. The Clyde pilotage situation continued.

Pilots National Pension Fund

The scheme – established in 1971 – two decades later, has a £200m deficit. The trustee sought to establish the extent of its powers to levy contributions on the ports that authorise pilots. A complex legal case concerning the funding of the Pilots National Pension Fund would be taken to the High Court. Richard Williamson (Chairman of the Pilot Trustees) explained that the case was solely to establish whether or not there was a liability. If, as anticipated, such liabilities were found to exist the specific liabilities of each party would subsequently be analysed and set. In the case of Trust Ports the port's trustees were unable to commit to payments unless required to do so by a court order. It was even possible that the Government may be liable in that it was the 1987 Act which had caused the problems in the first place. Because this case it unique, any outcome was impossible to predict but the hope was that it would result in a clear allocation of liabilities and that the pensions regulator would ensure that those liable would honour their commitments.

Azimuth Project

This means handling ships with azimuth pods. In November Gareth Rees and Nigel Allen (Southampton pilots) attended the inaugural meeting of the Azimuth Project part funded by the EU to study the operation of control devices when manoeuvring vessels in pilotage waters. This was to be a three year project put together and managed by Newcastle University comprised of naval architects, training establishments, simulator manufacturers and hydrodynamics departments with a major input from the UKMPA. There was a total of 15 partners each taking a turn by hosting a quarterly meeting. September 2010 was the UKMPA's turn. (See appendix 134.)

2009

Pilot transfer arrangements

The lobbying effect that IMPA had at IMCO, was amazing, the way that the brotherhood of the international pilots came together was not matched by any other organisation, group or delegation. The importance of having so many pilots on so many country delegations acting in a discrete and professional was very apparent and could not be overstressed. Anyone questioning the value of Membership of IMPA was seriously lacking ordinary brain power.

Pilot ladder problems continued and in the November 2009 issue a French pilot was reported to be severely injured when a brand new ladder parted at deck level; he and the remain of the ladder fell 8 metres into the water between the ship's hull and the pilot cutter. In June an Italian pilot suffered serious injuries when attempting to board via the pilot ladder and side door. Earlier in 2009 a Turkish pilot died when a ladder broke and he fell into the sea.

Brian Wilson, Chairman of the Technical & Training (T&TC) made a special point of explaining the inspection of pilot transfer arrangements under the SOLAS 1.

The inspection of Pilot transfer arrangements come under SOLAS 1, Regulation 8, surveying of lifesaving appliances and other equipment of cargo ships, (8(b), (i), (ii) and (iii) "provide for the survey and inspection of various life-saving and other equipment, including means of embarking pilots" to ensure that they comply with the requirements of the present regulations, are in satisfactory condition and are fit for the work for which the ship is intended.

The above is very important, it required that pilot ladders be surveyed and inspected at the above survey and periodically at port state inspections. The MCA were aware of that and Brian Wilson & the T&TC would be assisting them with their duty.

2010

Pilots National Pensions Fund – a new legal obstacle

22 January 2010. Over the years, there had been a substantial decline in membership, as port authorities have left the scheme and made other arrangements for their pilots. The action has therefore been brought as the scheme now has less than 200 active members and a deficit of over £200m (€228m).

At 31 December 2006, the scheme was worth £350.2m, but with such a large deficit against its liabilities the trustee felt it must seek a ruling forcing port authorities to help make good this deficit.

"There is now no way that the remaining active members can contribute enough to make up the deficit," said a representative the Port of Tyne Authority, one of eight defendants. "The trustees want to know how far they can force the port authorities to pay money into the scheme."

"Officials will have to examine who is an employer for the purposes of scheme-specific funding, and for the purposes of Section 75 debt. And the judgment could influence what employers have to pay if they try to leave behind their responsibilities to earlier scheme membership".

The defendants in the court action also include the Port of London Authority and Milford Haven Port Authority. The case itself became a test for the pensions industry, however officials believe it will not be a landmark ruling largely because of its membership. "While it is certainly going to be of use, its significance has been overplayed. In particular, 87% of the scheme's liabilities relate to self-employed service, which is a unique feature a real one-off [case]. Although it's a large case with multiple partners, I am not sure that it will have a wide impact on pension schemes generally, because it is not likely that there are many schemes with self-employed members."

The case was expected to take three weeks, with judgment reserved for up to several months afterward; legal costs estimated to run to between £10m and £15m.

AZIMUTH

Azimuth Project was hosted by the UKMPA in September, as the Association had no facilities in which to hold such a meeting, it was held on the *Independence of the Seas* the large Royal Caribbean Cruise Lines with podded propulsion during the four day cruise from Southampton to Cork and back. The funding for the project was from the EU via Newcastle University with a total budget of £1.2 million from which the UKMPA would receive a contribution proving a healthy surplus or the UKMPA.

The vessel departed Southampton in charge of Gareth Rees and with about 20 member of the project. For details of the cruise see pages 255/6.

122nd Conference Cardiff May

Membership stood at 459, but it is estimated that about 200 pilots working in the UK were not members. The UKMPA was making efforts to improve that statistic.

Joe Wilson in his chairman's report spoke of the history of the PNPF in which very UK pilot had been a member and in 1972 there had been 1,318 active members with 715 pensioners. But the

1987 Pilotage Act had resulted in new pilots tending to join their port's scheme and consequently the current membership stood at 181 actives and 1340 pensioners. Despite the low numbers, PNPF pilot trustees were still elected by the UKMPA which also dealt with general pensions enquiries for non PNPF members.

Insurance

The insurance presentation by Ron Watts, the treasurer, stressed that the Royal Sun Alliance legal protection policy for members was a unique policy tailor-made for pilots offering unparalleled protection for UK pilots. As a result of some cases currently being processed, the current highest cover of £1 million may need to be revised upwards. There were three major cases being handled by RSA insurance, one of which looked as if it would exceed the £1m cover. Another case which had been successful involved a pilot who had had his authorisation downgraded by his CHA, the policy had paid the difference to restore his salary.

The DAS policy didn't just cover pilots whilst piloting but also other members of their family. At less than £15 per annum it was extremely good value. There were also the benefits of the optional accident policy i.e. not restricted to accidents while piloting.

Rob Watts explained that he had given the insurance details in a talk to the EMPA Conference, with the result that many European members at that Conference asked for more information since it represented a level cover and protection which was considered to be "Gold Plated" by European standards

A motion proposed that insurance cover should not be compulsory requirement for UKMPA membership produced votes for 3 and 22 against.

Pilotage Exemption Certificates

This was a problem dating back to the 18th century and about 1895. The CHA's began to press for a liberal attitude to Exemption certificates. If the qualifications required for exemption were somewhat less stringent, the masters and officers would find it easier to obtain the certificate would also reduce the number of qualifying visits to the relative port. Relaxing the qualifications would allow multiple certificates and thus giving rise to a 'private pilotage service'. A ferry company would find it easy to transfer exemption certificate holders from ship to ship. The concerns of the UKMPA were expressed to the DfT, who although appeared to be sympathetic to pilots admitted they had little control of the CHA's.

PART FIVE

PART FIVE

A Rapidly Changing Scene

AFTER THE SECOND World War pilotage administration worked well under the existing legislation, the Pilotage Act 1913 that had been draughted after an irregular series of parliamentary inquiries instituted during the immense change in commercial shipping from the early 1800s. The peace of the post Napoleonic Wars covered the introduction of steam power. By mid-19th century the screw propeller improved the fuel consumption allowing larger ships ship to provide ocean passages at a reasonable price and rapid transport for people. Initially some shipowners claimed that steam power reduced the need for pilots.

But with the need for speedy carriage of mails, and to avoid mails being delayed the Cunard Line arranged for their steamers, based on Liverpool, to embark pilots at Irish ports on passage home (Cork & Londonderry). This was the first system of appropriate (choice) pilots. Further south, large steamers making for London embarked their pilots off Dungeness, among the many vessels passing through the Channel east and west, bound for northern European ports with potential collision situations.

The 'choice' pilot systems caused severe aberrations in comparing pilot incomes in the late 19th centuries. The introduction of the pilotage legislation 1913 immediately prior to WW1 allowed a sensible acceptance without strife. After the great depression from 1925 to 1935, there was pressure from the shipowners and most pilot groups were constrained to reduce their pilotage charges.

The years WW2 from 1939 to 1945 were not significant to the politics of pilotage. Due to the strains of war several local pilot groups left the UKPA to join the T&GWU. This caused some reorganisation. Pilot groups were concerned with covering the increased traffic immediately after the end of hostilities.

From 1950 larger, faster passenger vessels appeared transatlantic traffic resumed pre-war proportions. In 1953 the development of the jet engine allowed faster, cheaper transatlantic passenger flights and ocean passenger vessels turned to cruising. Large bulk carriers of grain, oil and ores carried cargoes increased by a factor of 6. The pilotage revenue for each port reduced proportionately: the income per pilot dropping quite severely. Then, in 1968, the six-fold increase of container traffic reduced the number of the individual pilots' services by a factor of six.

During the early part of the 1950s discussions towards a standard for pilots' earnings began to bear fruit. In 1956 the Ministry held informal talks with the pilots and shipowners, leading to an Inquiry, chaired by Sir Robert Letch, the report of which recommended that the earnings of pilots should be measured against the National Maritime Board Scales of Pay for Officers. To the "Letch Report" can be attributed the structure of pilots' earnings for the ensuing three decades.

The in the late 1960s the EEC demanded that cargoes from Europe to the UK were given preference. Cargoes from Scandinavia (Denmark, Finland & Sweden were not then members) were restricted and reduced, entering Britain through east coast ports such as the Humber and the Tees. The Thames ports, which over the centuries had been used for trade from the British Commonwealth countries, were left with severely reduced cargo imports.

There were now, too many pilots. Some vacancies on the Humber, Harwich, and at Southampton and Milford Haven were filled taking pilots from Liverpool and Manchester.

From 1951 the UKPA and the Union ports pilots were discussing mutual problems for negotiation with shipowners. From 1965 to 1970 Union pilots insisted on retaining links with the World Seafarers Organisation via their T&GWU a concept that would prove erroneous in a few years. In fact the Union ports' members were very slow in acknowledging the value of membership of the European Maritime Pilots' Association; the leadership of the T&GWU was concerned that their own importance could be eroded. In view of the problems, then appearing, the two pilots' organisations held joint talks and discussions with the Chamber of Shipping to take steps to provide improved pensions for all pilots. In 1969 there was an agreement to set up a National Pilots' Pension Fund using the then current Trinity house Pensions Fund as a base, the pilots being required a to pay a 15% contribution, meaning an adjustment in pilotage rates.

On the death of their permanent Secretary & Solicitor C.D. Griffiths, the UKPA appointed Edgar Eden as General Secretary in 1968. With previous links with port authorities he promptly realised that pilots needed a seat at higher levels in international matters. After talks with EMPA he approached the International Maritime Counties Organisation (IMCO).

At the 1972 EMPA conference in Italy the Committee members wanted to choose R,H. (Dick) Farrands (London north) as their president and were surprised and disappointed when he refused. They were concerned that the Union ports pilots were against any such proposal. As I (the author) attended the conference unofficially and as an observer, a number of the EMPA Committee approached me, asking if there had been opposition to Dick. I was able to assure them that the Committee of the Union ports pilots had spent some time urging Dick to accept. He refused for personal reasons.

At his first UKPA Conference, Edgar Eden warned UK pilots against any precipitate action linked to the Letch report. But the pilots as a body were angry; in spite of an annual 10% increase in the cost of living there had been no increase in rates. And in conjunction with the union pilots all pilotage work ceased for 24 hours on 26th January 1971, when almost every pilot (1,600) attended. This convinced the Government and the Chamber of Shipping that there was an urgent need for a new approach to pilotage administration and the responsible government departments in particular deemed it necessary that there should be a change of authorities.

From 1956 through to 2001

For the next couple of decades developments brought change in the nature and advance of shipping which affected pilotage administration in way quite unforeseen. Arriving as important events – nodal points: national pensions 1969, standard rates of pay (Letch) (1957), transfer to other ports and pilots for exchange (1976), new comprehensive Pilotage Act, change of port authorities (1988) early retirement (1988). the *SEA EMPRESS* (1996) disaster and the Humber contracts dispute 2000 to 2003. Both of the two latter having major, unanticipated, effects on UKPA affairs that are best appreciated from the excellent reports by Barrie Youde, a barrister and former pilot, at the end of this summary.

1973

SCOP

Realising that the current legislation regarding pilotage was out of date and inadequate to handle the modern pilotage systems a Steering Committee on Pilotage was (SCOP) instituted. All ports large and small were visited and systems, personnel and equipment studied.

The topics covered relationship to the master, shipowner and port; pilots' remuneration; qualifications and mobility; pilotage dues; central pilotage board; compulsory pilotage and pilotage certificates; nationality questions; large and small ports; survey of pilotage craft. The recommendations in the appendix appeared in 1974 (p. 109).

The Human Factors Study

Under the auspices of the Research Division of the National Ports Council (NPC) representatives from Birkbeck College, London School of Hygiene and Tropical Medicine, the UKPA, TGWU, Trinity House and the NPC met in March 1973 to consider the practicalities of a research proposal project for Human Factor Study on Maritime Pilots submitted by Pat Shipley, Lecturer in Engineering Psychology.

Many pilots were concerned at their conditions of work and how it was affecting their handling of the large vessels which continued to increase in size. Accident statistics were indicating a greater likelihood of incidents with larger vessels in pilotage waters.

Recent medical evidence had suggested a comparatively high number of incidents from a particular British pilotage district. The study was funded by the National Ports Council, Department of Industry, the Shipowners through the Pilotage authorities and the pilots' organisations themselves. Commenced in October 1975 and to report in 1977/8.

ACOP 1977

The Advisory Committee on Pilotage was established to promote parliamentary legislation based on the recommendations of SCOP in

1974. One recommendation was to form the Pilotage Commission which lasted from 1977 to 1991. See the letter of David Robinson (p128).

The Merchant / Shipping Act 1979

There were a mere few sections of the Merchant Shipping Act 1979 affecting pilots. A major section established the Pilotage Commission – a paid body. The ordinary members received £1,250 per annum, plus expenses covering the various ports visited.

But new pilotage legislation enacted as the Pilotage Act 1987 was undergoing the Parliamentary procedures from May 1986 although its provisions came into effect the following year. The wording of the Act ensured that UK Government departments no longer had an obligation to take action where there was a dispute between Pilots and the former pilotage committees. The retiring chairman of the Pilotage Commission foresaw the problems that were to appear. (See Appendix B.)

The current pilotage authorities i.e. Trinity House and the local authorities were eliminated from pilotage administration. The ports of the day, mostly commercial public companies, were required to apply to become Competent Harbour Authorities taking responsibility for employing pilots as employees or as contracting personnel. Licences were no longer issued; suitable persons were 'authorised' to pilot vessels in their respective areas.

This dangerous legislation may in future bring considerable difficulties in pilotage administration. Financiers buying into various ports companies may also see that the several parts of a specific port can be sold off 'for development', breaking up a Competent Harbour Authority without consideration of safety and or safety aspects.

In the 1980s

In the late 1970s the UKPA arranged group accident and health insurance for members. After a couple of years, and in a few instances, the claims were considerably higher than the insurance companies had estimated and premiums, particularly for permanent total disablement, were increased, It was mentioned that London pilots claims were higher than the average for the UK as a whole.

The DAS legal insurance £40 per year with 50% discount for £80 annually represented good value.

During the 1980s significant changes were to appear in the administration of pilotage, caused by the new legislation often using advice provided by the SCOP and ACOP committees.

From late 1982 the Humber pilots, already busy with extra work, brought larger and unusual import traffic carrying coal to several sites along the Trent and Ouse building stocks to combat coal strikes in 1983/4. There were many such strikes and most failed completely. There would be no major industrial action affecting the whole of the UK.

In 1976 the pilots at Great Yarmouth were covering the work of 25 pilots with only 12 pilots and thought that the traffic would continue for another ten years. The rate of work was far too heavy to carry on for long and the ship-owners objected to the earnings generated for the pilots and another four pilots were taken on.

The UKPA had already agreed to a free flow of pilots from one district to another.

Three transferred from the Thames and one from Sunderland although they were all over 40 and did not merge easily into the wages regime, but were accepted per the UKPA policy. Then, in 1980, a sudden and unanticipated edict from the Norwegian Government virtually stopped the passenger trade to the oil rigs in the area. One third of the port's trade ceased overnight. One year undermanned, next year they were over-manned. They began to look for transfers for the three pilots over 40: their former districts refused to accept them back (due to the age limit of 40). The UKPA policy of free flow of transferees did not have a happy effect in all cases.

UKPA(M)

The newly founded UKPA (Marine) came into being six weeks after a ballot count, on the 31st January 1986 under the stewardship of Mr John Connolly, the National Secretary of Dock Workers and Inland Waterways, the office of the UKPA (M).

The Association executive began working on the question of reducing the number of pilots overall. The change permitted by the 1987 Act allowed pilots to take over shore positions.

In this year the three Humber pilots districts stopped work for 24 hours to discuss the systems proposed by the CHA. Pilots from the major UK and European ports were invited to attend.

At the first Conference after the introduction of the 1987 Pilotage Act the following resolution was passed by the assembly: that the use of a strong national organisation with the TGWU is essential to co-ordinate, maintain, and enhance the pilotage profession, mandates the Section Committee to do all in their power to assist local pilots in furtherance of that objective. Long debates took place on (1) compensation, (2) lump sum payment, (3) guidelines for future employment of pilots.

1988

In the first year regulation action came under the 1987 Pilotage Act 317 pilots retired, of which 250 had enhanced pension benefits for early retirement. With UKPA(M) membership in January 1986, 1,300, there were 807 total pensions at the end of the year, 53% employed, 47% self-employed. Negotiations began on reducing the number of London Pilots from 109 to 36 (London 36 pilots and 3 temporary pilots). On 1st October approximately 823 pilots remained in the profession, with 167 pilots not being authorised and consequently being entitled to the Lump Sum and Linked Enhanced Early Pension scheme.

The 'Early' Early Retirement Scheme launched at the beginning of 1988 released sixty-five pilots from Liverpool, Manchester and the Clyde, easing the situation at those ports. But this also meant that the UKPA M had lost 65 members.

The Liability of Pilots and the ability of the CHA's to vary Agreements was the main discussion topic; the amount of legal advice needed over the past year. Arbitration had been necessary in Aberdeen, Liverpool and the Clyde. The arbitration agreement at Aberdeen had not been implemented, and the Clyde had an on-going problem. The end of the fourth year since the 1988 implementation of the Pilotage Act brought several legal battles with CHAs who were trying to vary their original agreements. It was very difficult to stop any CHA changing their Pilotage Directions except where such action would create a safety problem. The Government deemed it not to be their problem under the 1987 Pilotage Act.

1996

The UKPA(M)'s legal efforts had made exceptional demands on the membership. The result of arbitration was, on the whole, in Aberdeen pilots' favour, but had involved a long hard and expensive battle with the hostile CHA. Two ports, Falmouth and King's Lynn, had been asked to look at self-employment and the UKPA(M) had engaged their solicitors to draw up suitable contracts with an emphasis on the pilots' terms, and to be presented to the respective ports. Liverpool was considering a self-employed option as, possibly in the longer term, the Medway would also achieve.

SEA EMPRESS

An incident at Milford Haven occurred that would have a significant effect on pilotage administration. A pilot taking a ship out of port, was expected to bring another vessel transferring from one ship to the other off the entrance to the Harbour. Unfortunately the inward bound vessel, a Russian tanker, approached far too near the entrance while waiting for the pilot. The master was not familiar with the port. As the pilot arrived on the bridge there were language difficulties and the tanker was too close to the shore before the pilot could obtain control, it grounded and subsequently was lost and the oil-damage devastated the coasts for miles away.

The pilot, a salaried employee, had been directed by the Harbour authority to bring the inward bound ship into the harbour. The use of one pilot for the two vessels in rota dispensed with another pilot thereby reducing the port fees. The authority found the pilot to blame and imposed penalties on him – however the Courts and the Government removed any blame from the pilot who was re-appointed. (see the legal commentary by Barry Youde later)

1998

After the review of the Pilotage Act 1987 was published, a meeting of all concerned was held by the DETR, with CHA's port authorities, Chamber of Shipping, tug owners, pilots, Nautical Institute. Andrew Burr of the Dept. confirmed that there was no prospect of a further Shipping Bill. The concerns of the several parties were stated – Mr Burr attended the UKPA(M) Conference at Middlesbrough in November. The Labour Government was very concerned over standards of port safety: a matter of public interest and especially over the statuary powers granted to CHA's and the absence of accountability for the stewardship of the public interest within the 1987 Act. A seminar on the Review was held by the Nautical Institute, a week later and chaired by Peter Russell, President of the Nautical Institute (London pilot).

The need for improvement in the provision of pilot ladders, correct positioning and standards of manufacture of the ladders and allied equipment became the content of Merchant Shipping notices: a new instrument adjusting existing legislation in excess of SOLAS requirements. Non-compliance with regulations of merchant vessels due to hull design arose as a particular area of concern. The Technical & Training Committee had discussions with the Ministry of Defence re the pilot ladder arrangements on the HMS *Penzance* class of mine-hunter. The Committee visited the vessel and founded improvements but arrangements were still non-compliant.

2000

The First Decade of the 21st Century

This period had a series of problems for the Section Committee; they were becoming involved with a growing number of organisations and several government departments: Maritime and Coastguard service (MCA), Department of Trade (DfT), Advisory Committee on Protection of the Sea (ACPOS), UK Major Ports Group, Associated British Ports (ABP), Nautical Institute (NI), Chamber of Shipping (COS) among several others including the International and European Pilots' Associations, Transport & General Workers Union (TGWU). The SC members not only had to attend meetings but coordinate their attendances between rota duties as pilots in their respective ports additional to numbers of ports in the UK and Europe.

The wish of the CHA's to increase the number of pilotage exemption certificates was causing concern, as was any reduction of the standards of training and allowing multiple vessels named on the certificates.

Boarding and Disembarkation

The efforts re arrangements for boarding and disembarking by IMPA, EMPA and the UKMPA the many improvements sought, proposed and tried yet there was no end to the number of new problems arising. New ship-owners, using more minor countries as flags of convenience, continued to ignore the regulations promulgated in the World's maritime press. And UK Government Departments needed pressure to take measures to ensure safety.

Vessel Traffic Services

A few experts in this decade, looking at trials of electronic apparatus, the so-called pilot boxes, proposed that pilotage was possible by personnel in the Vessel Traffic Services. At the same time several electronic devices for a pilot to carry on the ship. One of the devices was to be used with a laptop computer. One of the problems arising with laptops appeared when the laptop was positioned on a secure flat surface inside the navigation bridge. In an incident in Moreton Bay, Queensland, Australia, (the approaches to Brisbane): the pilot, making a critical turn had to walk several metres to consult the laptop and during the few seconds the turn was delayed and the ship grounded. Where is the pilot expected to place the laptop ready for use?

2000

The true effect of the provisions of the Pilotage Act 1987 became evident as the Millennium arrived. The wording of the Act ensured that UK Government departments no longer had an obligation to take action where there was a dispute between Pilots and the former pilotage committees. The retiring chairman of the Pilotage Commission foresaw the problems that were to appear. (See page

124). The provision, operation and management of pilot services was left entirely in the hands of the Competent Harbour Authorities (CHA's), that is companies both public and private. The CHA was to delineate the pilotage, recruit, train and direct pilots according to the needs of the harbour and provide challenges for the pilots.

Extraordinary Meeting 7th December 2001

This was held in the Hull Guildhall for all pilots who were not working. In fact, with the off-duty Humber pilots, almost 250 pilots, including representatives from the Netherlands Germany and Italy, filled the hall to overflowing.

The deputy Mayor welcomed the assembly and expressed the hope that the discussions could resolve the dispute between HPL and APB and ensure the on-going prosperity and safety for Kingston-upon-Hull. The UKMPA chairman Norman McKinney pointed out that the Pilotage Act of 1987 introduced a poor piece of legislation in the mistaken belief that costs to shipowners would be reduced. But it also transferred responsibility for pilotage to the CHA's who became prosecutor, judge, jury and executioner over pilotage matters without accountability.

The assembly were convinced that the ABP failed to support the Port Marine Safety Code and that the Government department responsible were powerless to interfere.

2002

After an increase of subscriptions members asked what was covered. Chairman Joe Wilson explained the costs in terms of percentage of the several categories: Insurance, TGWU, IMPA,EMPA, (service) training.

2003

The ruling of the employment tribunal dismissed the claim by the HPL that they had been illegally and unfairly treated by the ABP It was apparent that the outcome had proved very costly for the UKPA and the PNPF too. Without the services of the TGWU it would have been impossible for the HPL to take their dispute this far.

2004

Insurance

Paul Haysom was able to arrange a replacement of the N&G policy with the Royal & Sun Alliance to cover members in 2005. New rules by the Financial Services Authority meant that a 'group' policy was not allowed but a similar policy had been taken on offering a discount on premiums for named individuals. With the new policy members were able to choose from two cover options available for £250,000 and £500,000. It was found that employed pilots were not covered by the Harbour Authority's insurance. With the growing 'blame culture', the validity of the £1,000 limitation of liability under the Pilotage Act might be subject to a legal challenge: Cover is essential for all pilots.

117th Conference Eastbourne

After short debate the delegates, by a narrow majority, voted to dismantle the Pilots' National Committee for Pensions, a very successful forum that had worked well over the past 3 decades. The UKMPA President, Lord Tony Berkeley, stated that MP's lack of interest in shipping meant no Government port's strategy, by holding up development of ports, the UK would become a feeder outpost for Europe!

The MCA, expected to monitor the individual ports' compliance with the Port & Marine Safety Committee (PMSC), appeared had been 'got-at' and were unenthusiastic in a thorough investigation into honesty, effectiveness, safety and competence of port administrations. Again, the MCA claimed they could not investigate and take action whenever an offence against the use of pilotage exemption certificates (PEC's): it was a matter for the CHA. The CHA stated that they were not required to monitor any possible false use.

For the first half of the year the UKMPA dealt with the renewal of contracts in the self-employed districts of Poole, Gloucester and Dundee and in the employed districts of the Tyne and SE Wales and various employment matters in Belfast involving a ballot for industrial action over TWGU recognition.

At 30th Sept. the membership stood at 493 from 47 districts, this figure represented reduction of 8 over 2003. Neath district had withdrawn from membership. Dundee had reduced from 5 to 3 but the other two pilots had transferred to Perth thus creating a new District. The other 6 pilots were from ports where pilots had retired and were not replaced.

Barry Youde, barrister, presented delegates on several legal options available to HPL members against APB and David Fortnum confirmed that HPL members were taking the first steps to launch a legal challenge.

LEGAL: Mark Foden, of Blake Lapthorn Linnell (BLL) solicitors detailed the work undertaken on behalf of pilots during 2005, reviewing contracts for both employed and self-employed pilots, unfair dismissal and also with the London pilots, advising on the proposed new arrangement for Local Navigation Certificates for watermen.

Limitation of Liability

Section 22(1) of the 1987 Pilotage Act had provided valuable protection for pilots and had thus kept the number of claims against them low. This legal protection was now being challenged and Mark thought it was only a matter of time before a test case claim was made against an individual pilot. The Act just covers civil liability for negligence but not criminal misconduct which is covered under Section 21.

In the case of a negligence claim against a pilot although 22(1) provides a maximum personal financial liability of £1000 the pilot would also be likely to have his authorisation suspended or removed and he would then be responsible for his own legal defence costs in fighting the suspension and potentially the costs of the claimant. The limitation also only applied when a pilot was undertaking his duties as a pilot. It did NOT apply to criminal cases brought following an incident under the other Acts such as the Water Resources Act or if manslaughter charges are brought following a fatality in which a pilot may be implicated. For this reason that Mark considered pilots needed to ensure they had adequate insurance.

2005

118th Conference at Maidstone (jointly London/Medway) November

The Conference was busy in that the following acronyms appear in the reports: PNPC, MFR, MNPA, IMPA, TWGU, MCA, DfT, BLL, PMSC, GLA, H&SE, MAIB, NRA, DESMERALDA, IALA, P&I, VTS, IMO, CHIRP, NMAST, a bewildering number that displays a fair idea as to the spread of the work covered by the Section Committee members.

CHA's problems for the future

It appears that investment (private equity) companies, if they bought port plc's, would be able to gain control over pilots and pilotage without accountability. This is disturbing.

2007

119th Conference Harrogate

This Conference was put back from November to May in order to make attendance more attractive for delegates and their wives. Peter Wylie was congratulated for arranging the more central venue for a well-supported and successful conference. Membership was stated to be 492 pilots from 46 districts. The speakers were Michael Grey of *Lloyd's List* and presentations from Stephen Meyer (Chief Investigator MAIB), James Weedon (Head of Ports division Dft) Geoff Stokes (Port Liaison Policy Leader MCA) and Kevin Austen (HPL pilot and solicitor, Barlow Lyle & Gilbert).

Another speaker, Andy Kirkham of the International Group of P&I Clubs, had a very hard task to explain the use of the term "pilot error" to the assembly who let him know that they were by no means happy with the wording. However those present left with a far greater understanding of the work and the P&I Clubs. Andy Kirkham also agreed that the aims of the UKMPA and the P&I Clubs were the same, acknowledging that high standards in pilotage reduce incidents and therefore claims.

2008

121st Conference on board HQS Wellington

39 Pilots attended from 15 districts: the membership was 493 from 45 districts.

The TGWU and the union AMICUS were preparing to amalgamate into UNITE.

It was suggested that employed pilots were subsidising the self-employed pilots with their premiums – a myth – in reality the insurances were currently being required by more employed pilots than self-employed pilots. The policy was more relevant to employed pilots.

2009

Pilot transfer arrangements

This was still the most dangerous part of Pilotage. The lobbying effect that IMPA had at IMCO, was amazing, the importance of having so many pilots on so many country delegations acting in a discrete and professional was very apparent and could not be overstressed.

Pilot ladder problems

A French pilot was severely injured when ropes parted at deck level he and the ladder fell 8 metres into the water between the ship's hull and the pilot cutter. An Italian pilot suffered serious injuries when attempting to board. Earlier a Turkish pilot died when a ladder broke.

Pilots National Pension Fund

The scheme – established in 1971 – in 2009 had a £200m deficit. The trustee sought to establish the extent of its powers to levy contributions on the ports that authorise pilots. A complex legal case concerning the funding of the PNPF was to be taken to the High Court. Richard Williamson (Chairman of the Pilot Trustees) explained that the case was solely to establish whether or not there was a liability. If, as anticipated, such liabilities were found to exist, the specific liabilities of each party would subsequently be analysed and set. In the case of Trust Ports the port's trustees were unable to commit to payments unless required to do so by a court order. It was even possible that the Government may be liable in that it was the 1987 Act which had caused the problems in the first place. This case is unique and any outcome impossible to predict, but it is hoped that it would result in a clear allocation of liabilities and that the pensions regulator would ensure that those liable would honour their commitments.

Court proceedings took place in February 2010 lasting several weeks, with the judgement announced in June the same year and which was favourable in many respects for the Trustees of the PNPF. The CHA's were liable to contribute to the Fund thereby make up the deficits.

Although the 1987 Act was intended to direct the administration of pilotage away from national Government towards the local port authorities, the many commercial and service pressure groups compelled the several departments to enter into exchanges with each group. The S.C. spent a considerable amount of time and energy assisting the ports with difficulties re pilots' contracts, but was increasingly involved with a growing number of committees. The members have to reconcile pilotage work with home life and, in addition, attend meetings often at irregular dates and venues.

Criminal proceedings

In the past few years there have been attempts to bring criminal proceedings against pilots in actual marine spheres, in Canada, Hong Kong and Australia. The prosecutions have been brought in none-marine courts without experienced lawyers and judiciary. This disturbing trend is likely to appear in the UK. The Section

Committee, aware of possibilities, are keeping in touch with government departments and IMPA.

Barrie Youde

I am extremely grateful to be invited to report some observations made since 1976. At that time I was a licensed pilot at Liverpool, having been granted unrestricted status that year following an apprenticeship which began in 1959 and service as a junior pilot which began in 1966. Some of my observations are from personal experience as a licensed pilot and others are from later experience following call to the legal Bar at the Inner Temple in London in 1990. I have been in legal practice since that date.

There is no doubt that in 1976 pilotage in the United Kingdom was in a state of some flux. There were dramatic and obvious changes in the pattern of trade and concern was widespread as to how the governance (and therefore the laws) of pilotage were to be maintained in the future, in light of an obviously diminishing requirement for the numbers of pilots whilst an equal (if not increasing) volume of sea-borne cargo needed to be the subject of import to (if not export from) the United Kingdom. Her Majesty's Steering Committee on Pilotage was in full flow in its deliberations, change was clearly in the air and the awaited results were quite unpredictable.

In the meantime the 1913 Pilotage Act remained in force and pilots, for the most part, went about their daily lives. The vast majority of pilots were self-employed and were not party to any contract of employment with any harbour authority. This had been the position since time immemorial for reasons which were soon to become clear but which, in 1976, were not as clear as they are today. In 1976 it was widely imagined that, in future, pilots would become the employees of harbour authorities as a matter of administrative neatness if nothing else. In 1976 when the matter was discussed at all it was frequently proposed that, if a pilot were to become the employee of a harbour authority, then the harbour authority would become liable for the negligence of the pilot (in any case where negligence might be shown), on the ordinary principles of vicarious liability which apply to any employer whose employee might be found negligent. It was said that, for that reason, harbour authorities were understandably reluctant to engage pilots as employees as the potential liability of a negligent pilot was plainly vast.

The 1913 Act was to remain in force until 1988. Before that date, however, events of considerable significance occurred; all of which call for some examination but it is helpful first of all to recite the facts of each event in chronological order. In December 1978, the tanker *Esso Bernicia* was inward-bound to an oil-terminal at Sullum Voe in the Shetland Islands, with tugs in attendance. When the vessel was approaching the berth the head-tug caught fire in her engine-room and, in the emergency which had clearly arisen, let go from the tanker. Deprived of head-tug assistance the vessel collided with the oil-terminal and damage ensued to both the vessel and the jetty. The vessel was under pilotage but, unusually at the time, the pilot was an employee of the harbour authority, Shetland Islands Council. The owners of the vessel sued the tug-boat interests (alleging inadequate design in the tug-boat) and also the harbour authority, alleging vicarious liability for the negligence of its employee. As is the nature of such litigation it took several years before any conclusion was to be reached in Court. The conclusion will be examined further below.

In the meantime in December 1980 a self-employed pilot at Liverpool was subjected to disciplinary proceedings for his wilful disobedience of an order issued by his harbour authority. He was penalised by way of both fine and reprimand. The facts were that he had piloted a Greek ship to an anchorage at which pilotage was not compulsory and had been discharged from the ship by her master, who did not wish to pay for any non-compulsory service whilst lying at the anchorage. It was the ship's intention to remain at the anchorage for almost twenty-four hours in accordance with her own Docking Orders. An official of the harbour authority ordered the pilot to wait in unpaid attendance to the ship throughout that time and the pilot refused to do so. I was the pilot. By convention, most pilots would simply have waited in compliance with the order and probably I would have done so, too, in normal circumstances. The order was, however, clearly unlawful as far as I could see; and the fact that it was Christmas-time gave me the necessary courage to make a stand and to challenge the harbour authority. The process of challenge took some time and the harbour authority held its ground.

In 1983 in Parliament the Pilotage Act of 1983 became law. This instrument was introduced as a consolidating Act which incorporated the Act of 1913 and other relevant legislation. A significant provision of the 1983 Act was, however, that it granted to a harbour authority the power to employ pilots, with the added rider that the power should be deemed always to have existed. The introduction of this provision created the misconception in some circles that a harbour authority had somehow been given the power to impose terms of employment upon pilots against their will, which was not the case. The imposition of employment terms against a person's will is otherwise known as conscription. A significant provision of the Act of 1913, which remained in force, was (as in all previous pilotage legislation) that pilots who were subjected to disciplinary proceedings enjoyed a statutory right of appeal to the County Court.

In 1983 correspondence with the harbour authority in my own disciplinary case (above) eventually ground to a halt and the only logical further step was to exercise the statutory right of appeal to Liverpool County Court. The case eventually came into Court in June of 1986, almost five and a half years after the facts had arisen. At Court, the harbour authority made the submission to His Honour Judge Frank Nance that there was a chain of command extending from the chairman of a harbour authority down through every stage of pilotage administration to the serving pilot at the very bottom: and that the pilot was obliged to obey any order issued by a harbour authority. At this point the Judge exploded, "Not when the discharge note has been signed! The pilot is self-employed, isn't he? He pays his taxes under Schedule D, doesn't he?" There followed quite the most embarrassing silence which I have ever witnessed as Counsel for the harbour authority was obliged to admit the matters which had until that point been overlooked. The Judge delivered the coup-de-grace with the question, "Why do you come to Court so badly prepared?" The ultimate judgment was that the order had been unlawful and the appeal was therefore allowed, with costs awarded in my favour. My relief at being exonerated by the Judge was spoiled only by the knowledge that so much opposition had been shown by others who had at least as much interest in pilotage as I had. But that is beside the point.

A little more than two years later, on 1st October 1988 the Pilotage Act of 1987 became law and the Act of 1913 was repealed. An immediate effect of the new Act was that all pilotage licences were withdrawn. At face value, this measure left the United Kingdom without a single licensed pilot. At the same time, however, in order that pilotage services should be maintained a new instrument known as an "authorisation" was issued to those pilots willing to serve under the new regime. The difference between an authorisation and a licence is extremely difficult to identify and the need to do so has not yet arisen. It is sufficient here to point out that each one both creates a permission and grants the ancient privilege of conducting vessels under statutory pilotage to persons who would not otherwise have that privilege. Another significant provision of the new Act was that each harbour authority became obliged under Section 4(2) to offer terms of employment to pilots. At most ports, pilots accepted the terms of employment which harbour authorities offered. At other ports the pilots opted, in exercise of the statutory option granted by Section 4(2)(b), to reject the terms of employment offered and to remain self-employed. To that extent the new Act was to have far-reaching repercussions but in other respects the new Act created very little change.

In the remaining days of 1988 the long-fermenting case of the *Esso Bernicia* at Sullum Voe reached the House of Lords. As indicated above, the facts of the case had arisen some ten years previously and the case was therefore considered under the provisions of the 1913 Act which had been in force at the time. This small point was to have repercussions later. The case itself had taken the whole of the interim period to pass through the Scottish courts without finality acceptable to the parties concerned and had thus found its way into the House of Lords as the finis litium point of the United Kingdom legal system. Their Lordships conducted an extensive review of previously decided cases of pilotage law since the early nineteenth century. Points of law confirmed with approval by the House were that a pilot who has become duly qualified following examination by persons qualified to examine him becomes a public servant. The case of Holman v Irvine Harbour Trustees (1877) was cited with approval, in which it was said that a licensed pilot serves the public and the public is his master; and that the legal position of a pilot is similar to that of a notary public or a messenger at arms. The House was then obliged to consider the position of a pilot who had accepted terms of employment from a harbour authority or other public body, as this was the unusual position which existed at Sullum Voe in 1978. Their Lordships gave careful consideration to an Australian case where the point had arisen in 1917. At length, the House of Lords delivered their judgment that a pilot is an independent professional who serves a ship as a principal and not as the servant or agent of any general employer. To that judgment could have been added the words "if he has one"; but as in the case of the *Esso Bernicia* there clearly was a general employer the addition of those words would have been superfluous. The surprise to the legal world was the establishment at the highest legal level in the United Kingdom that, even in cases where a harbour authority does employ pilots, the harbour authority itself continues to enjoy protection from liability for the negligence of any pilot which it might licence or authorise; for the basic reason, as explained, that a pilot is an independent professional who serves as a principal and not as an employee.

In 1993 an unsuccessful challenge was made to the decision of House of Lords in the *Esso Bernicia* case. The new facts had arisen after October 1988, and therefore during the currency of the 1987 Act. Within the London pilotage area the vessel Cavendish, when under pilotage, had collided with a fixed navigation mark and damage had been caused. (At this point it might be worth recording that the American word "allision" crept into common usage in cases of collision with fixed objects, in distinction from the word "collision" which has somehow become restricted to the meeting of two moving objects. The owners of the Cavendish sought to hold the Port of London Authority (PLA) liable for the negligence of the pilot on the basis that the pilot was directly employed by PLA. The case was heard in the High Court in London (fully two tiers of litigation below the House of Lords). It was submitted on behalf of the owners of the vessel that the introduction of the Act of 1987 had altered the position as the House of Lords had found it to be in the *Esso Bernicia* case under the 1913 Act. Mr Justice Anthony Clarke QC (as he then was) had no difficulty in rejecting the submission. A close examination was made of the meaning of Section 16 of the 1987 Act which provides that: "The fact that a ship is being navigated in an area and under circumstances in which pilotage is compulsory for it shall not affect [i.e. SHALL NOT RELIEVE – B.Y.] any liability of the owner or master of the ship for any loss or damage caused by the ship or by the manner in which it is navigated."

It was held that Section 16 makes a pilot the servant of the shipowner for all purposes connected with navigation. Accordingly, a harbour authority as employer of a qualified licensed or authorised pilot is not responsible to the owner of a ship damaged by the pilot's negligence while under pilotage. It was observed that the harbour authority takes no part in the pilotage and its own obligations are satisfied merely by the provision of a pilot of a proper standard of competence. When delivering judgment, Mr Justice Clarke went further and cited the biblical observation that no man can serve two masters and therefore that, once it was established that a pilot is for some purposes the servant of the ship, he cannot at the same time be the servant of anybody else. It is noteworthy that although the judgment is a first-instance judgment (i.e. not a Judgment of the Court of Appeal or still less of the House of Lords) it has now stood without successful challenge for almost twenty years. There is no realistic prospect of any successful challenge.

Three years later in February 1996, disaster struck at Milford Haven when the tanker *Sea Empress* struck rocks when under compulsory pilotage inward bound. Widespread pollution occurred. A significant legal issue which arose was that of the criminal liability of a harbour authority rather than any civil liability. A major investigation began.

In the meantime in 1997 there were two events which arose directly from the ten-year-old provisions of the Act of 1987. Those provisions required some further and closer interpretation, particularly at Section 4. At Liverpool, where in 1988 it had been widely understood that the harbour authority was given ultimate power to determine the employment status of pilots, the pilots elected in 1997 to exercise the statutory option provided by Section 4(2)(b) and to revert to the self-employed standing which had previously been enjoyed. The pilots had grown to realise that the burden attaching to any contract of employment with the harbour authority far outweighed any perceived benefit which might have arisen: and in point of fact the penny had dropped that, for pilots, there was no benefit whatsoever in being an employee of a harbour authority.

As though to underline the point, there was a case on the Clyde in the same year (1997) in which an unfortunate pilot had placed himself in breach of his contract of employment with the harbour authority and the harbour authority had thereupon revoked his authorisation, as it was empowered to do under Section 3(5)(d) of the Act. There was no issue as to the competence of the pilot or as to any misconduct affecting his ability. He was not at fault on either of those two points. The pilot had simply ventured to express an opinion to the harbour authority and in consequence his entire career at the Clyde was brought to an end.

In searching for a remedy for the Clyde pilot it became apparent immediately that the statutory right of appeal to the Courts against interference with a pilot's licence or other disciplinary matters which had been expressly enjoyed under earlier legislation no longer applied; and that the only remedy appeared to be the common law remedy of making application to the High Court (or Scottish Court of Session) for Judicial Review of the relevant decision taken by the harbour authority. The procedure of Judicial Review is not a matter of right. It is for the discretion of the Court to determine, as a preliminary step, whether there is merit in the application for review. In the case of the Clyde pilot, the Court of Session observed that, because the pilot had accepted terms of employment from his harbour authority, the first step which he should have taken was to appeal to an Employment Tribunal on the basis of a claim for unfair dismissal. As this step had not been taken, the application for Judicial Review of the revocation of the pilot's authorisation failed. This was a salutary lesson for all pilots as to the burden which is undertaken when accepting terms of employment from a harbour authority.

Matters at Milford Haven following the *Sea Empress* incident of 1996 eventually came to Court in 1999. The Department for Transport via its subordinate Environment Agency brought a criminal prosecution against the harbour authority under the pollution legislation and not specifically under the Pilotage Act. The relevant provisions of the Pilotage Act were, however, considered at great length in determining to what extent, if at all, criminal liability for the pollution might lie. Legal matters were eased considerably when the port authority pleaded guilty to the criminal charge of causing the pollution. The matter to be determined then was not guilt (which was expressly admitted and therefore established) but an appropriate sentence in respect of the guilt. In other words, how bad was the pilotage and to what extent was the harbour authority culpable for the faults?

The case was of such public significance that the Judge appointed to determine matters at Cardiff Crown Court in 1999 was Mr Justice David Steel who was (and remains) the presiding Judge of the Admiralty Court in London. Standards of qualification and experience came under close scrutiny; including the local regulations which applied to the necessary experience required in relation to the vessel in question. It was shown that by a reckoning of the experience of the pilot against the size of the vessel the pilot was qualified in accordance with the regulated standards but only just so. His actual experience of ships the size of *SEA EMPRESS* was minimal. As at most major ports, standards of experience at Milford Haven were and still are maintained by reference to the "time of service" to be determined by a harbour authority pursuant to Section 3 (2) of the 1987 Act. The matter of lack of experience is an obvious standing problem in the maintenance of any regulated standards of experience. The history of the last two hundred years records that the only resolution available to a harbour authority acting in the public interest is to increase the amount of experience required in the lower standards of pilotage before granting licence/ authorisation/permission to a pilot to undertake the pilotage of larger ships. The Judge found expressly that he did not make any determination of negligence on the part of the pilot and neither did he find incompetence; but he did find (in holding the harbour authority liable) that the experience which the harbour authority had required of the pilot was inadequate. In specific terms, the standards maintained by the harbour authority were inadequate.

In imposing a heavy fine upon the harbour authority Judge Steel said, "The significance of these matters is all the greater in the context of a scheme of compulsory pilotage. Shipowners and masters must needs engage a pilot. They have to take the training, experience and expertise of the pilot provided at face value. While the master remains nominally in command, it has to be recognized that the pilot had the con[duct of the navigation] and a master can only interfere when a situation of danger has clearly arisen. The port authority imposes a charge for pilotage but in the same breath has the added advantage of the pilot being treated for purposes of civil liability as an employee of the shipowner. All this calls for the highest possible standards on the part of the port authority."

The harbour authority, having pleaded guilty in Cardiff Crown Court to the offence of causing pollution through failing to maintain adequate standards of pilotage, appealed to the Court of Appeal against the severity of the fine imposed. In April 2000 the harbour authority was able to satisfy the Lord Chief Justice in the Court of Appeal that its standards of required experience had been raised and that the concern of Judge Steel in the Crown Court had been addressed and that there was therefore scope to reduce the fine to the lesser sum of £750,000.00 (reduced from £4million) in answer to the Appeal. In doing so, the Lord Chief Justice both confirmed the propriety of the principle enunciated by Mr Justice Steel and acknowledged that the harbour authority, subsequent to the offence, had shown itself willing to comply properly with the principle. The principle that a harbour authority is obliged to maintain the highest possible standard in all respects in compulsory pilotage areas was therefore both identified and established clearly at common law. It is a principle which arises automatically wherever compulsory pilotage exists and it seems unlikely that the principle could be challenged by anybody.

In those circumstances it was surprising, to say the least, when very little more than twelve months later (June 2001) a harbour authority in a compulsory pilotage area gave notice of revocation of authorisation to all of its pilots within a time-scale (eight months) which precluded any possibility that the local existing standards of experience could be maintained. This is what happened at the Humber, where regulated standards of experience required of pilots were no exception to the common law requirement that a period of several years of experience was required from initial qualification for the pilotage of smaller ships to unrestricted qualification for the pilotage of any ship. The requirement operates at major ports throughout the world to the present day.

At the Humber, however, the harbour authority issued notice of revocation in June to become effective in January the following year, 2002. In light of the consequences of the notice in terms of a clear disregard for the principle that the highest possible standards are required in compulsory pilotage areas, it seems likely that an immediate application for Judicial Review of the notice would have been successful. What actually happened was quite different. The Department for Transport remained wholly unwilling to intervene and the pilots who were subjected to the notice took no legal action of any kind to restrain the harbour authority in its intended course of action. In consequence in January 2002 there was de-authorisation en-masse of all pilots who had been given notice; and the regulated standards of experience were simply abandoned by the harbour authority. Where previously a standard of four years of experience had been required for qualification for the pilotage of most large ships in the Humber area, plus a further six years in addition in respect of the very largest, those established standards were abandoned and not maintained at all. Qualification for authorisation at the Humber today at any level is stated in Pilotage Directions to be "on the recommendation of the harbour master". The fact that in any major port the harbour master will probably never have qualified as a pilot might not yet have been given the full consideration which is properly required.

The pilots who had been disqualified in January 2002 did not take matters lying down. The Humber was one of the ports at which the pilots had not accepted terms of employment on the introduction of the 1987 Act and had continued to serve on self-employed terms until the harbour authority chose in 2002 to disqualify them. Supported by the Transport and General Workers' Union the disqualified pilots sought recompense. The advice given to them by lawyers instructed by the Union was that the terms of their self-employment were so restrictive that it might be possible to persuade an Employment Tribunal that they had in fact been employees of the harbour authority all along; and that they were therefore entitled to compensation for unfair dismissal. An application was therefore made to the Employment Tribunal and evidence was called over seventeen days on various dates between May 2002 and March 2003. The ultimate decision of the Tribunal was unanimous that the pilots were not employees of the harbour authority. The pilots appealed against the decision but their appeal was dismissed.

Nothing daunted, the pilots sought further advice, although financial support from the Union was by now exhausted. Any further action would need to be funded privately. A case was prepared alleging that on the part of the harbour authority there had been misfeasance in public office which, if it could be proven, should entitle the pilots to substantial damages. Proceedings against the harbour authority were issued out of the High Court in July 2006 in a representative action on behalf of eighty-eight of the one hundred and thirty pilots who had been disqualified. Expert Witnesses were instructed and the trial was eventually listed for hearing over four weeks in London in June 2008. The matter, however, did not reach trial. In April 2008 the harbour authority and the eighty-eight pilots agreed out-of-Court terms of settlement.

That same year, 2008, concerns were again raised at the Clyde when, through the disqualification of a very large proportion of the complement of senior manpower, another harbour authority placed itself in a position whereby it could not comply with its own regulated standards of experience for pilots. At one point, the Clyde harbour authority was unable to provide a single pilot whose experience was in compliance with the four years of experience necessary for unrestricted qualification on the Clyde in accordance with the standards which were not only applicable in 1988 but which were also confirmed by a fresh Pilotage Direction made on 13th July 2009. Again the Department for Transport was put on notice of the wilful non-compliance with the *SEA EMPRESS* principle and again chose to take no action whatsoever.

Barrie Youde
CH41 SEU

A Final Word from a shipowner: David Robinson

I feel duty bound to focus on one matter which loomed large throughout the discussions and debates on reorganisation and which will indeed always be with us. That is the conflict which can exist – and indeed on occasions cannot be avoided – between commercial pressures and safety of life and protection of the environment. This country's record with regard to safety and environmental protection has always stood high and I personally could never have been a party to promoting a change in the organisation of pilotage had I not been convinced that it would continue so to do. However we must recognise that under the old regime the pilot being a self-employed person probably felt in a stronger position to resist commercial pressure than he may do today as an employee. Whilst I have the fullest confidence in the ports of this country, they, and for that matter, the pilots also as their employees, must be constantly on guard to ensure that the high standards which have been maintained in the past are in no way eroded by the pressures of commercialism being allowed to outweigh the interests of safety of life and protection of the Environment.

APPENDIX

APPENDIX A

SCOP

SUMMMARY OF MAIN FINDINGS AND RECOMMENDATIONS OF THE REPORT "MARINE PILOTAGE IN THE UNITED KINGDOM"

Relationship of the Pilot to the Master, the Shipowner and the Port (Chapter 3).

While the respective roles of pilot and master are very difficult to define, we reaffirm that the pilot conducts the navigation of the ship while the master retains supreme authority on board and may, where essential for safety, override the pilot. Rec 1 – On balance, we *recommend* against attempting to spell out this relationship in a new Act. Rec 2 – We also *recommend* that the provisions of the 1913 Act regarding the pilot's liability to the shipowner should be left unchanged though it might be desirable to remove the need to execute a bond. Rec 3 – We further *recommend* that selective pilotage should be continued where the parties concerned favour it. While pilotage should, as now, usually be administered independently of the port, there should be the closest co-operation between the two.

Pilots' Remuneration (Chapter 4)

Most pilots value their self-employed status though it has some characteristics of salaried employment. Advocates of salaried status believe it would achieve greater efficiency and security. Rec 4 – We *recommend* against making a change from self-employment but believe that the new legislation should keep open the possibility in the light of increased efficiency secured by reorganisation. Rec 5 – We further *recommend* that central machinery should seek to secure equitable remuneration including application of work indices and that a central fund should help to compensate pilots for losses of earnings outside their control.

Qualifications, Training and Mobility (Chapter 5)

Most pilots are recruited from the merchant service while the remainder come through apprenticeship schemes. Except for certain small pilotage districts. Rec 6 – we *recommend* that a master foreign-going certificate should be the minimum qualification in future, subject to fulfilling obligations to apprentices and perhaps continuation of arrangements for prospective pilots to have an early identification with pilotage. Rec 7 – We also *recommend*, partly to facilitate mobility, a nationally agreed training programme for pilots possibly including simulator training, with special training in respect of an individual pilotage area.

APPENDIX

Compulsory Pilotage and Pilotage Certificates (Chapter 6)

The existing requirements for compulsory pilotage are anachronistic and need review in the light of present-day risks. Rec 8 – We *recommend* that, as a general principle, pilotage should be compulsory subject to carefully considered local exemptions for areas, small vessels and experienced personnel where these can safely be given and certain general exemptions, eg in respect of HM ships. Linked with this recommendation, Rec 9 – we *recommend* a liberal attitude to the issue of pilotage certificates to masters or chief officers of ships which use a port frequently and can demonstrate their familiarity with it by examination; and that those ships should meet a portion of pilotage costs. Rec – 10 We also *recommend* more stringent requirements for communicating estimated times of arrival or departure with penalties for infringement. Rec 11 – We further *recommend* that there should be arrangements to require a pilot to be taken in cases of special risk.

Nationality Questions (Chapter 7)

The Pilotage Act places no nationality restrictions on granting pilots' licences but many byelaws restrict them to British subjects. With the exception of certain longstanding ferry services, the Act prohibits the issue of pilotage certificates to aliens. These provisions may need to be considered in the light of EEC obligations; general provisions on nationality matters in a new Pilotage Act might be activated by Commencement Order. Bearing these questions in mind Rec 12 – we *recommend* that the automatic restriction of pilotage certificates to British subjects should be removed though all certificate holders should have fluent command of English and appropriate qualifications. This recommendation is subject to consideration of the effect on demand for pilots and on pilotage finances, measures to ease possible redundancies in certain ports.

as well as the scope for reciprocity. We see no special merit in nationality restrictions on pilot licences for which a UK master's foreign-going certificate would be required.

Assistant to the Pilot (Chapter 8)

Mainly for very large ships but also in certain very difficult waterways there is a need for a pilot to have an assistant. Rec 13 – We *recommend* that a new Pilotage Act should enable byelaws to be made which would make it compulsory for an assistant to be taken on a vessel for which a need had been established.

Pilotage Dues (Chapter 9)

While there is a good case, supported by practice abroad, for levying a basic charge whether a pilot is taken or not, the need for this may be less in view of the proposed extension of compulsory pilotage and Rec 14 – we *recommend* that a central organisation should review this question. Rec 15 – We also *recommend* that the basis on which pilotage dues are levied should be studied centrally and that charging and accounting arrangements should be simplified and rationalised. Rec 16 – We further *recommend* that a new Act should specify penalties in the event of dues not being paid within a given time.

Future Organisation (Chapter 10) Larger Ports and Estuaries

More than 1400 of some 1600 UK pilots are concerned with piloting vessels into and out of the major ports and estuaries of the UK and the organisational solution adopted must ensure an effective and efficient service. Rec 17 – We *recommend* that responsibility and authority be given to local pilotage authorities representative of shipowners, pilots and ports together with some independent members who could, contribute additional navigational and management experience. Rec 18 – We further *recommend* that the areas covered by such authorities should allow a single pilot to pilot a ship from the seaward boundary of the district to its berth and vice versa, subject to considerations of fatigue and the required expertise in internal dock systems.

Central Board

Rec 19 – We *recommend* that a Central Board be established with specified functions on a continuing basis and the authority to play a part in reorganisation through membership of local reorganisation committees. While its general field of operations should be specified in legislation, flexibility to vary its functions in the light of experience should be allowed. Rec 20 – We *recommend* that the Chairman and Board members should be appointed by the Secretary of State and would include shipowners, serving pilots, port operators and others with a nautical, financial or administrative background. A full-time staff of perhaps 20-30 would be required.

Smaller Ports

Rec 21 – We *recommend* that the possibility of including smaller ports in larger pilotage districts nearby or of amalgamating with other smaller districts should be considered. Alternatively, the Central Board might have a small ports section or some small ports might continue with their present administration for some time to come.

Future Role of Trinity House London

While Trinity House itself would cease to be a pilotage authority for larger ports. Rec 22 – we *recommend* that it should continue to provide a source of independent navigational advice at local and national level which has proved of great value in the past. It would probably have a special responsibility for a number of smaller ports. Rec 23 – We also *recommend* that its pilotage staff should be absorbed into the new system, that the Central Board should be housed initially at Trinity House and that Trinity House might have responsibilities for the surveillance and maintenance of pilot boats.

Other Issues (Chapter 11) Provisional Licences

Rec 24 – We *recommend* that pilotage authorities should be able to issue provisional licences to meet transient needs subject to strict limitations on their number and with the right of appeal.

Pilotage to the Berth

Rec 25 – We *recommend* that pilotage jurisdiction should cover berthing and dock movements and that, in due course, all dock pilotage should be within the control of the pilotage authority.
River Thames. Rec 26 – We *recommend* bringing all Thames pilotage under one control while safeguarding the position of existing Thames watermen and apprentices and maintaining the local knowledge and skills required.

APPENDIX

Compensation

Rec 27 – We *recommend* that legislative provision be made for compensation in the event of redundancy.

Penalties

Rec 28 – We *recommend* that the penalties in the 1913 Act be brought up to date.

Surveying of Pilot Craft

Standards of pilot craft vary and Rec 29 – we *recommend* that consideration should be given to responsibility for survey being taken either by the Department of Trade, the Central Board or Trinity House.

APPENDIX B

Pilotage Commission

Pilotage Commission

It was all too clear at a very early stage in the life of the Commission that the 1979 Merchant Shipping Act as a vehicle for the reorganisation of pilotage throughout the United Kingdom was defective. It was truly a poor and ineffectual compromise arising from the SCOP Report of 1977 which failed to accept the recommendations of the ACOP Report of 1974. The Pilotage Commission being set up as little more than advisory body was not given the necessary powers to effect the much needed reorganisation of pilotage in Britain. Overall pilotage suffered fundamentally not (as many chose to dunk) from the quasi-self-employed basis on which the great majority of pilots operated under the 1913 Act but from the fact that the conflicting interests of the shipowners, the ports, the independent pilotage authorities and the pilots themselves, coupled with the ultimate over-riding hand of government, made for an outdated bureaucratic system offering the worst of all worlds. The Commission, as constituted, was powerless to effect change in the face of this system and in 1982 informed the then Parliamentary Under-Secretary of State, Mr Iain Sproat, that the only feasible remedy and certainly the only one likely to be acceptable to the Government of the day was to place responsibility for pilotage in the hands of the port authorities. Indeed this proposal made even more sense as time progressed due to the considerable changes in the pattern of international trading which resulted from containerisation, North Sea oil and the UKs entry into the EEC. All of these factors coupled with advancing technology led to a reduction in the number of ships trading worldwide and also a contraction of the ports industry. The Commission further submitted to Mr Sproat its proposal for compensation and early retirement arrangements to cope with the surplus of pilots which would inevitably result from a realistic reorganisation of the pilotage service.

The Commission's proposals for compensation and early retirement were however not accepted and in August, 1982, Mr Sproat appointed Samuel Montagu & Co. to examine the whole question of compensation and early retirement and submit a scheme. After considerable discussions with all interested parties and the Commission, the Montagu proposals were finally put forward on the basis of a draft Scheme at the end of 1983 and the Commission had the task in January, 1984 of trying to obtain agreement of all the interested parties. Regrettably this proved impossible, due to the many parties and interests involved, culminating in the total refusal of the GCBS to accept the compensation proposals. It must be remembered that under the old regime the shipowners exercised a considerable influence on pilotage affairs nationally as one of the parties to the Letch Agreement which governed the level of pilots' earnings and also locally through representation of Local Pilotage authorities.

In June, 1984 I wrote to Sir David Mitchell, who was at that time the Under-Secretary of State, again urging that the only way to achieve a reorganisation of pilotage throughout the United Kingdom was to place the responsibility with the port authorities. The Commission however as I have already indicated could do nothing to effect such a change under the 1979 Act; only Government had the power to initiate and introduce the necessary legislation.

By the end of 1984 the need for a radical change in the old regime had become more widely accepted and in consequence the Government in December, 1984, published a Green Paper on Pilotage Reorganisation as a discussion document. In line with that the responsibility for pilotage should be placed in the hands of the port authorities.

During the discussion process the need for compensation and early retirement arrangements inevitably emerged as one of the keys to the success of any reorganisation. Accordingly on 10th February, 1986 the then Secretary of State, the Rt. Hon. Nicholas Ridley, asked me on a personal basis – quite apart from my capacity as Chairman of the Commission – if I would endeavour to negotiate a compensation and early retirement scheme with the parties in view of the failure of the Montagu proposals to gain acceptance. By this time the ports and the pilots were clearly the two principals in the ring and I was able to report to the Secretary of State on 10th April, 1986 that the British Ports Association, the United Kingdom Pilots' Association, and the Pilots' National Pension Fund, had all accepted the scheme for compensation and early retirement which I had negotiated with them. This was announced to the House of Commons on 23rd May, 1986 by your predecessor, the Rt. Hon. John Moore.

The Pilotage Bill was introduced into the House of Lords in November, 1986 and became law on 15th May, 1987 as the Pilotage Act, 1987 with the appointed day for the port authorities (designated Competent harbour Authorities under the Act) to take over pilotage being subsequently fixed as 1st October, 1988. It would be trite for me to reiterate the arguments which led to the many amendments and safeguards which were written into the Bill as introduced. These can all be followed in Hansard and are in any event now part of history. Suffice it to say that the Act when it finally reached the Statute Book was an improvement on the Bill as originally introduced – albeit in the light of experience not perfect. This has been borne out by the difficulties which have arisen under the Pilots' Compensation Scheme.

The 1987 Pilotage Act heralded the end of the need for the Pilotage Commission. However before being swept into the annals of history, the Commission was charged inter alia with the task of obtaining agreement on compensation for pilotage authority staffs. In addition, as an independent body, the Commission undertook the administration of the Pilots' National compensation Scheme. The major task however given to the Commission under Section 24 of the 1987 Act was the preparation of proposals, to be embodied by you in Schemes, for the reorganisation of all 77 active pilotage districts throughout the country. This involved the transfer of the relevant property rights and liabilities (including in particular former staff) and also the arrangements to be made as regards the transfer of staff of former pilotage authorities. In the case of the 39 Trinity House Districts it was necessary to identify and evaluate the many Trinity House Funds and physical assets by way of property, boats and equipment with a view to the division of these assets (and also an apportionment of ultimate liabilities amongst the several port authorities [CHAs] assuming responsibility for pilotage in the former Trinity House Districts) as from 1st October, 1988. Furthermore the pilotage staff of Trinity House had to be safeguarded – not only those declared redundant as a result of the reorganisation but also former staff already on pension (a large number of whose pensions were wholly or partially unfunded), and future deferred pensioners. The cost of securing and funding pensions for the Trinity House pensioners amounted to some £1.9 million. The final distribution of the funds and assets of Trinity House in accordance with the Schemes, will require some port authorities to pay in to the Liquidation Fund to meet their share of die outstanding liabilities, whereas others will benefit from the

APPENDIX

Liquidation Fund by sums ranging from fairly small amounts to over £2 million in the case of the largest share. As at 31st May, 1990 there was approximately £2 million in the liquidation fund bank accounts earning interest

As you are aware, the reorganisation of pilotage has been achieved at no cost to HM Government and hence no burden on the taxpayer. Compensation monies have been provided (and will continue to be until 30th September, 1991) by the ports (CHAs) and the early retirement costs are being met by the Pilots' National Pension-Fund. It is to the credit of both sides that reorganisation went ahead with no Government financial support unlike the docks industry which required considerable financial aid from Government to enable the winding up of the Dock Labour Scheme. The use of a large part of the Pilots' Pension Fund actuarial surplus has inevitably delayed certain hoped for improvements in pension benefits and also a possible reduction in contribution level.

Having completed all the tasks assigned to it the Commission will go into liquidation on 27th September and hopefully the final accounting by the Liquidator of the Commission's assets can be speedily completed. All CHAs throughout the country will share in a distribution of the Commission's net assets.

It would be ungracious of me if at this juncture I did not pay tribute to the principal parties involved in making a success of the reorganisation of pilotage, namely, the port authorities, the majority of whom assumed responsibility for pilotage for the first time, and the pilots themselves, who collectively and as individuals faced a traumatic change in their working ethos. The fact that on 1st October, 1988 the pilots entered the new era in a spirit of trust, co-operation and goodwill speaks volumes for their sense of duty as professional seamen.

Before concluding I feel duty bound to focus on one matter which loomed large throughout the discussions and debates on reorganisation and which will indeed always be with us. That is the conflict which can exist – and indeed on occasions cannot be avoided – between commercial pressures and safety of life and protection of the environment. This country's record with regard to safety and environmental protection has always stood high and I personally could never have been a party to promoting a change in the organisation of pilotage had I not been convinced mat it would continue so to do. However we must recognise that under the old regime the pilot being a self-employed person probably felt in a stronger position to resist commercial pressure than he may do today as an employee. Whilst I have the fullest confidence in the ports of this country, they, and for that matter, the pilots also as their employees, must be constantly on guard to ensure that the high standards which have been maintained in the past are in no way eroded by the pressures of commercialism being allowed to outweigh the interests of safety of life and protection of the Environment

While the end product in the shape of the present reorganisation under the 1987 Act was not envisaged when the Pilotage Commission was constituted in 1979, the Commission can leave the scene in the knowledge that without its consistent and positive input from 1982 in promoting the need for a total, and in those early days revolutionary, reorganisation under the Port Authorities, the old regime may yet be with us and reorganisation still no more than a continuing debate.

Finally, I would wish to record that I have been honoured to have to have been able to serve on the Commission from its inception in 1979, initially under Dr Denis Rebbeck and since November, 1983 as its chairman. During my period of about 7 years as Chairman I have been well and ably served by a small staff and I have worked with a total of 16 Commissioners appointed from time to time.
David M. Robinson

APPENDIX C

Helgoland pilotage

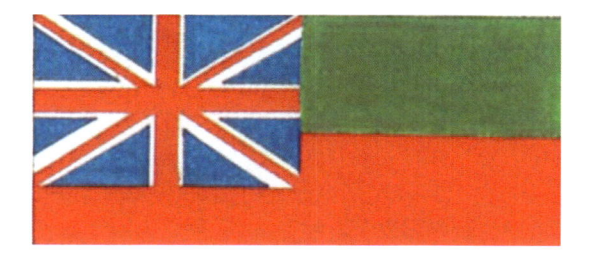

IT IS NOT generally known the Helgoland the island at the edge of the German Bight was once in British hands for over 80 years. When the Napoleonic forces took over the whole of the north European Coast, The British Navy took possession of the island in 1807 encouraged the island population to enrage the French by smuggling and, in general, become a nuisance. The Helgolanders were mainly fisherman, but often they were asked to pilot the ships to the Elbe. There those temporary pilots thoroughly annoyed the Elbe pilot when by-passing the outer cutter and entering the river. The Islanders for the last few decades of the 19th century considered themselves as British and even after the island was exchanged with Germany for Zanzibar. Most of them held on to a British passport until the Nazis came to power. Recently a former Elbe Pilot proudly told me that his grandparents had British nationality. I mentioned that the Helgolanders used to pilot ship in the approaches to the Elbe. His indignant reply was "They often stole our work !" The following story was researched by Günther Spelde, former Weser Pilot.

On 10th September 1820, the brig, NEW MINERVA, under Captain Richard Shaldon of Liverpool with a crew of twelve, bound from Pernambuco to Hamburg, made a course to pass close to the island of Helgoland (30 miles north of the German Coast) during good weather and possibly take a pilot for the Elbe. The wind was from WSW. The island was about 2½ miles off bearing E by N, the course leading towards the reef off Nathurn Brunn. The pilot boat with the pilot-captain Michael Luhrs and with nine pilots rowing went alongside the brig. They called to the Captain steer his ship to the southward. This done, Luhrs boarded and asked for £21 for pilotage to the Elbe. The Captain refused, offering f5. The pilot-captain pointed to nearby reefs and left the ship. The pilot boat passed the NEW MINERVA and sailed towards the deep water. Initially the captain followed with his ship, but as the English charts showed no reefs, Shaldon altered the course to East.

Many of the inhabitants of the island including the Governor stood on the higher land to watch the inevitable stranding occur. Shortly afterward the ship touched the ground, but came free again. The pilot went back aboard knowing the Captain now wanted his assistance, and demanded £168 pilotage fees. The captain again refused the offer. Pilot Luhrs then returned to the island and on looking back saw the brig hard aground again. At 1800, the pilots again offered assistance. The Captain believed, however, he could free the ship himself.

The following morning the NEW MINERVA was flying the pilot signal. The pilots went out and pilot Luhrs called for £1,000 for the freeing of the ship and the subsequent pilotage. The Captain then offered £100. There was no 'accord', and in an excited state the Captain threatened Luhrs with a pistol.

Next the pilots went ashore, followed by the Captain. He complained to the Governor Sir Henry King, who could not help him, but made a proposal . . . . to leave the acceptance of assistance and fees to the Hamburg Arbitration Board. Both parties accepted this. The Captain then chose two pilots who carried out the anchor and at high water attempted to heave the ship free. Two attempts failed. As the east wind swung north and increased in strength the pilots saw no possibility of saving the ship and advised the Captain so.

The Captain again went ashore and, in the courthouse, read the written salvage laws of Helgoland. He noted that the salvors could, after bringing in the salvaged cargo, claim one third of the goods. Nevertheless, he sought assistance from the Governor again, who repeated that he could not help. The Captain's only choice was to give up a third, either of ship or cargo or lose everything. On 12th September, he ceded ship and cargo for salvage under protest, leaving proceedings for the Hamburg insurers. The Governor lifted the normal legal rights, handing the whole to the inhabitants of the island. The salvors demanded a third of the cargo and brought the cargo ashore without a break over a couple of days, using their own boats. As soon as the vessel was lightened they floated it free from the reef. The Captain now argued without success that the terms were unfair.

Now the aged Richard Shaldon on this, his last trip, realised he had lost his wealth in the form of the freight of the cargo ... everything. A few days later he used his pistol and committed suicide in his cabin.

The total value of the ship and cargo amounted to £51,000. The insurers complained against the allocation of a third for the Helgolanders. The Hamburg Court decided however, that the contract between the Captain and Helgoland community was completed and complied with.

APPENDIX D

AZIMUTH Project

THERE ARE 15 partners in the EU AZIPILOT Project with each partner taking a turn at hosting a quarterly meeting. This presented a problem for the UKMPA since we do not have the resources or infrastructure to support such a meeting. Originally our thoughts turned to hosting a meeting in London at HQS Wellington, but this would have presented some expense and logistical gymnastics to organise as the UKMPA representatives in AZIPILOT are not based in London. But then we had a brainwave – why not host our' partner meeting on a podded cruise ship?

After surveying various brochures, we identified a short cruise out of Southampton to Cork and back at the end of August aboard the Independence of the Seas.

Our partners were immediately enthusiastic and, once the EU Project Officer gave the green light, the cruise was on! We then had to build a structure to our four nights aboard the cruise ship. As this ship is a regular visitor to Southampton we had already made preparations with one of the Masters, Captain Arnolf Remo and although Captain Remo was going on leave the day we joined his relief Captain Teo Strazicic was the perfect host for the voyage

Through Liam Dempsey, Dublin Pilot, we were able to set up some arrangements for our time in Cork and by the time we boarded, we had a reasonable itinerary organised. It had been arranged that Gareth would pilot the ship outwards from Southampton and Captain Strazicic kindly granted permission for all of us (around 20) to be present on the bridge for departure!

The Captain expertly manoeuvred the ship from Berth 101 and we all stood on the opposite bridge wing to observe the complete manoeuvre as the synchronous controls moved before us, as if by magic.

The Independence of the Seas (338.8 m loa 38.6 m beam) has 3 pods, 1 fixed and 2 azimuthing and 4 massive thrusters (4 x 3400Kw) which enabled the 13015 sq. m. of windage to be safely manoeuvred in 40 knots of beam wind without any tug assistance.

One of the areas the project has focused upon is the operational restrictions imposed by the engineering constraints of the pods. Central to this are concerns about bearing failure on the pods – the propeller on a pod pulls the ship through the water, unlike a conventional propeller that pushes the ship through the water. Bearing wear is most critical when there is no thrust on the propeller. Hence, the term 'positive thrust' i.e. try to keep some positive thrust on the pod. With two or more pods a neutral effect can be achieved by vectoring the pods and opposing thrusts.

This was displayed to good effect whilst leaving the berth and the group were privileged to remain on the bridge as the ship sailed down Southampton Water into the Solent. The next morning we commenced our project meeting followed in the afternoon by the arrival at Cork where once again we were invited to the bridge for the passage inwards. Two Cork Pilots boarded (one was on a familiarisation trip) and we swung a little upstream of the berth in a dredged box 400 metres across which provided a challenging restricted space in which to swing the ship which showed off the capability of the Captain, Pilot, the bridge team and of course the ship and its array of modern equipment. No tugs were necessary.

The ECS display shows the ship shape swung within a predetermined turning circle, which is within the oval-shaped dredged box. Note the speed of the bow and stern, the Rate of Turn at the time was over 30 degrees a minute! Our friends in Cork had arranged a morning visit to 'their' Simulator at the National Maritime College of Ireland (Coláiste Náisúnta Mara na hÉireann) in the morning, followed by a visit to the recently opened Spike Island in the afternoon.

What became apparent in the Simulator was the degree of planning that Cork Pilots had done prior to this ship arriving for the first time a year earlier. They had the ship modelled on the Simulator and when we repeated the previous day's arrival it was clear that the Cork Pilots had visual marks and passing distances all detailed in support of the electronics that the ship'and staff were very familiar with. Cork Pilot Aidan Fleming had liaised with us prior to our visit and we are very grateful for his and Gerry Cahill's help in arranging our visit to the Simulator.

Deputy Harbour Master (previously a Pilot} Paul O'Regan kindly arranged the visit to Spike Island. The Island has only recently opened as a tourist destination and we learned about its fascinating history.

At sea, on the return leg we continued our partner meeting in one of the conference facilities on board and were privileged that Captain Teo and his Staff Captain answered many questions posed by the group which was followed by another bridge visit where Captain Teo then explained how he operated the bridge controls.

This was followed by the Chief Engineer escorting the group to the engine Control Room, a visit to the Port Pod Room and answering the many questions. We are indebted to Captain Teo for the time he gave us to explain very comprehensively the manoeuvrability of his ship to the group. As is the custom on these occasions, on behalf of the UKMPA we hosted a partner dinner on board on the last night in the "Portofino' Restaurant – all concluded that this trip had been the highlight of the project. To see the operation of pods for real and have them explained by the ship's staff was a one off experience for most of the partners!

We also hosted a meal on board the ship in the 'Chops Grill' Restaurant for our new Irish friends in thanks for their considerable efforts in helping to arrange a fantastic visit.

The Author

HARRY M. HIGNETT, born in Merseyside in 1927, obtained a masters (fg) certificate in 1954 after 11 years at sea, the latter seven serving in Shaw Savill Lines. In 1954 entered the Manchester Pilot Service as Helmsman and in 1960 was appointed pilot. From 1974 to 1981, the Choice Pilot for Clan Line. Contributor of special articles for *Journal of Commerce,* 1970 to 1990. 25 articles on maritime history for SEAWAYS – (Nautical Institute). In 1972 was awarded a Travelling Fellowship by the Winston Churchill Memorial Trust, spending four months in major ports and waterways of Europe and North America studying vessel traffic systems. On these travels he acquired an interest in the history of the respective pilot services and in 1975 began serious study of pilotage history world-wide. Vice-President of Liverpool Nautical Research Society and member of the Nautical Association of Australia.